cu   795

D0961212

It Don't Worry Me

It Don't Worry Me

The Revolutionary American Films of the Seventies

Ryan Gilbey

ff Faber and Faber, Inc.

An affiliate of Farrar, Straus and Giroux

New York

Faber and Faber, Inc.
An affiliate of Farrar, Straus and Giroux
19 Union Square West, New York 10003

Copyright © 2003 by Ryan Gilbey
All rights reserved
Printed in the United States of America
Originally published in 2003 by Faber and Faber Ltd., Great Britain
Published in the United States by Faber and Faber, Inc.
First American edition, 2003

Library of Congress Control Number: 2003104955
ISBN: 0-571-21486-X

Designed by Jonathan D. Lippincott

www.fsgbooks.com

10   9   8   7   6   5   4   3   2   1

To Diane

Contents

It Don't Worry Me

Introduction

Last night I took another look at *Easy Rider*, the film that helped liberate American cinema. That's quite a burden for any one movie to bear, so perhaps we shouldn't be too hard on it. Yes, it's impossibly earnest, and as a manifesto for budding rebels, it has all the authentically subversive tendencies of an *American Beauty*, a *Shirley Valentine*, a *G.I. Jane*. Like those films, its concept of insurrection is placatory and consoling – it can conceive of rebellion only in crowd-pleasing, banner-waving terms.

And still none of that matters, because it is possible now to watch *Easy Rider* without actually seeing a frame of what Dennis Hopper shot. Here is a work that you are moved to applaud more for the movies that it made possible, than for what the film itself is or ever was – which at the very least is more than future generations will feel able to say about the likes of *American Beauty*. In short, *Easy Rider* may be bogus, but it got the job done.

Other films had, in turn, made Hopper's picture possible. Its immediate forebears were the down-and-dirty biker movies churned out by Roger Corman's exploitation empire along with numerous other sensationalist or opportunistic quickies. The enterprising Corman wasn't given to jumping on bandwagons so much as trying to out-run them: if the major studios had struck gold in a particular genre – the gangster flick, say, or the monster movie – then Corman would flood the market with imitations that, while not twenty-four-carat by any means, had a garish glimmer of their own. If a studio picture did attract glory that he felt was rightfully his, you could sometimes hear the gnashing of his teeth above the sound of chiming cash registers. 'I made movies about interplanetary adventures when George Lucas was still in grade school,' he griped some years after the success of *Star Wars*.[1] Those that Corman hadn't made with his own hands, he had adapted for an English-speaking audience, having developed in the early 1960s a profitable sideline in re-dubbing Russian science-fiction movies with new dialogue written by, among others, Joe Dante (*Gremlins*) and Francis Ford Coppola.

Lucas himself conceded that *Star Wars* was essentially a Corman picture with better production values, and indeed most modern blockbusters share something of that B-movie spirit, where a recipe of stock ingredients is prepared for viewers who are so fluent in the genre conventions that they could probably write the script for themselves. What Corman neglected to mention in his complaint was that the popularity of those young film-makers whom he felt had purloined his trade gave him the opportunity to return the compliment – and to milk some profits of his own out of their triumphs. The late Corman productions *Piranha* and *Alligator* were affectionate and gory replays of the first two *Jaws* pictures, while *Battle Beyond the Stars* was a witty rehash of *Star Wars*. All three movies – homages, cash-ins or reclamations of what rightfully belonged to Corman, depending on your point of view – were scripted by the young writer-director John Sayles, part of the last generation of budding film-makers to have been inducted into the film industry by Corman.

In this respect, it wasn't really the films at all that made Corman the pivotal figure in the new wave of young American directors – it may even be that the films were the least interesting thing about him. The wide-eyed movie buffs who served their apprenticeship under Corman provided cheap and enthusiastic labour on productions for which the phrase 'shot on a shoestring' suggests a misleading degree of luxury. But Corman's decision to pump young blood through the arteries of his production company looks now like an act not exclusively motivated by financial considerations. There is altruism mixed in there, foresight too.

In 1973, after the likes of Coppola, Martin Scorsese, Peter Bogdanovich and Jack Nicholson had flown the Corman coop, Michael Goodwin observed: 'The thing that makes Corman-produced . . . exploitation product superior is very simple: he tends to hire young, talented film-makers who, in turn, tend to hire young, talented writers, musicians and actors. Everybody seems to have fun making movies for Corman – and a lot of good film-makers have come out of the process.'[2] And synchronicity played its part: Corman captured a DIY spirit – punk before punk was patented. 'You should just start working wherever you can,' Scorsese reminded wannabe directors in 1975. 'Drive counts. This is Hollywood.'[3] Steven Spielberg, a contemporary of Scorsese's, though not one of Corman's crop, offered similar advice. 'It's so easy to make a picture on 16mm today without a lot of bread, and get a lot of help, because the major studios are looking for new people,' he observed. 'You'll finish a picture and screen it, and you'll get the studio heads storming the projection room to hear if it's good.'[4]

Which brings us back to *Easy Rider*, the film that made this situation viable. It was conceived and executed by two men who were part of Corman's vast extended family. Hopper was itching to direct, having shot second-unit footage for Corman's cautionary tale of psychedelia, *The Trip*, written by Jack Nicholson. Peter Fonda had played the lead in that film, and in Corman's 1966 biker movie *The Wild Angels*, and it was the latter picture that gave him the idea for a movie about two modern-day cowboys roaming America. Columbia Pictures became interested in the *Easy Rider* script (by Fonda, Hopper and Terry Southern) after the project's natural home, American International Pictures, was ruled out because Samuel Z. Arkoff of AIP had vetoed the idea of Hopper assuming both acting and directing duties. Jack Nicholson advised that Hopper and Fonda should take the movie to the production company Raybert, run by the director Bob Rafelson and the producer Bert Schneider, who were at that point making the Monkees' movie *Head* (co-scripted by Nicholson). Raybert had family ties to Columbia, which is how Hopper and Fonda's cheaply made little road movie ended up being backed by corporate muscle. Not that anyone considered it a sure thing. But by the end of 1969, it had grossed over $19 million and become the fourth-biggest hit of the year.[5] In the climate of uncertainty, with once-dependable spectaculars like *Sweet Charity* and *Hello Dolly* proving to be an increasing liability, this success had a refreshing zing.

Hollywood was not the safest industry in the 1960s. Conglomerates had engulfed many of the majors, and the end of the decade brought catastrophic losses for the likes of MGM (down $35 million) and Warner (down $52 million). Only Disney, whose four-wheeled family comedy *The Love Bug* had been the biggest hit of 1969, outran the curse.[6] Audience attendance figures had slipped. No one seemed quite sure who the audience was any more. *Easy Rider* answered that question for the foreseeable future.

In the wake of its success, movie executives restaffed the industry with young bucks who knew how to relieve the burgeoning youth market of its pocket money without performing a similar raid on the studio coffers. Directors were no longer required to earn their stripes in television or theatre; the seasoned old pros were out. Of course, there were initial tensions in some director–studio relationships. George Lucas's *THX 1138* and Brian De Palma's *Get to Know Your Rabbit* were both meddled with by Warner Bros executives who had had their fingers burnt too recently by the counter-culture freakiness of Nicolas Roeg and Donald Cammell's *Performance* to let these new pups off the leash.

But for the most part the experiment was an unheralded success. The decadent, star-stuffed extravaganzas didn't disappear overnight; *Airport* was the highest grossing film of 1970, while *The Poseidon Adventure* took that honour in 1973.[7] Both pictures squeezed numerous bejewelled and overfed celebrities, major and minor, into a cramped space and invited the audience to take bets on the order of their demise. But by the close of the 1970s, the five highest-grossing films of all time – *Star Wars, Jaws, The Godfather, Grease, Close Encounters of the Third Kind* – had all been made by directors under thirty-five years old. The DNA of modern movies had been dramatically altered too. Whereas theatrical or literary roots had often promised a film Oscar glory prior to the 1970s, that hereditary tradition began to lose its validity. Between 1939 and 1949, popular novels had been the basis for eight out of the eleven movies that walked off with the Best Picture Oscar, but by the 1970s that was down to three, with the statistics for stage-to-film adaptations similarly diminished (from five top Oscar-winning films taken from plays in the 1960s down to zero in the following decade).[8] What all these figures point to is the emergence of cinema as an autonomous art form, rather than the adjunct to television, theatre or literature that it had frequently fallen into being.

Audiences came to realize that they could find in movies elements that television could not accommodate or countenance. Genre itself served as a concerted snub to televisual values: as hit movies like *M*A*S*H, American Graffiti* and *Alice Doesn't Live Here Anymore* were pulped into TV shows, horror, crime and porn movies reminded audiences that there were some things that would always remain incompatible with the demands of the 8 o'clock sitcom. The new cultural dynamic also

made accessible to English-speaking viewers the exotic vocabulary of world cinema; Corman's company New World had
bought many of those pictures for US distribution, which
meant that the latest works by Fellini, Truffaut or Kurosawa
were ushered on to American screens by the words 'Roger Corman Presents . . .' Then there was the scope and scale of the
movies; the opening shot of *Star Wars*, or the closing spectacle
of *Close Encounters*, could not be contained within the television frame. Or else this newly uninhibited medium could simply provide less highfalutin' pleasures. You might witness a flash
of nudity, a burst of violence; you might hear the word 'fuck'.

In January 1972, when audiences first saw Malcolm McDowell
drain a long, chilled glass of milk-plus and fix the camera with
his long, chilled stare at the start of *A Clockwork Orange*, I
was six months old, hanging off my mother's breast, glugging
my own milk. When Robert De Niro sauntered into a bar in
Mean Streets to the throbbing accompaniment of the Stones'
'Jumpin' Jack Flash' – a song that articulated what was going
on in his hips as much as what was going on in his head – I was
two, and taking cocksure steps of my own. On the same day
that *Taxi Driver* was released, and its writer Paul Schrader was
wandering over to a New York cinema to witness for himself
the opening-day queues, I was four years old, and impatient to
set eyes on my sister, who had been born early that morning.
Yes, I was the ideal age to absorb the first wave of *Star Wars*
hysteria. But when George Lucas's long-nurtured project *Apocalypse Now* finally reached the screen under the authoritative,
if less than steady, hand of Francis Ford Coppola, I could only
stare dumbly at the intimidating poster, where the title had
been slashed across an image of Marlon Brando's face which
seemed to be burning, melting, into teardrops of wax.

All of which is to assure you that I don't have any stories to
spin about how swell it was to be elbowing my way to the head

of the queue at the Bleecker St. cinema on the opening day of *Nashville*, or to be sipping cocktails with Martin Scorsese and Brian De Palma at Julia Phillips' housewarming. In a way, that is the point of this book: you don't need to have been there to have your life enriched by the energy and creativity of those years; you don't need to ascertain the colour and potency of the pills that were being popped during the making of *Taxi Driver* in order to be seduced by that picture's vivid, nightmarish romance. Those movies burned into the screen, and into our memories and imaginations, and they burn on. Of course, the stories exist if you want them. There were abundant portions of drugs and sex on offer to the artists who were in the process of rejuvenating cinema. And undoubtedly the climate of excess fed back into the work. It's hard to imagine that the film-makers who conjured visions as heady as *Apocalypse Now*, *The Long Goodbye* or *Taxi Driver* could have done so if a puritanical sensibility had found them in bed by ten each night with only a P. G. Wodehouse for company. But for anyone who did not experience the shock of those movies when the prints were still wet, when the names Scorsese and Spielberg were associated with potential rather than achievement, the gossip and scandals and salacious conjecture are just so much gift-wrapping: however distracting, however titillating, it all means nothing once you have reached the prize within.

I didn't know who the producer Robert Evans was the first time I saw *The Godfather*. I didn't know of his stormy private life (which he has celebrated too frequently in his own book and film, *The Kid Stays in the Picture*, to be allowed to spill on to these pages). And now that I do – now that I am familiar with his drug intake, his mental breakdown and the names of all his girlfriends – I find that this information neither enhances nor sullies the regal texture of Coppola's film. The fact that Woody Allen titled *Annie Hall* after the real name of his lead actress Diane Keaton, and that the movie itself was a fictionalized account of their relationship, are intriguing footnotes but I didn't know all that when I first saw the movie and marvelled at its mix of moods and styles and flavours. As for George Lucas's divorce, or who Steven Spielberg wanted to marry . . . well, it doesn't alter what is up there on the screen, and it certainly isn't what drives people to movies and keeps them there. That's down to the work. How that work altered the landscape of modern cinema is a more edifying and miraculous story than any amount of anecdotes about what the cokehead film-maker did with so-and-so's wife and her lesbian twin sister up at the *Playboy* mansion.

For most of us, irrespective of age, the movies of the past are not movies of the past at all. I hope this book will be a reminder of that. It isn't intended as a historical text. And it certainly didn't feel like one – only in the course of preparing the book did I see some of the rarer De Palmas, or a few of the out-of-circulation Altmans, for the first time. So if it occasionally feels as though I'm writing as the end credits are rolling – well, that's exactly what happened. To have regarded those works from a lofty, retrospective vantage point would have been fraudulent, not to say inappropriate. If there is one thing that most of these movies have in common, beyond the nationality of their creators, beyond the role they played in advancing cinema, it is that their power remains undimmed.

By the same token, it would be absurd to pretend that every film made in the 1970s by a young American director was touched by the hand of God. Readers may find cause to argue with a few of the names singled out for commendation in these pages, or to regret some of the omissions. Jonathan Demme gets his own chapter, but no comparable space is devoted to Peter Bogdanovich; Stanley Kubrick finds favour despite not having made a film in America since 1960, but the likes of William Friedkin and Hal Ashby are left out in the cold. Partly this comes down to personal bias, and partly to the effect that time has had on the work of those directors.

In the case of William Friedkin, it's both. He seems to me a man who happened to be in the right place at the right time, twice, and has spent the rest of his career trying to work out how he managed it. *The French Connection* and *The Exorcist* were hit movies that exploited cinema's new explicitness. But have you seen them lately? The finest directors communicate the medium's lightness along with its profundity. Watching a William Friedkin film is such a slog that you can just imagine the long hours, the on-set squabbles, the equipment being lugged out of the trucks each day. It's not art or entertainment; it's hard labour.

The years have been almost as unkind to Ashby. *The Last Detail* and *Shampoo* retain a tartness more easily ascribed to the writer, Robert Towne. But while preparing this book I watched again his fondly remembered *Harold and Maude*, and realized how perplexing and irrelevant it seems in the light of Jim Jarmusch and Hal Hartley, Wes Anderson and Spike Jonze, David O. Russell and Alexander Payne. This would-be stab at taboo material lacks the courage to remove the dagger from its sheath.

There is no chapter devoted to Peter Bogdanovich, because, for all the affection and craftsmanship of his first four pictures, he never fulfilled their promise. (And I say that as someone who can recite the script of *What's Up, Doc?* backwards.) It's true that George Lucas also failed to match the achievements of *THX 1138* and *American Graffiti*. But whereas the likes of *The Last Picture Show* and *Paper Moon* were skilful homages, Lucas's early pictures were important and influential works in their own right – and pivotal in understanding the evolution of *Star Wars*, a picture that for all its deficiencies irrevocably transformed movies and their audiences in ways that continue to impact on cinema today. And if there is one criterion determining the choice of directors assembled here, then that is it.

Demme is included because he made two of the most intriguing and inventive films of the 1970s (*Citizen's Band* and *Last Embrace*), and would proceed to repeat that accomplishment in the 1980s (with *Melvin and Howard* and *Something Wild*). Kubrick might have fled America, but he remained a

dominating figure in world cinema, and I would argue that the
brace of features that he made in the 1970s (*A Clockwork Orange* and *Barry Lyndon*) are as pertinent as anything by Coppola or Scorsese to the cinematic movement that is the focus of
this book. No one could debate the inclusion of Altman and De
Palma, Spielberg and Malick, but the book is intended to illustrate the cross-pollination of these film-makers, and how they
contributed in concert to this new American revolution.

Cinema is a treasure trail: everything leads somewhere; everything opens up new worlds. It's one of the things that sustain it.
When you stumble across a movie for the first time, it becomes
irrelevant when it was made. If a movie feels urgent to you – if
you daydream about it at your desk, your stove, your steering
wheel – then its history becomes superfluous. It may as well be
a freshly struck print; it may as well be opening at a cinema
near you next Friday.

The first time I tasted Robert Altman's 1970s work was in a
triple bill at a dank and underheated London repertory cinema
in the late 1980s. *McCabe and Mrs Miller*, *The Long Goodbye*
and *Thieves Like Us* – the best £5 I've ever spent. I had scam-
pered in from a blizzard: I was wearing a shawl of snow on the
shoulders of my coat, my ears were crisp and red, I had lost the
feeling in my fingers. I nursed a coffee in my front row seat and
thawed out. At least, that's the way I remember it. But I wonder
now if it had even been snowing that day, or if I had simply
fallen under the spell of that wintry first movie, *McCabe and
Mrs Miller*. When you're watching a film that's so sensual that
there ceases even to be any distance between you and the
screen, how can it matter when it was made? *McCabe and Mrs
Miller* was released in 1971, the year I was born. That afternoon it was as real and alive and immediate to me as the
snowflakes that – I maintain – were melting off my boots and
dangling from my eyelashes.

1. Francis Ford Coppola

In the films of Francis Ford Coppola, size matters. This robust Italian-American ogre, with a protuberant beard beneath which small children might seek shelter from the rain, has throughout his career tamed projects bigger than himself, or inadvertently trampled those too delicate for his extravagant tastes. Size itself often seems the subject of his work, and the motivation for his choices. When his movies were small, he was thinking big. But when a studio tried to pressgang him into an ostentatious project such as *Mame*, he instead rushed into something more modest, like *The Rain People*, before the spectre of that bloated pay-cheque made him crazy. 'By just starting to do [*The Rain People*], I'll prevent myself from succumbing to all these other offers,' he told himself.[1] Couldn't he see that those offers would always be there, and that they were as crucial a part of his film-making apparatus as cameras and boom mikes?

The story of Coppola in the 1970s is characterized by polarities and conflicts often of his own making. While *The Rain People* was being mistreated by its distributor and ignored by audiences, Coppola was winning the Best Screenplay Oscar for co-writing the hyperbolic screenplay for the 1969 film *Patton*. When he accepted the commission to direct *The Godfather* in

Making *The Conversation* (1974): Gene Hackman confers with Francis Ford Coppola. (© Paramount Pictures)

The Conversation: Gene Hackman as Harry Caul. (© Paramount Pictures)

1971, it was only because his idealistic San Francisco studio American Zoetrope was floundering. Between shooting the first two *Godfather* films – scuzzy but expansively scaled crime melodramas – he crafted *The Conversation*, a weirdly internalized thriller that aspired to a European arthouse aesthetic. The latter picture even contains the line, 'Since when are you here to be entertained?' – ostensibly delivered by the hero to his assistant, but sounding more like a warning to anyone in the audience who has the temerity to expect a good time. A pattern of perpetual struggle was set in motion. Down on his luck, he would grudgingly accept hacks' work, and breathe fire into it. Overburdened with armfuls of Academy Awards, he would sniff out something downbeat or dangerous. His restlessness became compulsive, and fruitful.

Each film seems partly a response to its predecessor, partly an ongoing effort to locate a suitably proportioned canvas. Some, like *The Conversation* and *The Godfather Part II*, which both opened in 1974, seem to have evolved by osmosis, a Watergate-fresh paranoia and dread seeping from one to the other, encouraged by the fact that both feature prominently an actor (John Cazale) who resembles Nixon reborn as a ventriloquist's dummy.

And yet the 'big' films are no less personal than the 'small' ones. If anything, there is a shortfall in passion on more modest projects like *The Conversation* and 1983's *Rumblefish*, as though Coppola requires a generous expanse of screen and story to give him room to manoeuvre within his characters' world. This director is prone to contradictory impulses: he's a gregarious loner, naturally inclined toward the hubbub, but compelled to seek out the loneliness and isolation at its centre. Nowhere is he more at home than at the wedding party in *The Godfather*, moving from the sun-kissed revellers and excitable whippersnappers, to the shadowy chambers a mere breath away where men's lives are being mapped out or curtailed. Such contrasts keep his movies alive, which could be why parts of *The Conversation* seem fog-headed. It's as though there isn't enough in that slender mystery to hold his fascination – nothing to compare with the ambition and dexterity required to conceive of the crosscutting at the end of *The Godfather* and *Apocalypse Now*, and throughout *The Godfather Part II*.

After finishing *The Conversation*, Coppola had told fellow director Brian De Palma, 'What I hope to do in the future is make only personal films – but in such a way that even my big projects will be what you would call personal films.'² Like Werner Herzog, he needs that friction to survive: he needs projects like *Apocalypse Now* and *Megalopolis* that are conceived not just as movies but myths in their own right. But unlike Herzog, it hasn't overtaken his desire to simply hammer out a good yarn. You can still discern in Coppola the industriousness that characterized his work for Roger Corman. Sometimes it is mangled by his failure to correctly assess the scale of a project; you can feel him fighting for clarity among the necessary ambiguities of *The Conversation*, whereas in *Apocalypse Now* you wait in vain for him to rediscover precisely that instinct, that purity. But even if his instinct for storytelling is in conflict with the material, it's in him – it's there.

Coppola got his first directing job from Corman, on the 1963 horror cheapie *Dementia 13*. He also directed parts of *The Terror* (1963), but then there weren't many people from the Corman stable who didn't: Monte Hellman and Jack Nicholson were among the numerous other directors on a picture that was shot, says Corman, 'in two days without a finished script because I hated to see the wonderful gothic sets for *The Raven* go to waste when we wrapped'.³ (Coppola had wasted no time appealing to Corman's instinct for recycling: he had landed the job on *Dementia 13* by convincing his mentor that they might as well knock off another picture while they had the equipment unpacked anyway to shoot *The Young Racers*.)

Gradually, Coppola accumulated writing assignments that

helped him inch forward within the industry. 'Coppola at that time was my shining star,' said Steven Spielberg, 'because here was a student from UCLA, who was writing professionally, who was making a living from his writing, and just starting out as a director . . . Francis was the first inspiration to a lot of young film-makers, because he broke through before many others.'[4]

He shot a laboriously zany comedy, *You're a Big Boy Now*, in 1966, and the clunky but sweet-natured musical *Finian's Rainbow* the following year. The long-awaited realization of his pungent road movie *The Rain People* – which he had first written in 1960 under the title *Echoes* – inspired Coppola to establish American Zoetrope, named for the revolving light-and-picture contraption that predated the movie projector. 'The basis for what Francis wanted the company to be was friendship and exchange of ideas,' said Bob Dalva, who edited Carroll Ballard's 1979 Zoetrope film *The Black Stallion*.[5] Within this idealistic collective Coppola gathered together like-minded writers and directors – among them George Lucas, who dreamed of making movies that were 'experimental, plotless, technically engaging',[6] and the writers Matthew Robbins and Hal Barwood (who later wrote *The Sugarland Express* for Steven Spielberg, as well as doing uncredited work on *Jaws* and *Close Encounters of the Third Kind*) – in the hope of creating artistic independence from the studios. However, with Zoetrope soon relying on financing from Warner Bros, this quickly became a fragile conceit.

Warner Bros donated $600,000 so that Coppola could take American Zoetrope through the leap from film company to full-scale studio in its own right. But the film giant became jittery about the scant commercial potential of the scripts that Coppola provided in exchange for the funds, and was soon demanding its cash back. A viewing of *THX 1138*, the disturbing futuristic thriller that Lucas had made for Zoetrope, only confirmed the studio's fears. It was, however, keen to retain two of the screenplays which it believed had commercial potential. One was *The Conversation*, which Coppola had written between 1967 and 1969; the other was *Apocalypse Now*, Milius's loose adaptation of Conrad's novel *Heart of Darkness*, which Lucas was planning to shoot as a 16mm, on-the-hoof quickie. Coppola, who cherished both screenplays, had to swallow his pride and buy them back. Milius emerged unscathed: Warner Bros had been so impressed with *Apocalypse Now* that they bought one of his earlier screenplays, *Jeremiah Johnson*, and sent him to work on *The Life and Times of Judge Roy Bean*. But Coppola had no choice but to accept the humbling task of directing *The Godfather*.

The most spectacular clash in *The Godfather* is between the dimestore grubbiness of the material, and the top-dollar gloss of its presentation. Mario Puzo's Mafia sleazefest could rightly be called a page-turner, if those pages weren't gummed together with the sweat and saliva that oozes out of its titillating prose. Like Peter Benchley's *Jaws*, Puzo's novel adhered so purely to the exploitation formula that Corman himself must have been forced to tip his hat in admiration. And just as Carl Gottlieb filleted and refined Benchley's book for Spielberg's film, so Coppola chiselled away at the grime on *The Godfather* in order that it might be passed off as a throwback to the comforting glamour of the Hollywood melodrama. The movie looks dignified in that way that makes the movie industry feel good about itself; 'it has even been called the *Gone with the Wind* of gangster movies,'[7] proclaimed one magazine.

It was the perfect con. Of course, the picture *does* look magnificent. Maybe too magnificent – the grandeur can work on the viewer like a moral anaesthetic, as it clearly has done on Coppola, and the film gives you precious little enticement to tempt you out of that awestruck slumber. Even the swathes of shadow that earned the cinematographer Gordon Willis his nickname, the Prince of Darkness, have a decadent, chocolatey allure. The rows of Studebakers snoozing in the Corleone family driveway, gleaming in the afternoon sun, are like cockroaches that you would happily keep as pets. But the movie's sumptuous surface makes possible its intrinsic commentary on modern American mores, its enquiries into the efficiency of justice, the shortcomings of patriotism, the dynamics of father–son relationships. It's a work that assumes the iconography of the past for the business of questioning the present.

In 1972, the subject matter benefited from topicality; its release, noted one writer, 'coincided with a grisly Mafia carnival in New York (bodies stuffed into auto trunks or thrown into rivers – that sort of thing)'.[8] And there was a more deliberate pertinence in its unresolved torment over the patriarchal family structure, which neatly coincided with the new movie culture that was preoccupied with challenging convention. Coppola's ethnic background made him affectionately predisposed toward the Corleone family's rituals of camaraderie, and there were enough traces of dissent to suggest the potential for a more corrosive investigation.

But only just. The editorial distance that Coppola forged between himself and the Corleones' romanticized self-image is negligible. Even the crosscutting between the baptism of Michael's son and the murders that are being carried out at Michael's behest is a touch too masterful to be properly appalling. In fact, any sign of a critique on Coppola's part can be narrowed down to one image: when the Mafia boss Vito Corleone (Marlon Brando) learns that a plot to avenge his attempted assassination was instigated by his son Michael (Al Pacino), whom he had believed would be unsullied by the family business, his eyelids mournfully and involuntarily clamp shut. In that ripple of grief, Brando gives us a hint of emotions too hazardous for Coppola to confront, at least in this picture. Until that moment we have received no sign that Vito Corleone feels anything but pride and contentment in his life. And yet here he crumbles at the possibility that Michael is continuing the cycle that he himself began. There is self-disgust in that

gesture, as well as dread, disappointment and helplessness –
Vito's affronted eyes, his downturned mouth, point toward the
words of Michael's wife Kay (Diane Keaton) in *The Godfather
Part II* as she justifies to Michael the abortion of their child: 'I
wouldn't bring another one of your sons into this world . . .
I had it killed because this must all end.'

We have been adequately prepared for Kay's exclusion from
the Corleone family from the moment that Michael uses a pay-
phone to find out about his father's condition, and forbids her
from entering the inner sanctum of the phone booth; she's
forced to loiter outside, peering in, trying and failing to discern
from the vaguest signs what is going on in the life and the mind
of the man she loves. As a hint of how their life together will
progress, or rather not, it's as damning as it is conclusive. But
Vito's own admission of dissent is more disturbing, and there's
a case to be made that the entire second instalment of the *Godfather* series is founded on that fleeting expression, that moment when he realizes that none of his offspring will succeed in
escaping the family curse – that each of them will at some point
be clasping themselves as he now does, wracked with the agony
of foresight.

Brando's physical appearance in the role is an inventive mix
of majesty and disintegration that corresponds with the film itself. He has passed imperceptibly into stock material for comics
and impressionists – an entirely natural progression given the
close proximity of physical comedy to Brando's conception of
Vito. Even now, you can feel how hazardous his playing is. The
long face culminates in a bulldog mouth: the mouth is like a
black hole, into which the rest of his features are sucked; from
somewhere in that hole comes the kind of voice that suggests a
lifetime of sword swallowing topped off with a deathbed dose
of morphine. Damaged but drowsy, he is trying to make sense
of a world that from the moment we meet him he is on the
verge of exiting. Coppola would use Brando as the bait at the
end of the river for both the hero and the audience of *Apocalypse Now*, and *The Godfather* inverts the same gimmick.

When Vito Corleone is gunned down early in the narrative, we feel a shock disproportionate to our empathy with the character. It's more the case that Brando has been such a commanding presence, we can't conceive of how the film will continue in his absence. And so Coppola exploits our selfish investment in our own pleasure – that is, our desire to savour more of this exquisite actor – in order to intensify our involvement in the narrative. Simply by keeping Brando alive, even if he is off-screen in a hospital bed, Coppola is guaranteeing our commitment.

Brando's size, coupled with the scale of his past achievements, also plays its part in imprinting him on our memories. Harry Lime in *The Third Man* would not have carried quite the same mercurial charge if he had been played by, say, Fred MacMurray as opposed to Orson Welles. What Welles had at that point, and what Brando had when he played Vito Corleone – and later Colonel Kurtz in *Apocalypse Now* – was a uniquely volatile kind of celebrity. These men are troublemakers, not gameplayers. If Brando, more obviously suited to the howling-at-the-moon passions of Bertolucci's *Last Tango in Paris*, seemed like a risky choice for *The Godfather*, which was released in the same year, then no such uncertainty hung around *Apocalypse Now*. By the time that movie opened in 1979, it seemed possible that Brando might one day establish his own barbaric colony in a corner of unpolluted jungle – that would at least be more beneficial to his reputation than the prospect of a future filled with soulless star cameos like his one in *Superman The Movie*.

The Godfather and *Last Tango in Paris* provided Brando with a nutritious feast after suspicions that – with a few exceptions (such as John Huston's 1967 *Reflections in a Golden Eye*, for which Coppola had written the first draft) – he had been getting by on titbits ill-suited to his diet (like Michael Winner's *The Nightcomers*). With the revival of the Hollywood movie – and in 1972, when *The Godfather* opened, cinema admissions did climb steeply – came the return of this wayward giant.

Coppola's eye for iconic casting is astute. Besides trading on the tarnished glory of Brando for *The Godfather*, and his unassailable cult following for *Apocalypse Now*, there is the use of Dennis Hopper too in the latter picture, as a photojournalist festooned with cameras and too full of chatter. Hopper had acted, on and off, in the eight years since *The Last Movie* – his reviled 1971 follow-up to *Easy Rider* – was made. But most viewers must have looked at him playing Kurtz's court jester in Cambodia and thought, 'Oh, so that's where he's been all these years.' (Many more might have willed his return to obscurity after witnessing his mannered performance, bizarrely encouraged by Coppola.)

And who else would have had the good sense to foresee the decrepit menace that Lee Strasberg would bring to the vinegary crime boss Hyman Roth in *The Godfather Part II*? Strasberg had been director of the influential Actors' Studio since 1949, and a tutor to, among others, Al Pacino, James Dean and Marilyn Monroe. As played by Strasberg, Roth's physical frailty only accentuates his mental agility. All that power in the hands of a man too unsteady to aim straight at the urinal! And still we can see his brain fizzing with bloodthirsty plots that he is too broken to implement personally. The idea that Pacino is now wrestling with this gorgon, his former teacher, under cover of reverence, lends a suspenseful poignancy to the battle of wills between Michael Corleone and Hyman Roth that provides *The Godfather Part II* with some of its keenest flashes of social embarrassment.

That movie must seem a curious kind of sequel for anyone weaned on *Rocky*s and *Terminator*s, *Omen*s and *Airport*s. Its connection to its predecessor more closely resembles the relationship between *Cat People* and *Curse of the Cat People*, or *The French Connection* and *French Connection II*, two sets of movies that use brand familiarity as a means of ambushing the audience, persuading them to accept something they might otherwise consider peculiar or unpalatable. If *The French Connection* had included those same, gruelling scenes of heroin addiction and cold turkey that constitute a significant part of the sequel – well, then there might not have been a sequel.

The Godfather Part II pulls off an even more audacious trick. Our familiarity with the characters is not just a way for Coppola to confront us with a more complex picture than we might otherwise accept. Familiarity actually becomes part of the subject of the film itself, through the contrasts between this movie and our memory of the original, and between the two interlocking story streams: one strand scrutinizes Michael Corleone as he rots on his new throne; the other follows Vito from his childhood in turn-of-the-century Sicily to his escape to America after his parents' murders, and his ascension through the ranks of a neighbourhood protection racket in Little Italy.

The movie superficially resembles its predecessor. Gordon Willis again shot much of the film in a virtual blackout. (When Vito unscrews the lightbulbs prior to performing his first assassination, it's as though he is moonlighting as Willis's assistant.) Only now the darkness isn't just deep and rich, it has an aggressive physical presence. The black recesses of Michael's study look plush, like something into which you could sink your fingers. The atmosphere itself is like leather upholstery, the air in that room impedes the characters' movements. It takes an age to raise a glass, or to advance a few steps. The darkness gathers in Michael's hollowed cheeks like pools of oil, just as it did in his father's eye sockets. Dean Tavoularis once more designed the sets, which seem to have increased in austerity. It would be less plausible in the new Corleone residence for something as frivolous as the deflowering of a bridesmaid to take place, as it did in the original picture. The oppressive gloom rules out anything more hot-blooded than necrophilia.

Coppola retains most of the characters from the first instalment, though each appears in a dramatic state of decay or disfigurement that confounds the hint of family reunion inherent in most sequels. Michael Corleone looks in graver need of a good mortician than his dead father: the formerly boyish Pacino has calcified; he moves more slowly than ever, like a pall-bearer doomed to perpetual procession. When he lunges to strike his wife, or dives to the floor to dodge gunfire, it's like seeing a corpse rise suddenly from the slab. Even the Brylcreem in his hair looks like it was smeared there to snare wayward flies; you can imagine him counting his gold bars in the wee hours, and reaching into his hair for a midnight snack. (Coppola's 1991 film *Bram Stoker's Dracula* was inevitably handicapped by having had its thunder stolen in this picture by Pacino: he's Nosferatu and Renfield both.)

Evil is a cinch to play. The true potency of Pacino's performance is in the lightning flashes of panic that he reveals in Michael, when a moment's eavesdropping confirms Fredo's betrayals, or when Kay tells him that she had their child aborted. In the second that the confession leaves her lips, we fear for her – all that arctic macho pride that he lugs around on his back like a Charles Atlas globe will have to fall somewhere, and we brace ourselves for the damage it will wreak. But we may also cheer this little death, for it confirms that all power over mortality does not reside in Michael's hands. Kay fights back in the only manner available to her now that Michael has got her cornered. If she can't get at him out there, she's going to do it in here – in her womb, the only province over which he has no dominion, and the one most pivotal to his plan for supremacy.

Michael's sister Connie (Talia Shire) now has a complacent, druggy stupor to match her brother's malaise. Fredo (John Cazale) has a sharply receding hairline, but one that actually seems to be receding as you look at it, along with his moral fortitude. The comely beauty of Kay (Diane Keaton) has hardened too, and now she resembles a first lady who understands too well that she is anything but first in her husband's affections. That knowledge has aged her: in the first film, she wore a quizzical summer hat that suited her quizzical summer manner – she seemed always to be pleasantly reclining in a sunbeam; now she looks most at home bent over the sewing machine. She is fraught with introspection – you can read in her face the long evenings spent alone gazing out over Lake Tahoe, forbidden from leaving the house, not knowing where her husband or her life have gone. And now she must guard herself even against her own children. When her eldest son, Anthony, whispers to Michael, who is leaving on a business trip, 'I could help you,' those words are not merely a child's innocent request to accompany his father to the office, but a reminder of the cycle in which Kay has dramatically interceded. Yes, he could help him, just as soon as he is old enough to inherit his daddy's shark-eyes and his shark's taste for human blood.

The sense of waste in Kay is surprisingly forceful. You could put it down to the baggage that Keaton brings to the film in the form of her collaborations with Woody Allen. When the time came to reprise her role as Kay, she was on her way to becoming Allen's regular sparring partner, and his equal in comic vim; they had appeared together on stage and film in *Play It Again, Sam*, and in Allen's movie *Sleeper*. Immediately after *The Godfather Part II* she was at her most effervescent in *Love and Death*. Coppola's instincts were bang on the money. What better way to articulate the despair of a woman crushed by her dictatorial husband than to hire an actress renowned for her champagne fizz and then force her to play flat?

Only the Corleones' lawyer Tom Hagen (Robert Duvall) remains unchanged in the sequel. But then Tom is the eternal shock-absorber for the atrocities perpetrated by the Corleones; he cleans up the corpses that they leave in their wake, and he doesn't speak out of turn. (He's a man ahead of his time: he would have made a hell of a spin doctor.) Whatever horrors his kindly, stoical face glances upon are absorbed into his blood and bones, leaving no trace of remorse, no ripple of disgust. I wouldn't like to peek inside him. With Michael and Connie and Fredo, the corruption is plainly visible in the rigor mortis pallor of the skin. But who knows what condition Tom Hagen's body is in, after decades of playing host to the family's gnawing, cancerous secrets?

Coppola's masterstroke in *The Godfather Part II* is to intermittently provide relief from the suffocating mausoleum of the Corleone residence with the oxygen of scenes in Sicily and Little Italy. This is an improvement over the first picture, where the audience's respite from the ultra-noir setting was provided by Michael's escape to Sicily, which had the slightly artificial ring of a film-within-a-film. In the later picture, the scenes more fruitfully cross-pollinate one another, and the textural levity of the passages featuring young Vito in turn removes the burden of tonal variation from Michael's various trips. The pressure to 'lighten up' the movie for the audience's eyes does not therefore rest on Miami, which looks as fittingly sad and seedy as Hyman Roth, whom Michael is visiting there, or Havana, where the sleaziness of a sado-masochistic stage show introduces a shrill note of carnal menace into the Corleones' sexless universe.

As well as the Sicilian sunshine, the grubby vitality of Little Italy, and the subtle changes in costume and colour, Coppola can bank on Robert De Niro's measured but zesty performance as the young Vito Corleone to temper the malignancy of the latter-day scenes. It says something about Coppola's insight, and foresight, that he could look at the unkempt, ramshackle De Niro in Martin Scorsese's *Mean Streets* and locate within that tornado of hair and fists the precise poise and patience it would take to create Vito. Pacino's beauty has drained by the first scene of the second film; his whole body seems to hang off that set of cliff-edge cheekbones that look sharp enough to sever a horse's head. The life that thrummed in Pacino in the first picture has passed here to De Niro, with his soulful eyes, his strong arms, the bohemian beauty spot that suggests ink impetuously flung from a quill.

Both actors are working from the model of Brando in *The Godfather*. Pacino's shoulders have risen to meet his ears. He has the hunched sluggishness with which Brando was afflicted in the first film. Meanwhile, De Niro studies Brando's performance and works backward from it: whereas Brando's voice was coarse to the point of being unintelligible, De Niro takes us

back to a time when the vocal chords weren't quite the texture
of sandpaper, when his voice suggested five miles of rough road
rather than fifty. In one scene, he even manages to imitate
Brando's swollen face by making movements that suggest he's
chewing on his own tongue.

The juxtapositions between these three actors form part of
the repertoire of contrasts employed by Coppola to stimulate
our imagination, and our sense of irony. He uses dissolves between the film's time-frames, rather than cuts, to emphasize
how the characters flow into one another. One stunning transition, between Michael learning of (what he believes to be)
Kay's miscarriage, and Vito helplessly looking on at young
Fredo wracked with pneumonia, makes it appear that Michael
is actually being absorbed into his father's body. In *The Godfather*, Coppola proved himself a master of crosscutting; here,
he fuses scenes together, working against the cold grain of the
edit, so that the camera appears to transcend temporal and spa-
tial divides. The very concept of a sequel, the ceaseless rapport
between past and present, becomes the spark for the film's emotional life, a spark that would be extinguished were the scenes
to be arranged in chronological order (as they were in Coppola's re-editing of the first two films for a TV version: without
the profound mutual nourishment that the scenes of Vito and
Michael gave to one another, it played like an above-average
mini-series based on a departure-lounge bestseller).

The modern sequel has become very much like the modern
film trailer, with its glossy packaging of thrills, selling-points
and plot-signposts designed only to reassure us that our price of
admission will not be risked on a rank outsider. *The Godfather
Part II* doesn't conform to those specifications; it may initially
look, feel and smell like the first movie, but its tone is uglier
and more remorseful, and the film has the air of a solemn re-
pentance for cinematic sins.

The Godfather Part II brings sharply into focus those moments of unresolved discomfort that we might have felt during

The Godfather, as when the film goads us into rooting for Sonny and shuddering at his death (his demise is so melodramatic that he himself might have choreographed it), or encourages our beaming approval every time another character promises to make an offer that can't be refused. Just as no one seems capable of uttering that catchphrase without succumbing at least partly to a self-satisfied smile, so *The Godfather*, seen without the mordant riposte provided by its sequel, accelerates the pop-culture transformation of ghouls into vaudeville entertainers and matinee idols – the volatile defender Sonny, the ineffectual Fredo fumbling with his gun as his father is assassinated, the dashing and good-mannered Michael proving altogether too keen to demonstrate that an Italian-American's gotta do what an Italian-American's gotta do. The family is excessively appealing, and the Corleones' weakness in the face of attack only increases our empathy; our hearts swell at the sight of these bloodthirsty bullies and murderers facing the threat of being usurped.

But the second film makes bitter sense of the first. Without it, *The Godfather* would not have weathered the years so well. It might even have aged as graphically as *Dirty Harry*, another celebration of male power that also uses the vulnerability of a borderline-anachronistic hero to solicit our goodwill for old-fashioned, uncomplicated violence. While that picture's four sequels simplified and compounded the brutality of the initial concept, *The Godfather Part II* brings illuminating shadings to the existing text, providing another example of the beneficial interplay between past and present. *The Godfather* is altered, enhanced and redeemed in its presence, just as Michael's descent into Hell, which would on its own be chilling, becomes genuinely heartbreaking when seen through the gauze of his father's ambitions. It would diminish the movie to say that it adheres to a flashback structure; on the contrary, the two eras appear to be unfolding simultaneously, each informing the other.

Likewise, the landscape of the second film casts dramatic shadows across its predecessor, and our responses to it. Take Michael's boast from the first film, for instance: 'My father made him an offer he couldn't refuse.' How the audience warms to the ease with which liberty and violence are rendered synonymous. We imagine ourselves the beneficiaries of this deal, never the ones whose 'brains or signature' will be on the contract in question. 'When the courts fail you,' noted Coppola, 'and the whole American system fails you, you can go to the Old Man – Don Corleone – and say, "Look what they did to me," and you get justice. I think there is a tremendous hunger in this country, if not in the world, for that kind of clear, benevolent authority.'[9] That key word 'benevolent' betrays the failings of that first *Godfather* film. When the Corleones' business methods are visualized for our delectation in the film's most notorious scene, the merest hint of jeopardy is eliminated by the swooning horror of the brutality (a horse's head deposited in a man's bed) and the calculated arrogance of the victim, who had thought himself beyond the Corleones' influence. The horror doesn't impinge on us any more than the on-screen blood stains our clothes. The man's bestial screams, together with his silver bouffant and sullied silks, make him as repugnant as the severed head itself. Every possible measure is taken to forestall our sympathy and disgust, so that we interpret the scene as a glorious display of power, rather than an act of squalid violence.

This is generally consistent with the tone of the first movie. Kay represents the slim hope of redemption, first when she visibly winces at Michael's anecdotal recollection of his father's violence, and later when she is physically and symbolically barred from family business by a closing door. Only in that shot, which ends the film, does Coppola appear to have grasped the extent to which he has made the audience culpable. Kay is excluded, but from the position of the camera – inside the darkness of Michael's study, looking out at her – it is we who are excluding her. We are in that study with Michael, sipping from his dustless tumblers, colluding in his miniature apocalypses. We have succumbed, like weak politicians bending to the favour of a despot. We should be ashamed of ourselves.

And, in *The Godfather Part II*, I think we *are* made to feel ashamed at last. There is a scene midway through the film when a senator who has previously expressed his hatred of Michael is forced to kow-tow to him, to publicly and humiliatingly flatter him. What we are feeling must be very close to what Michael feels: what a worm, what a wretch. We experience Michael's luxurious sense of superiority flooding our own veins, and we feel swollen with smugness. This senator is every man by whom we have ever been wronged or badmouthed, presented here before us, grovelling on his knees.

Then it happens: the bad penny drops. The only reason that the senator is grovelling is because Michael is responsible for having made an ugly situation vanish – the murder, apparently by the senator, of a prostitute in an establishment owned by the Corleones. Of course, it was Michael himself who created that ugly situation in the first place. And now, as we realize that our gratification has been cruelly engineered, and our self-righteousness grossly misplaced, an earlier line of dialogue returns to us like buried grief. As the slaughtered prostitute lay sprawled among the blood-drenched sheets, her corpse engendering in us no greater compassion than we had felt at the sight of that horse's head, Tom had perused the scene. And like a macabre magician, he had assured the senator, 'It'll be as though she never existed.'

How abominable, we might have thought, that a life can be swallowed into thin air. And yet we are the ones who have made it happen. We have helped to cover the Corleones' tracks, to prepare the unmarked grave, simply by forgetting that woman's murder long enough to congratulate ourselves, and Michael, on the senator's metamorphosis from tormentor to foot soldier. Tom was right: it is, indeed, as though she never existed.

The ability of cinema to implicate us in wrongdoings of which we would never be capable in our waking lives is one of this art form's fundamental appeals. We have all committed thousands of murders there in the dark, just as we have all conducted thousands of love affairs and bank robberies, and died a thousand deaths. But the unique capacity of *The Godfather Part II* is to tangle up our guilt with compassion and remorse. Plenty of film-makers can persuade us to identify with a monster. Rarer are those who cause our sympathies and allegiances to fluctuate within the space of a single scene, a single shot.

I am still trying to unpick my feelings about the scene where Michael disowns Fredo ('You're nothing to me now') and warns him not to approach their mother without first giving a day's notice. It's a quiet scene; but how it deafens. We despise Michael, but we feel his outrage at Fredo; we pity Fredo, but we have witnessed Michael's wrath. And we know that this puny rag-doll of a man will barely be able to withstand his brother's scorn, let alone face the bottomless reserves of cruelty which Michael has discovered in himself since filling his father's chair. The men are no more than silhouettes set against the merciless brightness of Lake Tahoe in winter. It's cold out there, in the snow, in the icy water, but inside it's colder. Michael enjoys his stillness, his mastery over his own body language, while Fredo – awkwardly reclining in the lounger like a mortified patient anticipating the dentist's drill – can't stop his arms from flailing, his body from convulsing. Out there, in the water, is where he will eventually die. Perhaps he can feel it; perhaps that's why he can't keep still.

The scene is tough in the guise of tenderness. It's the threat of murder issued with one unfaltering eye trained on discretion and etiquette, like when Tom visits Frankie Pentangeli in prison and cryptically urges him on to suicide. As that conversation ebbs along, the two men savour their cigars and bask in the sunshine. They might be discussing the shortcomings of the seventeenth hole, or boasting of grandchildren.

Death is sometimes terrible in these films, but it can always be mastered by euphemisms and lowered voices. What's really frightening is the prospect of something uncontrollable – a drunken fracas, a round of fisticuffs, anything that suggests human behaviour disrespectful of strategy. It isn't right, surely, that the Corleone men are more visibly disturbed by the sight of a drunken woman causing a disturbance on the dance floor than by virtually anything else in the picture. Part of their panic can be attributed to the fear of women that permeates the movie. Women function here as pawns to give the family leverage, whether it's the prostitute whose murder implicates the senator, or Kay herself, whose function has simply been to bear Michael's heir. Any woman who doesn't fit that category must be forcibly removed, and is. Women symbolize the threat of vulnerability: to get close to a woman, you must first remove your holster, or at least put down your gun, and no Corleone is ever going to agree to that.

Before the second *Godfather* film, Coppola had made *The Conversation*, and in that too the threat of intimacy is synonymous with the prospect of defeat and self-annihilation; more than that, it becomes the whole subject of the film. That picture's protagonist, Harry Caul (Gene Hackman), is a taciturn surveillance boffin who keeps himself under lock and key. Even his appearance – his clipped little moustache, his rain-mac, his trim spectacles – suggests a disguise picked up in a joke shop. The prevailing irony of Coppola's concept is that Harry has nothing to guard. 'I don't have anything personal,' he confesses. 'Nothing of value. Except my keys.' Even those keys provide access to an apartment that contains only Harry's privacy. Which is the film's point: Harry imagines himself vulnerable to some physical or emotional violation, but in his paranoia he perpetuates that vulnerability. It may even be his reason for living. He enjoys visiting his girlfriend (Teri Garr) less than the prospect of discovering her with her trousers down, or her hand in the cookie jar ('You think you're gonna catch me at something,' she bleats). Without the threat of intrusion Harry wouldn't know how to function: penetrating other people's lives, and protecting himself from those who would do likewise to him, gives him his only purpose.

The world he inhabits is barricaded with deterrents and warnings, but they are no more reliable than the simple 'Private' sign that we glimpse on an office door. That sign in turn is as ineffectual a provision against external forces as the paper seal on the hotel toilet is against the blood that will come gushing out of that bowl. But even those defences are sturdier than Harry's protestations of ignorance in the face of the consequences of his work. He doesn't notice that the squeal of the reels on his tape machine is indistinguishable from a human scream. He fails to see how his actions implicate him in the big picture. Like Captain Willard (Martin Sheen) in *Apocalypse Now*, who only gradually comes to understand the symbolic nature of his mission to kill the renegade Colonel Kurtz, Harry must be brutally tutored in the relationship between personal and political.

It's a stark idea, and one that Coppola has some difficulty animating, or rather not animating. Part of the film's problem lies in the suspicion that he views Harry's downfall as a weird kind of triumph, a fulfilment of the masochistic austerity to which the movie itself is in thrall, but to which it can never completely surrender. The ending, in which Harry destroys his own apartment – even in one still-shocking gesture breaking open a statuette of the Virgin Mary – is a challenge to audience expectations of resolution; it's also consistent with the self-questioning mood of early 1970s cinema that contributed to the hero's disillusionment in *The Long Goodbye*, his defeat in *Chinatown*, his death in *The Parallax View* and the assassination in *Nashville*. It wasn't just that writers and directors were plumping for unhappy endings: the creative and political climate made possible and necessary endings that were in a sense not endings at all, but lunges into the unknown. Cataclysmic modern events like Vietnam and Watergate had temporarily relieved society of the comfort of good guys and bad guys and happy-ever-afters. Films like *The Conversation* tended to a new need, not so much for answers as for an acknowledgement that such commodities were hard to come by.

It's a measure of how desperately the film needs its inconclusiveness – played out in the equivocal punctuation of its final scene – that when Harry turned up twenty-four years later in Tony Scott's movie *Enemy of the State* (under the name 'Brill', but again played by Hackman, and to all intents and purposes Harry Caul) there was a sense of betrayal. We could be forgiven for feeling disappointed that the character was still alive, or at least not eating his meals through a straw and wearing a nappy. We had witnessed Harry's disintegration: to find him in a fit state to play grouchy sidekick to Will Smith was a slight on the finality of Coppola's movie, and an in-joke too far.

Although *The Conversation* needs that ending, I would like to see it savoured a little less. I think Coppola has trouble knowing how to scale the movie, so the destruction of the apartment becomes climactic, when in fact the movie doesn't need a climax. It's a small picture for Coppola; he has at his disposal a handful of actors, a few cramped and chilly sets, and an ephemeral enigma that hinges on nothing more than the stresses in a single sentence. (Few movies, with the obvious exception of Derek Jarman's *Blue*, can have depended for their success on the audience's ability to simply listen.) But without the opportunity for sweeping contrasts provided by the *Godfather* films, his work feels caged. While that might seem an ideal quality to bring to a movie as claustrophobic as *The Conversation*, it actually has an adverse effect: Coppola's fussiness, his compulsion to embroider every corner of the frame, every page of the script, with mystery or back-story, deprives the picture of its necessary sense of desolation. It's a chamber piece visibly troubled by its own minimalism.

The detachment discernible occasionally in the camera does not appear to be shared by the man behind it; he's making an arthouse thriller, as self-consciously as Woody Allen would later make *Interiors* an arthouse melodrama, but unlike Allen he wants to give the audience more than the material demands. In several scenes, the camera appears to be set to motion-activated autopilot; it moves to follow Harry, or searches for him when he has vacated the frame. It's a splendidly cold technique, and you can't help wondering how the film would have fared if Coppola had been brave enough to resort to it more often – to see, as Stanley Kubrick did, that form need not confine itself to the comfort of the audience. Indeed, *The Conversation* is most convincing when all traces of human interference have been expunged; when the plaintive, tinkling piano motif has been replaced by a hideous electronic gurgling that suggests an android's death rattle; when the camera seems to stop dead.

Coppola has confessed to having difficulty thinking himself into his hero's head. Referring to those memories which he used to elucidate Harry's past, and which were borrowed from his own youth, he candidly admitted, 'I could never feel anything for the character . . . That was almost a desperate attempt to give him a real character that I could relate to.'[10] The scene in the confession box and Harry's dream are Coppola's concessions to the audience's demands for an explanatory back-story, and to his own. Without the wealth of information that Harry is unlikely to voluntarily surrender, Coppola is lost; with it, the viewer can feel overburdened. If the trend for expanding movies subsides, if directors cease equating the definitive cut with the longest possible one, then let there also be a turn toward fine-tuning from which *The Conversation* could benefit; toward removing those scenes that were inserted to comfort the audience, so that we might feel something of the chill of unexplained abandonment that you get in the bravest work of Chabrol or Antonioni (whose 1966 *Blow-Up* is an obvious precursor to Coppola's picture).

Each of the four movies that Coppola directed in the 1970s (and, to a lesser extent, his screenplay for the timid 1974 film

of *The Great Gatsby*) deals in some fashion with the disintegration or debasement of the American dream. *The Godfather*
launches this investigation with its opening announcement: 'I
love America' is the first line we hear, spoken by an Italian im-
migrant who has left his mother country seeking prosperity and
justice. He has not found it. And so he turns to Don Corleone
to redress the balance, since the Corleones have prospered in
America by establishing their own currency equal in power to
the dollar – a currency based on intimidation and violence, and
expressed in bizarre codes and totems with voodoo connotations (a horse's head, a dead fish). The sequel temporarily restores the purity of the American dream, only to complicate
it by confining young Vito's early sightings of the Statue of
Liberty to the view from his featureless quarantine cell. The
landmark, this orphan's adoptive parent, is no less cold and un-
reachable than the mother who lies buried in Sicilian soil.

The *Godfather* films and *The Conversation* broached America's failings obliquely. When the chance came for Coppola to
take the caribou by the antlers in *Apocalypse Now*, he seemed
paralysed by the opportunity. Yet despite the film's failure to
apply convincingly to Vietnam the enquiries into moral responsibility that it had inherited from Conrad's *Heart of Darkness*,
it remains a work sustained by its contradictions.

If any film needs to be liberated from the chaos of its production, and the self-imposed burdens of its own history, it is
this one. Perhaps we have grown weary of the overblown anecdotes about the making of the picture, or maybe *Hearts of
Darkness: A Film-maker's Apocalypse* (Fax Bahr and George
Hickenlooper's documentary) was not just a profound piece of
cinema in itself: it was also an effective, and much-needed, full-
stop on a shaggy-dog story that had lasted over a decade.
Whatever the case, by the time *Apocalypse Now Redux* was released in 2001, with an additional forty-nine minutes of unseen
footage, it had at last become possible to view that picture
without recourse to myth and footnotes and backstage tittle-

tattle – and to see how naked, and how simple, it looked without the garnish.

Here is a wild, sprawling, sometimes silly film that is almost torn apart by its attempts to fill unbridgeable gaps. Coppola's propensity for indulgence jars sharply with the picture's eloquence about the indulgences of others. Its commentary on the American military's actions in Vietnam would be more persuasive if its glee at recreating the spectacle of those actions were not so blatant; if we could only feel 'the horror' that lingers on Kurtz's lips; if the movie could only have communicated the ghoulishness contained in his account of the Viet Cong soldiers who hacked off the arms of freshly inoculated children. But it doesn't – not nearly. Liberal outrage becomes a screen upon which to project the flickering lightshow of boastful destruction.

Common consensus identifies the script's fluid political stance as attributable to the contrasting politics of the right-wing Milius and the liberal Coppola, but there is a schism too in the very texture of the images. The battle at Do Lung bridge has the joyful visual and aural punch of an MGM musical, while the *Playboy* Playmates stageshow is a sustained and appalling mirage of humiliation as much for the soldiers watching as for the women timidly performing. Cinema has never been shy of conjuring images for our eyes to feast on, or images from which they yearn to recoil. Few film-makers manage to simultaneously stimulate these opposing impulses.

The film's odd mix of repulsion and attraction is personified by Colonel Kilgore (Robert Duvall), who with his vivid yellow neckerchief and dead-eyed shades has a pleasant whiff of Truman Capote about him. Kilgore is the picture's most charismatic figure; we miss him when he vacates the screen, and in the *Redux* version our ears are pathetically appreciative for his extra lines, booming out of the sky like the voice of God. He's the only character who provides that same emotional charge that you get from the film's set-pieces. Kilgore is the showman that the picture needs; he's like a ringmaster presiding over Vietnam as his own personal circus. He has the movie's funniest details: absent-mindedly snatching from a dying man's lips the canteen that he had generously offered a moment earlier; and addressing a disconsolate soldier squatting in the midst of a bombed-out village with the blithe advice, 'Cheer up, son!' He's so thrilled to find himself in the presence of the surfer Lance Johnson (Sam Bottoms), it not only feels plausible that he would lead an attack to liberate a beach rumoured to offer the choicest waves, you can also believe he might have staged the entire Vietnam war just to provide a suitable context for his own outsized PT Barnum personality. (He's so bombastic that when he speaks through a loudhailer, he sounds quieter than ever.)

Without Kilgore in the film, Kurtz would be a crushing disappointment. And if Kurtz had Kilgore's rambunctiousness, it would unbalance the film. Coppola gets that part just right. Kilgore is a shot in the arm for the film, and the audience, but he also makes sense of Kurtz's rebellion. Faced with a world where power resides in the hands of men like Kilgore, Kurtz's withdrawal into darkness becomes suddenly justified. If our eventual introduction to Kurtz feels like an anticlimax, all the better. An all-singing, all-dancing Kurtz would be a discredit to Conrad. In a picture that is pumped up, often irresponsibly, as one climax after another, the simplicity of Kurtz's scenes – and the audience's corresponding sense of deflation – represents the only element of the movie that doesn't feel conflicted or compromised.

Whereas the *Godfather* films and *The Conversation* are introspective pieces in which beauty or spectacle is only permitted so long as it is accidental, everything about *Apocalypse Now* is ostentatious. The movie is all surface, all effect; the magnificent visual ambition and handsome set-pieces only point up how unfocused the film is. It advances as cautiously on its target as Willard and his crew inching up the Nung river toward Kurtz.

For all its verbosity – and in its *Redux* incarnation, it plays more than ever like the work of loudmouthed men with runaway typewriters – it spends a lot of time talking around the issue. Colonel Kurtz turns out to know his T. S. Eliot, but a good hour before he begins reciting from 'The Hollow Men', audiences may have called out at the screen that insistent refrain from *The Waste Land*: 'HURRY UP PLEASE IT'S TIME'.

It can be kinder on the movie to wonder whether Willard's journey isn't taking place entirely in his head, as he suffers a protracted mental collapse to the sound of The Doors. Don't the dissolves in the opening sequence make it appear that entire forests are burning in the palm of his hand, just as the helicopters seem to be hovering over the surface of his face? Isn't he advised, during his briefing, that 'This mission does not exist, nor will it ever exist'? Then there is the coloured smoke – mustard yellow, candy-cane pink – coughed out across the river by flares, from which in one shot Willard's boat emerges like something produced by a demented sideshow conjuror with an 'alakazam'. And there is more hallucinatory imagery – the burning chopper lodged in a tree, the complaining cow being airlifted over a Vietnamese village, the forest of silver birches that transpires to be Kurtz's Montagnard tribesmen – to support the thesis that this movie is a story rendered in the language of a damaged sensibility. But a director whose best work on a film can be described as 'hallucinatory' should beware: that can easily be a backhanded compliment applied to a vision too feeble to survive the glare of the auditorium lights.

Apocalypse Now casts a spell, but it is one that's quickly broken. The film's importance as a contribution to the cultural dialogue about Vietnam is less easily dismissed, just as its value may be brought more sharply into context by the approbation heaped on Michael Cimino's masochistic drama *The Deer Hunter* in the same year. Both films, along with Oliver Stone's *Platoon* (1986) and, to a lesser extent, Kubrick's *Full Metal Jacket* (1987), have become part of 'Vietnam' as we now understand it. That word signifies less a war or even a country so much as a montage of cinematic imagery: the Russian Roulette scene in *The Deer Hunter*; Sergeant Elias running for the helicopter to the sound of Barber's 'Adagio for Strings' in *Platoon*; the chopper raid played out to Wagner's 'Ride of the Valkyries' in *Apocalypse Now*. This interpretation is so familiar now that any movie that contradicts the idea of Vietnam as a war fought in the haze of marijuana smoke and the fizzy colours of an LSD trip – such as *We Were Soldiers* (2002) – can for all its conservatism look unexpectedly radical.

As the first war that was shaped by cinema before the shells were even cold on the ground, Vietnam has been claimed by American film-makers. It's their war. The irony of the part played in this by *Apocalypse Now* is that its least convincing passages are those that attempt to address directly the political context of Vietnam. The plantation scene in the *Redux* edition, for example, in which Willard and his French hosts discuss over dinner the colonial history of Vietnam, and the war's implications, is typical of Coppola's literal-mindedness; it's the kind of dialogue that sounds underlined when you listen to it. The photojournalist at Kurtz's compound complains, 'I wish I had words.' The movie, with its narration written by Michael Herr in the style of a drone and dutifully delivered as such by Sheen, has too many. It finds Coppola flummoxed by the requirements of authentically marrying grandeur to intimacy – the same fusion that he had miraculously performed in the *Godfather* films – just as he still struggles with the contradictory impulses which led him in 1972 to remark: 'My romantic idea is to be part of an American New Wave . . . But I'm in a real state of transition now because ever since I was a little kid, I was raised to be successful and rich.'[11]

What you take from *Apocalypse Now* is not the babble of that narration, or the procrastination of the plantation scenes, but a mood here, an image there: the tranquillity surrounding Lance when he drops acid, paints his face and cradles in his arms a puppy saved from slaughter; Willard and the droopy-moustached Chef (Frederic Forrest) embarking on a search for mangos; Kurtz's oversized hand, big as a baseball mitt, patrolling the surface of his bald, bowed head. Quiet moments in an overcrowded film, from a director who could use a more devout faith in stillness.

Making *Star Wars* (1977): George Lucas on location. (© The Kobal Collection/ Lucasfilm/Twentieth Century Fox)

THX 1138 (1971): LUH 3417 (Maggie McOmie) and THX 1138 (Robert Duvall). (© Warner Bros)

2. George Lucas

A few derisory chuckles ricocheted around the auditorium at the press screening of *Star Wars Episode One: The Phantom Menace* – chuckles laced with dread. I know, because I was laughing. The cause of amusement and apprehension could be traced to the film's prosaic opening credit crawl. It read: 'Turmoil has engulfed the Galactic Republic. The taxation of trade routes to outlying star systems is in dispute.' And you thought to yourself: Could there be a less enticing sentence with which to begin a movie – any movie, let alone a flight of fantasy designed to stimulate the daydreams in schoolboy skulls?

But looking again at George Lucas's 1971 debut feature, *THX 1138*, I wonder how this bum note at the start of *The Phantom Menace* could have surprised anyone. Not that there is much at all wrong with *THX 1138*. It's an exceptional work, intellectually and visually riveting, and governed by a cruel rigour that never slackens. But there's no getting around the fact that it is a movie driven by an unfaltering respect for sound business sense.

If there is one word that has come to fit George Lucas like a Darth Vader glove, it is entrepreneur. Few people think of him as a film-maker any more, despite the fact that he has directed the most recent instalments of the *Star Wars* series (*The Phantom Menace* and *Attack of the Clones*). Interestingly, for someone whose first two films gently commented on the relationship between human beings and machines, the process of directing actors fails to stimulate him so much as the technical requirements of film-making. After handing directorial duties on *The Empire Strikes Back* to Irvin Kershner – his former tutor from USC, and the man who talked over with Coppola the idea for *The Conversation* way back in 1966 – Lucas was enthusiastic about his own role on the *Star Wars* sequel. 'I get to do the fun part,' he said. 'The director has to do the terrible part. The fun part is coming up with the designs for the creatures or the equipment, designing the toys and editing.'[1] You can feel in his words the relief of the tortoise as it retreats into its shell.

More than any other modern director, Lucas has succeeded in reducing the number of variables involved in film. Actors in the newest *Star Wars* pictures are likely to find themselves performing in a void, with effects, locations and sometimes even co-stars to be tweezered in later by men in laboratory coats. (As of 2002, *Attack of the Clones* drew more heavily on digital post-production than any non-animated movie before it.) This way there is less spontaneity to deal with, fewer of those pesky human beings. No wonder Lucas has publicly declared his admiration for the innovative computer-animation company Pixar, even bestowing upon its film *Monsters, Inc.* the much sought-after honour of having its US screenings preceded by the teaser trailer for *Attack of the Clones*. I'm sure he admires the wit and invention of a Pixar production, just like the rest of us. It wouldn't be too much to suggest, after *Attack of the Clones*, that he also craves Pixar's ability to produce smoothly realistic images without recourse to human contact. Even that notorious perfectionist Stanley Kubrick had to deal with wild cards that no computer programme could foresee – an unaccommodating or unsuitable performer, or the reflection of a stray cameraman in *Eyes Wide Shut*.

No such blunder would escape Lucas's scrutiny: even on his second film, *American Graffiti*, there was certitude in the way he went hunting for the unscriptable details of real life, the fluffs and tics that would ordinarily have been easy prey for an editor's scissors. 'There are lots of mistakes,' remembers Charles Martin Smith, who played the movie's bumbling Terry the Toad. 'It seemed to me that every mistake we made, he would cut into the picture.'[2] Sometimes, as in the scene where Terry has to catch a bottle of liquor, Lucas would go for take after take, not resting until the catch had been fumbled, the bottle almost smashed. He wanted the perfection of imperfection. I wonder why he can't countenance such priceless human error in the *Star Wars* films. A line reading that has been stumbled over, or a slight misstep by an intergalactic princess, would leak precious oxygen into that airless universe.

Lucas has always been heading in the direction of absolute control. There is a sense that he has simply been waiting for technology to catch up with his way of doing things, or to make his way of doing things possible. Just after completing *Star Wars* in 1977, he admitted, 'If I left anything for a day, it would fall apart, and it's purely because I set it up that way and there is nothing I can do about it. It wasn't set up so I could walk away from it. Whenever there is a leak in the dam, I have to stick *my* finger in it. I should learn to say, "Somebody else go plug that up."'[3] Now technology has reached the stage where the dam is leakproof, and Lucas, surely, cannot be happier. But it would be unfair to write him off as the unfeeling businessman; or it would be unfair to underestimate the worth of his good head for business, or to forget that the very real, raw talent that he displayed in the early 1970s was inseparable from those entrepreneurial skills. Even as he was building the Skywalker Ranch, his empire-cum-hideout in northern California, on the profits from *Star Wars*, he was still planning to use the place to make 'my little films' which, he insisted, would 'show emotions'.[4] That idea clearly got misplaced along the way. But it is not the case that George Lucas threw in his lot as an artist to become an accountant with a camera; rather that the accountant has constantly been there in the background, making his own unique contribution.

The first thing that hits you as you watch *THX 1138* in the twenty-first century is that it is an astonishingly well-planned film, built to last and perfectly insulated against the vagaries of time and fashion. Every character, except for the black-suited robot cops, is shaven-headed and dressed in blemishless white. Ostensibly this is a mark of the austerity of the film's futuristic fascist state, where all citizens are required to remain mildly sedated for maximum obedience, and sexual activity is forbidden. But Lucas must have known that nothing dates a film faster than a period-specific hairstyle or costume. And visions of the future are especially prone to the ordinary wear-and-tear of passing time, their apocalyptic predictions so easily reduced to quaint crystal ball-gazing the moment that the years catch up with them. How many science-fiction films have been betrayed by a wardrobe of silver-foil jumpsuits or a fleet of pod-cars? Better instead to interpret the future as a mangled version of the past, as in Terry Gilliam's *Brazil* or Michael Radford's 1984 film of *1984*, or else to divest yourself altogether of any notion of time, as Lucas does here.

The sole traces of *THX 1138*'s place in the chronology of film come in its early incarnations of figures who would soon become more familiar: the scavenging Shelldwellers who are obvious ancestors of the Jawas from *Star Wars*, or the chrome-faced cops who could be brutal forerunners of C-3PO; even the dome-headed children lost in their complicated playground games point to the excitable extraterrestrials at the end of Steven Spielberg's *Close Encounters of the Third Kind*. But the scenes in a borderless prison cell, where the white-clothed inmates are just disembodied heads and hands floating in the white void, more accurately reflect the rootless tone of this peculiar movie, which might have been made decades ago, or yesterday, or tomorrow.

Lucas had already shot the film, or a version of it, in 1967 at the age of twenty-three, while at the University of Southern California. Spielberg, then aged twenty, had caught the fifteen-minute short *THX 1138 4EB* (later amended to *THX 1138 4EB: Electronic Labyrinth*) at a student film festival, and had been 'jealous to the very marrow of my bones'[5] at Lucas's achievement. Spielberg later used the short as inspiration for 'LA2017', a futuristic episode that he directed in 1971 for the TV series *The Name of the Game*.

THX 1138 4EB had won Lucas a scholarship that entitled him to a six-month placement with Warner Bros, where he struck up a friendship with Francis Ford Coppola, who was busy shooting *Finian's Rainbow* on the Warner lot. Coppola hired Lucas as an assistant, just as Roger Corman had put Coppola on the payroll years earlier. What this amounted to for Lucas was serving as everything from dogsbody to impromptu production manager on Coppola's next film, *The Rain People*, while shooting a documentary about the film's production. Coppola had pencilled him in to direct *Apocalypse Now*, while also pitching to the Warner Bros brass the idea of a full-length *THX 1138*, which Lucas had been writing on and off.

As a first film, *THX 1138* could happily share a shelf with other distinctive debuts like David Lynch's *Eraserhead*, Darren Aronofsky's *Pi* or Lynne Ramsay's *Ratcatcher*, so comprehensively does it contravene traditional modes of storytelling. It's also interesting to view the picture in the context of low-budget film-making, since the paucity of funding seems as palpable here as the abundance of money is on Lucas's later work. Not that the film looks undernourished; rather that money is so much a part of what it is about – 'Buy and be happy!' runs the blandly intoned mantra of the film's consumerist society. When a young film-maker produces a movie on the cheap, a certain crumminess can be a large part of the charm. Think of anything from Roger Corman's assembly line, or Kevin Smith's *Clerks*, or Roberto Rodriguez's *El Mariachi*: each, with greater amounts of money, would perhaps have been a lesser film (an argument that was borne out when Rodriguez remade his film in 1995 on a larger budget as *Desperado*). In *THX 1138*, this is also true, but for a different reason.

The photography is clean and crisp, each shot measured with care and deliberation, with the only visible indication of financial restrictions being the minimal sets that are now so integral to the picture's identity. But this is a low-budget film to its core, a film preoccupied at a fundamental level by financial considerations. Lucas's script is vividly aware of cost, and of the role that finances and logistics would play in any future society. (In *Clerks*, when a character remarks that the destruction of a half-completed space station in *Return of the Jedi* would have resulted in the deaths of thousands of innocent contract workers, it's the kind of observation that might have come straight from the mouth of the ever-businesslike Lucas; in fact, you feel vaguely disappointed that it didn't occur to him.) As a result, *THX 1138* is one of the most level-headed science-fiction movies ever made.

A more inviting way to put it might be that Lucas never loses his grip on the reality within the fantasy. Certainly, he didn't consider the picture to be a hostage to the genre to which it bore a cosmetic allegiance. 'Everyone else calls it science fiction,' he said. 'I call it documentary fantasy.'[6] THX 1138 himself, played by Robert Duvall, is the film's hero – though 'hero' might be inappropriate given that his rebellion only results from inadvertently skipping doses of state-prescribed sedatives. After being imprisoned for having sex with his female roommate, THX escapes, only to discover that the prison itself has no security to speak of: it's merely a white expanse that unrolls in every direction. The prisoners are kept there by an erratic patrol of guards, but mostly by the fact that they believe themselves to be prisoners – it's a state of mind. Consequently, the prison breakout is almost lackadaisical; the escapees simply wander off into the hazy distance.

Once THX goes on the run, he has a greater chance of survival the longer he succeeds in protracting the chase. His pursuers are limited by a budget, and once they hit that financial ceiling the hunt will be abandoned. In the midst of this unconventional narrative there is one cursory concession to formula, in the form of a countdown. The thrills promised by any countdown have never been terribly sophisticated: it's a signal to the audience that the final act is underway, and as a staple part of most action movies it has in recent times become a lazy way to introduce tension that might not otherwise have been generated. But even here, Lucas won't let his audience take their simple pleasure unimpeded. This countdown monitors the funds remaining in the state coffers – the resources allotted to the task of recapturing THX. The audience's involvement in the countdown is therefore a complicated one. A lifetime of rooting for the good guy – that is, the top-billed, the photogenic one who gets the most close-ups – tells us that we should be willing THX to outlast his pursuers, but as the state's finances dwindle away, we realize that the film is inching ever closer to that most blasphemous of conclusions: the climax without confrontation; the climax without climax.

There is still tension in the pursuit of THX, but it is now inverted, and if we feel an urgency rather than a relief as the 'credits' begin to diminish, isn't that a subtle indictment of our inbuilt bloodlust? What is missing from *The Running Man* or *The Prize of Peril* or any of the other science-fiction thrillers that borrow from *THX 1138* is this intrinsic sense of disapproval. While those movies cater for our basest appetites as consumers, by advertising and then executing acts of violence, Lucas's picture encourages us to examine our own desires. If we are disappointed at being denied a final violent showdown between THX and his hunters, are we really any better than the film's population, who settle down at their TV screens to meekly devour broadcasts of state brutality?

It can only be deference to the audience's need for instant gratification that has prevented this perversely plausible device

– plots with a budget – from being purloined by other screen-writers. What a different world it would be if Lucas's film had been a hit: subsequent James Bond movies would have ended with the villain abandoning plans for world domination be-cause he had exceeded his overdraft; Rambo might have run out of ammo. You can't help feeling, on the evidence of *THX 1138*, that if the young, stringently logical Lucas had got his hands on *Logan's Run*, part of him would have seen the economic sense in culling citizens the moment they hit thirty.

There are satirical undertones too in the way Lucas chal-lenges the attitude applied by the Western world to its vari-ous revenge operations, where no cost, human or financial, is enough to call off a hunt once the smell of blood is in the air. And as in life, so in cinema: few film-makers would be daring enough to establish a conflict and then have the whole thing simply evaporate. It seems odd in the light of *THX 1138* that Lucas would later peruse the rough cut of Scorsese's *New York, New York* – which Lucas's then-wife Marcia had edited – and, recalls Scorsese, advise that 'we could add $10 million to the box-office receipts if we'd give the film a happy ending and have the man and the woman walk away together'.[7] The same might have been true of *THX 1138*. Sure, its ending was peace-ful, but it didn't provide what studio executives go sniffing for in the final pages of every script – closure. By preceding THX's eventual freedom with a laser battle, Lucas might have added some box-office receipts of his own, albeit at the cost of his pic-ture's integrity.

When he made *THX 1138*, Lucas knew the rules without necessarily feeling that he had to adhere to them. Just as THX opts out of the society into which he was born, so Lucas flouts the regulations of every known genre to create a picture that looks like science fiction, promises the excitement of a man-hunt, but delivers something more ambiguous. As a chase movie, it barely gets off the starting blocks, while those viewers searching for the awestruck wonder of *Star Wars* will find slim pickings. Aside from his camera's brief interest in a bank of coloured lights sparking suddenly into life, Lucas is more concerned with the geometrical precision of his compositions, which keenly mirror the compartmentalized tidiness of the film's futuristic world, just as the slow dissolves between shots suggest a sedated demeanour. While THX's life is divided along the lines of work and home, and his foil dinner-tray is separated into sections for drugs and for food, so the screen is subject to corresponding partitions. One memorable shot has the frame carved into thirds, with THX occupying the far right side of the screen, a stretch of blank wall on the left, and a sparse bathroom visible in the middle. In this bizarre, minimalist triptych, so neat but so jarring to the eye, the toilet occupies the screen's central space, where the protagonist would traditionally be; it looks guilty and vulgar there, like the toilet in *Psycho* – which Norman Bates couldn't bring himself to mention ('That's the . . . it's in there,' he says, showing Marion Crane around her motel room) – or pregnant with menace, like the toilet that spews blood in *The Conversation*.

The whole film can be read as an attempt to recondition our eyes, to question where we should be looking, and what we should be looking at (right from the opening titles, which flow the wrong way – top to bottom – in the manner of *Kiss Me Deadly*). The same technique is at play in *American Graffiti*, Lucas's affectionate anthropological portrait of his teenage years, in which the camera moves wherever the fancy takes it: this couple may be on the verge of breaking up, but did you see that rollerskating waitress over there being pestered by a customer? Or else a shot might be framed so wide that the characters are huddled to one side of the screen; or the action, such as Terry the Toad's struggle with a disobedient moped in the opening scene, unfolds off in a far corner of the frame. Even *Star Wars*, which is a more technically conventional work, opens with images designed to create optical disorientation; the written prologue crawling slowly into the distance, giving the screen a depth that it has never had before, followed by the gargantuan space cruiser sweeping overhead, adding width to that depth.

Lucas's framing in *THX 1138* and *American Graffiti* rarely imposes any hierarchy. In the aforementioned shot from *THX 1138*, the camera doesn't encourage us to examine the toilet rather than the wall, or the wall rather than THX: they are all simply objects offered up blankly for our scrutiny. When an opportunity for tenderness presents itself, as THX and his roommate LUH (Maggie McOmie) make love, there is the same numbness, the same absence of commentary. The couple's bodies may be captured by the camera in a tight, cramped close-up, but there is no attempt to convey whatever passion may have survived these characters' regimented upbringing; they are just flesh. The chasteness that feels coy in *American Graffiti* and *Star Wars* here has more of a point: passion would disrupt the picture's sinister serenity, beneath which we can discern ugliness and anxiety. It's there right from the beginning, in the unforgettably disturbing shot of a black-suited cop leading a white-clothed, bald-headed child away from the camera, toward an elevator at the end of a long white corridor. (Like another of Lucas's sensibly understated choices – removing LUH from the story without divulging her eventual fate – the suggestive, unforced nature of this image haunts the movie.)

For some viewers, the film's refusal to provide possibilities for empathy or identification may be as problematic as its withdrawal from a conventional conclusion. But what could be more appropriate, in a film about a society of people withholding gratification from one another, and from themselves, than to withhold from the audience these basic forms of gratification? *THX 1138* is a film that ends perfectly and imperfectly, in complete loyalty to itself, and in calculated ignorance of its audience's demands. While this makes the picture radical, even by modern standards, there is the niggling suspicion that Lucas would spend the rest of his career trying to compensate for what he had failed to bestow upon the audience, perhaps not realizing that by frustrating our expectations he had actually given us something more precious and elusive than satisfaction.

There were signs of a more amenable sensibility at work in Lucas's next film, *American Graffiti*. In recent years, the movie has unjustly acquired a reputation as a simple nostalgia fest, a slow cruise down memory lane, which doesn't take into account how far it, like *THX 1138*, departed from the conventional narrative template of its day. The only other American film-maker at the time who was dealing in multiple narratives was Robert Altman, and at this point even he had yet to make *Nashville*, his most graceful juggling act. But here was Lucas, challenging the received wisdom that you couldn't flit between separate, tenuously connected stories and expect the audience to keep up. Decades later, this has become an acceptable mode of storytelling, underpinning films like *Dazed and Confused*, *Go* and *Groove*. There are also viewers now who judge *American Graffiti* harshly for inspiring the long-running and rather banal TV series *Happy Days*, which borrowed its approximate milieu, as well as one of its stars, Ron Howard (later a film-maker himself after being given the director's chair on *Grand Theft Auto* by Roger Corman, though he went on to more prestigious, but less exciting, projects like *Apollo 13* and *A Beautiful Mind*).

That show – like the TV spin-offs from Altman's *M*A*S*H* and Scorsese's *Alice Doesn't Live Here Anymore* – was a mark of television's determination to cash in on the images that had been seducing audiences away from the box, rather than anything inherently 'televisual' in the movie itself. From the lyrical opening shot of a drive-in diner, its neon rings like a pair of freshly landed UFOs set against the burnt pinky-orange sunset, *American Graffiti* is a film that invests its intimate setting with unexpected grandeur. Odd that so many people can look at Lucas's work through the misty gauze of *Happy Days*, and assume film and TV show to be brothers-in-nostalgia. Odd too that the movie's wall-to-wall, bumper-to-bumper soundtrack – carefully pieced together by Lucas (who wrote each scene to a specific song) and Walter Murch (responsible for the ongoing hum of noise in *THX 1138*) – can seem unexceptional now to our ears, accustomed as they are to the relentless pulse of music in mainstream cinema.

But listen carefully: those aren't just any songs piled together to flog a soundtrack album: these lyrics are actively implicated in the images. There's 'Love Potion No. 9', ringing out as a gang of thugs get drunk on their own camaraderie, while the words 'You're sixteen, you're beautiful, and you're mine' are gently intoned by Johnny Burnette as a man tries to shake off his persistent young companion by making advances which he knows will be unwelcome.

After *THX 1138*, Lucas was still something of an unknown quantity. He hadn't been completely satisfied by his debut – 'I like the movie, but it didn't get across emotionally what I was trying to do'[8] – and was unmoved by offers to direct the musicals *Tommy* (eventually made in 1975 by Ken Russell) and *Hair* (which Milos Forman took on in 1978). Instead, he responded to the encouragement of his friend and producer – 'Francis had challenged me to do something warm and fuzzy.'[9] When *American Graffiti* opened in 1973, with a tag-line – 'Where were you in '62?' – aimed squarely at its youthful target audience, it did indeed display those placatory characteristics. To modern eyes less familiar with 1960s youth culture, and so less readily flattered, it may be easier to respond to the film's lolling rhythms, and its undercurrents of existentialism.

Lucas was eager to capture on film a period of his youth that he feared had become obsolete – its music and iconography superseded by newer fashions, its innocent glow sullied by Vietnam. But he also evokes a palpable uncertainty that resonates far beyond teenage boredom and confusion. Lucas's handful of characters spend the single night during which the film is set simply drifting from one escapade to the next, and sometimes barely even doing that. The most endearing of the bunch is John Milner, named for John Milius (who was also a friend of Lucas's co-writers, Willard Huyck and Gloria Katz), and warmly played by Paul Le Mat with a cigarette packet twisted into the sleeve of his white t-shirt, and his half-hearted quiff smeared with Brylcreem.

Milner is the oldest of the film's group of friends. He has a job as a mechanic, and no real intention of leaving smalltown California, content as he is to cruise the streets, rising to taunts from other boy racers – like the enigmatic cowboy played by Harrison Ford under the halo of a Stetson, with one long arm dangling out of his jalopy window. Milner just drives and drives; he always seems to be stuck in the centre of town, and yet the road refuses to end. On and on it stretches, until you feel sure that he will soon be forced to begin driving again in the opposite direction. This is smalltown life: the road has no end, but no promise of escape either.

Milner clings to his role as wide-boy, just as the cop who harangues him feels safe settling the same old scores with the same young delinquents. The film's rambling structure conveys this feeling of comfortable aimlessness so acutely that there is something unconvincing about the yearning of Curt (Richard Dreyfuss) to make a break for college in New York; it just doesn't feel urgent enough to provide a feasible distraction from the life he is fleeing. And when Lucas does try to justify Curt's desire to leave – by having him meet a former acquaintance who spent a single semester at college before returning home to complacency – it feels like too much editorializing for such a freewheeling film to bear. The idiom of the movie is so truthful that the merest calculation – such as the eye-of-God crane shot that swoops down on Curt near the end of the picture – smacks of dishonesty.

The *Wizard of Oz* influence, on the other hand, is more convincing for passing unstressed. When Curt pays an after-hours visit to the studio of Wolfman Jack, the real-life DJ whose broadcasts provide an aural link between the characters' stories, he discovers that this local hero, prized for his improvisatory skills, has most of his zany links stockpiled on pre-recorded cassettes. 'It's a great big, beautiful world out there and here I sit, sucking on Popsicles,' complains the DJ, alienated from the teenagers who hang on his every quip, and with only a busted freezer for company. The plummet from wistful fantasy to earthbound reality is deftly handled, and in retrospect quite brave, as though Lucas had revealed that the Force, that patchwork 'religion' which permeates *Star Wars*, was nothing but a jumped-up breed of sleight-of-hand trickery. Curt's encounter with the real Wolfman Jack is comparable with the moment when Dorothy discovers the feeble puppet-master behind the fearsome Oz, but with one crucial difference: Dreyfuss has been directed to let the revelation roll over him, and what little response he gives is barely registered by the camera.

In the *Star Wars* series, Lucas would later succumb to the urge for endless reiteration, repeatedly playing out the same ideas, confrontations, even scenes, in case the point had not been properly taken. Perhaps in those cases this could be excused by the age of the target audience. In *American Graffiti*, such lapses feel more incongruous, like pleas to the audience to recognize the weight behind the wistfulness, pleas that can only diminish the film's serious intent. But I don't think Lucas's occasional overemphasis should be interpreted as condescension; at this stage, he was still feeling his way around the audience, wary of incurring the distaste which had dogged *THX 1138*, and eager to locate the middle ground between his reflexes as a film-maker and as an entertainer. Whenever possible, he disparaged the notion that he was an artist. 'I don't make a work of art,' he insisted when *American Graffiti* opened. 'I make a movie. If it does what I want it to do then somebody else can come along and figure it out.'[10] Already you can sense him modifying the abrasiveness of that experimental debut film, buffing down the sharp edges, and preparing the way for *Star Wars*. Only now, with his empire assured, can Lucas be heard to confess that *American Graffiti* was avant-garde for its time. In 1973, such an admission would have been unthinkable.

Back then, Lucas was a film-maker obsessed with forward motion. Each of the three pictures that he directed in the 1970s depicts the different stages in a young male's realization that to establish his own identity he must escape the stifling environment of home. THX only realizes that escape is possible at the end of the picture; Curt possesses that knowledge at the start of *American Graffiti,* and spends the whole film mustering the courage to utilize it; and Luke Skywalker's departure takes place within the first forty minutes of *Star Wars*, with the remainder of the movie charting his maturation. Three stages of emancipation; three different methods of telling the George Lucas story.

It might be, as some have claimed, that the much-mocked Terry the Toad is Lucas's closest alter ego. But there isn't much doubt that when Curt rises high above California in the final shot, gazing down from the aeroplane window (he is flying Magic Carpet Airlines) at the road that is now reduced to a fissure in the earth, he has become George Lucas, on his way to a bright future. A series of ill-fitting end titles inform us that Curt went on to become a writer, which feels like narcissism gone mad (the smugness in Dreyfuss must suit people's idea of how a writer should be – he had the same role in *Stand By Me*, another film accused, rightly this time, of indulgent nostalgia). The unmistakable subtext is: I got out, I broke free of my roots, but what about those ordinary Joes, whatever happened to them? What happened, those titles inform us, is that they went on to less glamorous futures – premature death, military service or, worst of all, selling insurance.

Huyck and Katz lobbied to have those explanatory titles removed. 'We didn't want that tag at the end,' said Huyck. 'We would always take [it] out . . . and George would put it back in.'[11] All of which made the tardy 1979 sequel (which Lucas executive-produced) a self-defeating exercise, since the fate of each character had already been signposted at the end of the original movie. Not that there weren't more blatant signs that the sequel had nowhere to roam: it was called *More American Graffiti* which, as a title, smacks of the same here-we-go-again weariness as *Another Stakeout* or *I Still Know What You Did Last Summer*.

The use of Curt as the narrative motor, and the insertion of that epilogue to lend the story finality, betrays a certain lack of faith in the film's momentum. What Lucas might not have appreciated, in his efforts to make amends for leaving audiences high and dry with *THX 1138*, is that the various skits and vignettes in *American Graffiti* create a cumulative power that keeps the movie ticking over; the story doesn't require any more stability than that. And aside from that handful of intrusive touches in Curt's strand of the movie, Lucas doesn't force anything, letting each scene roll along at its own pace until, before we even realize it, we have been charmed by these tales of no one in particular doing nothing much at all. Anyone who knows Lucas's directing style only from *Star Wars* or *The Phantom Menace* will be startled at how deftly he arranges his actors on screen, creating the kind of beautiful clutter that characterizes Roger Corman's compositions, and which Corman passed on to protégés like Scorsese and Jonathan Demme. There are flashes of audacious zaniness too, made all the more strange for passing apparently unnoticed by the characters – the huge 'ICE' sign looming over Terry the Toad's car, or the salesman perched on an oversized yellow kitchen chair that could be a prop from *Alice in Wonderland*.

And it isn't just that Lucas's eye is so perceptive; his ear is tuned in to those disposable flippancies that don't deserve to be thrown away – 'My ex is gonna be a presidential aide,' we overhear one minor character announcing proudly, clinging to her scrap of secondhand glory. Language also provides the intermittent glimpses of cruelty in this otherwise benign universe. There isn't any pain in *American Graffiti*, not really; even when a group of ruffians threaten to tie Curt to the back of their car, it's all a gas. But the film contains the occasional reminder that life wasn't automatically sweeter in the past. One girl is forbidden by her mother from listening to Wolfman Jack ' 'cos he's a Negro'. (A rare example of racism being acknowledged in a George Lucas film. Wasn't the introduction of the character Lando Calrissian in *The Empire Strikes Back* a response to complaints about the whitewashed galaxy of *Star Wars*?) Another character, who is planning to leave town like Curt, goes begging for sex from his girlfriend. 'Give me something to remember you by,' he pleads, adding, 'You don't want me to forget you, do you?' Suddenly these sweethearts, who had seemed to be made of pure apple pie, don't look so different from the sleazy, bullying teens that crowd the frame in De Palma's *Carrie*.

These cherishable flashes of social observation are sadly missing from *Star Wars*, where the sole opportunity for Lucas to demonstrate his ease with portraying camaraderie arises in Luke's pre-battle scenes with his fellow fighter pilots – a bunch of interchangeable nobodies who are marked from the outset as cannon fodder. It could be that the leisurely, fluid tone of *American Graffiti* simply wasn't in his bones; he has admitted that he finds the writing process arduous ('When I sit down I bleed on the page, and it's just awful.').[12] His co-writers Huyck and Katz improved his dialogue, he said, making it 'funnier, more human, truer',[13] praise which is borne out by other scripts from this husband-and-wife team (they wrote *Indiana Jones and the Temple of Doom*, the wittiest entry in that Lucas-produced series). He would have done well to place his *Star Wars* script in other hands – hands that might have worked toward a human richness to equal the technological splendour.

But then in many ways the film was purgative, and not only of the George Lucas who had gone before. Lucas had felt cinema to be lacking in the naïve, uncomplicated thrills that he remembered from swashbucklers and adventure movies, and with *Star Wars* he sought to locate this footloose glee within a strain of fantasy resistant to the academic science fiction of the day.

Science fiction had long been associated with feelings of dread and foreboding, and *Star Wars* feels now like a spirited reaction against what had become a genre governed by paranoid worrywarts, and an attempt to return it to its former state of purity. Everything was going wrong in the future: the robots in *Westworld* were malfunctioning, as was HAL the computer in Stanley Kubrick's *2001: A Space Odyssey*; basic human identity was under siege in *Planet of the Apes* and *Zardoz*; carnage was on the roads in *Death Race 2000* and the roller-rink in *Rollerball*, while an extraterrestrial visitor was destroyed by Western civilization in *The Man Who Fell to Earth*. (Lucas had of course made his own contribution to this downbeat trend with *THX 1138*.) But *Star Wars*, which he conjured up after thwarted attempts to acquire the film rights to Alex Raymond's Flash Gordon, was designed to replace the cynicism and fear with undiluted wonder. 'Once I got into *Star Wars*,' he said, 'it struck me that . . . a whole generation was growing up without fairy tales. You just don't get them any more, and that's the best stuff in the world – adventures in far-off lands. It's *fun*.'[14] To that end, Lucas even rewrote the form's traditional opening, 'Once upon a time . . .', to become 'A long time ago, in a galaxy far, far away . . .'

Its carefree exterior may not have emerged from that decade untarnished, but *Star Wars* undoubtedly fulfilled the fairy-tale criteria in 1977. Its garish lasers and exotic monsters, and its nippy little spacecraft that squealed excitedly as they hurtled into the black void, provided for many viewers a range of unsullied sensory pleasures, like that first taste of ice cream, that first handful of snow. In modern cinema, its novelty value has scarcely been matched – perhaps by *Toy Story*, another reimagining of reality through the filter of fairy-tale iconography, or in the computer-generated shots from *Terminator 2: Judgment Day*, where reality itself was treated as a minor inconvenience to be overcome. Lucas's skill lay in recognizing that only the cosmetic appearance of adventure cinema was in need of alteration; its heart and soul could be transferred intact, and audiences would still applaud the same things that their grandparents had whooped and cheered at in the swashbucklers and serials of the 1930s and 1940s. In *Star Wars* Lucas draws on film history and acknowledges his creative ancestry. That's why Han Solo (played by Harrison Ford in an unofficial continuation of his *American Graffiti* persona) politely pays the bartender for damages incurred during a fracas, just like James Stewart in *Destry Rides Again*; and it's why the film forces Luke, in the midst of untold technological advances, to cross a chasm by swinging on a rope, Tarzan-style.

But as well as establishing a dialogue with the past, Lucas was also wiping the slate clean, creating for new viewers a Year Zero in their cinema experiences – a point at which they could confidently say in later years, as many have, that this is when movies got better, or at least bigger. You can see the gameplan now, just as one can see the logic behind inserting infantile characters into *The Phantom Menace*: an insurance policy to snare younger moviegoers, who in a decade or two will be splashing out on the *Star Wars* DVD box sets. But it would be wrong to see Lucas's strategy as strictly commercial. It is genuinely apparent from the *Star Wars* series that he doesn't just want our money: he wants *Star Wars* to be held in the same esteem in which his generation held Flash Gordon. And he's achieved it – quickly, succinctly, if not quite deservedly. Although he heralded the picture as being 'on the same intensity level as a Roger Corman movie only a hundred times bigger',[15] it was actually even more rudimentary than Corman's most ramshackle rush-job, the better to broaden its commercial appeal. The characters were standard types: a eunuch hero (Luke Skywalker), a damsel who, for all her superficial feistiness, was still frequently to be found in distress (Princess Leia), a lovable rogue (Han Solo), an unambiguous villain (Darth Vader) and a platoon of wacky supporting characters distinguished by varying degrees of deformity, eccentricity and body hair.

Luke's journey, instigated by the massacre of his family, follows the example set by John Ford's *The Searchers*, though there could be no room in Lucas's effervescent fantasy for even a hint of the complexities of grief and vengeance found in Ford's film. That would only come with *The Empire Strikes Back*, where the revelation of family ties between Luke and Darth Vader echoes the blurring between good and evil in *The Searchers*. *Star Wars* isn't exactly in denial of death, but unlike the fairy tales to which Lucas aspires, the movie can only accommodate it under certain conditions. Like *Superman The Movie*, it incorporates the death of a leading character who is then effectively revived later in the story. Darth Vader murders Luke's mentor Ben Obi-Wan Kenobi, who returns as the boy's spirit guide courtesy of the omnipotent Force, just as Lois Lane's death is challenged when Superman reverses time, bringing her back to life.

These scenes deliver children to within a hair of death, without actually having to confront its finality. While that is a shortcoming, there is at least a real sense of physical danger in *Star Wars*, represented by an inventive gallery of gnarled miscreants and murderers. The squealing Tusken Raider, goggle-eyed, metal horned and with its face swaddled in decaying bandages like a refugee from an old Universal *Mummy* movie, terrorizes Luke in the desert. In a seedy bar, a man whose face appears to have received the attentions of a scalding iron intimidates Luke, while a walrus-faced creature looks on, much like any curious bystander in any disreputable watering hole. While these moments play on a fear of adult hostility, Luke's struggle with a serpent that pulls him underwater in the trash compactor neatly taps into the childhood trepidation about what might be lurking in those hidden spaces in the home – what's at the bottom of the bin, and what's that moving around in the bath? In their evocation of parochial menace, these memorably intense encounters are not only more chilling than Princess Leia's rather campy exchanges with Darth Vader and the purse-lipped Grand Moff Tarkin (played by Peter Cushing in the manner of a prissy Madam at a well-to-do brothel); they also generate a precious suspense which has vacated the film by the time we reach the climactic battle sequence.

It seems impossible looking at *Star Wars* that Lucas's reputation is founded on such sequences, since it is only in the smaller, intimate set-ups that he knows where to place the camera, or the actors. The showdown between Darth Vader and Obi-Wan Kenobi, for instance, is staggeringly clumsy, framed as if for the stage, with no attempt to exploit the more fluid space of the cinema screen. But the close-ups in that crummy bar are lovingly assembled, cataloguing two or three of the hideous clientele at a time, and driven by a child's instinctive, fascinated hunger for all things repulsive. Lucas shows us intergalactic jazz musicians with colourless, over-ripe snake eyes bulging from their heads, and rumpled folds of skin, like plastic surgery that hasn't been properly finished, and we want to see more. He shows us a hammerheaded ghoul whose skin has the texture of burnt pork, its accusatory eyes planted on either side of its T-shaped face, and still we want to see more. But when his actors are on screen, Lucas doesn't know what to do with them, and so there seems to be nothing there – just deep space.

On *THX 1138*, he had the characters' lives worked out to the last awful, deadening detail. The film was full of insights into how everyday life would be in the future – children being fed their daily lessons intravenously, workers unwinding with state-approved broadcasts of sex and violence. But how do the characters in *Star Wars* get their kicks when they're not dodging asteroids or swinging across chasms? Surely all those pent-up emotions can't be satisfied by the one leisure pastime that is glimpsed – a chess-like game involving live pieces. *Battle Be-*

yond the Stars might have had little except good cheer, but it boasted characters who knew how to keep themselves busy on their days off from rescuing princesses and vanquishing warlords.

It is not that Lucas has failed to imagine adequately the infrastructure of his fantasy. The geography of the *Star Wars* galaxy is carefully plotted, and Lucas contrasts its opposing corners to sometimes startling effect (how our eyes struggle to adjust to the spectacular shock of the vast white desert after spending ten minutes in the thick black depths of space). The corridors and catacombs of the film's motherships and space stations resemble intricate adventure playgrounds that every child yearns to investigate. But the human beings look lost in there, as though they have only recently moved in, and haven't yet adjusted to where everything is. Lucas seems insecure as a film-maker for the first time, having constructed the perfect, gleaming skeleton of a fine adventure film, but finding himself without the necessary resources to dress its bones. Of course, *Star Wars* wasn't just an immense success, as *American Graffiti* had been: it was *the* immense success of the 1970s, setting box-office records, sparking the merchandising revolution, providing a sanctuary for family audiences left out in the cold by the last (or rather first) big blockbuster, Spielberg's 1975 *Jaws*, and generally redefining mainstream cinema. Lucas got what he wanted: he brought to fruition his dream of innocent, escapist entertainment, in the process assuaging his bad memories of *THX 1138*. And really, he was never doubted again.

But *Star Wars* has not lasted. It looks brittle and hurried now, and no amount of digital tinkering – which Lucas instigated to create *Star Wars: Special Edition* in 1997 – can compensate for the movie's lack of heart and humour, those crucial ingredients which have helped preserve his earlier works. He created that new version to drag the special effects up to date, but it was never the effects that had hamstrung the film in the first place; that damage was done by misdirected actors, mistimed reaction shots, dialogue that followed no speech patterns in the known universe, and a director who had started second-guessing the audience instead of trusting his own instincts. As it turned out, he did know what the public wanted, and he very cleverly flattered their taste. Now that same public who swooned over the film on its original release continue to vote it their favourite movie of all time, and their unquestioning nostalgia will keep justifying the need for new versions, special editions, director's cuts, sequels, and other such backward steps.

In an attempt to articulate the differences between himself and Coppola, Lucas once said, 'Francis likes to go jump off cliffs, and I hug the ground.'[16] To the casual observer, there would appear to be a disparity between the director's earthbound description of himself and the fact that he has made his fortune from a cycle of wistful fantasies. But those fantasies have served a unique purpose, allowing him to withdraw from the experimentation of his early, inspired film-making – to hug the ground more tightly. He has created the world's most popular and persuasive movie franchise, and crawled inside it, unlikely ever to emerge again. 'George is probably not only the best film-maker of our generation, but he's also the best businessman,'[17] said Spielberg in 1978. It's a statement that is as half-true today as it ever was.

Steven Spielberg. (© MCA / Universal Pictures)

The Sugarland Express (1974): Goldie Hawn as Lou Jean Poplin.
(© MCA / Universal Pictures)

3. Steven Spielberg

Nearly six months to the day after *Star Wars* was released, another science-fiction movie provided an antidote to the earlier film's crypto-cynicism, a tonic after its parched imitation of pleasure, and an epiphany in the wake of its faithless fantasies. Steven Spielberg's *Close Encounters of the Third Kind* opened in the US in November 1977, which qualified it as an early Christmas present into the bargain.

The two films could not be more different. The concept of *Star Wars* might endure without its cast members, as the largely computer-generated prequels *The Phantom Menace* and *Attack of the Clones* have demonstrated. In Spielberg's movie it is the vitality of the human characters that makes sense of the technology. Some of the most breathtaking moments in *Close Encounters of the Third Kind* feature no special effects whatsoever – apart from underrated innovations like acting, compassion, vision, that sort of thing.

I'm thinking of the dance of moonlight and shadows on the side of a house, or on the plump hot face of a sleeping child; the barren Indian panorama that is interrupted by a hundred outstretched arms and pointing fingers shooting into view from the bottom of the frame; the giant globe being unhinged from its stand like God's own executive toy; Richard Dreyfuss kissing his wife, played by Teri Garr, but keeping his eyes on the heavens as he does so; and, later, Garr's face when she knows her marriage is over – the long, sorrowful look that she gives the sky, as though it is another woman with whom she knows she cannot compete. Find me a corresponding passage of human warmth in *Star Wars* and I'll willingly fall on my light-sabre; find me a scene that makes you tingle just to recall it, and I'll eat a Jawa.

From its opening shot, *Close Encounters of the Third Kind* sets out to disarm. What kind of science-fiction movie begins with truck lights blinking through a sandstorm, and progresses to the spectacle of a fleet of 1945 bombers scattered in the desert like discarded playthings on a nursery floor? The clue is in the title. It may be impossible now to disentangle the phrase 'close encounters' from our familiarity with it, just as 'the smell of napalm in the morning' and offers that can't be refused spring readily to our lips. But when the film was released it provided a fresh kink in the collective vocabulary. What exactly was a 'close encounter'? Was it related in some way to a brief encounter? It sounded sinister. Now that we know it denotes contact with extraterrestrials, another connotation remains: the hint of an encounter with something that is already right under our nose, right there in our living room. The most alien element in the film doesn't come from a galaxy far, far away. It's us.

The genius of the movie is that it filters its fantastical vision through humdrum domestic imagery and iconography. The effect of the otherworldly UFOs upon the blanded-out suburban neighbourhoods over which they swoop is meticulously quantified, right down to the nuts and bolts, the nooks and crannies – literally so in one sequence, when the camera becomes transfixed by the screws unfastening in an air vent, and the chatterbox clatter of a hyperactive cat-flap.

The special effects are a crucial part of the movie's magic, but it is important to remember that Spielberg bestows upon those screws, that cat-flap, and all the other details of mundane domestic life, the same eerie power exuded by the UFOs. It doesn't take too much skill to loosen our jaws at the sight of a colossal spaceship docking in a darkened landscape. That's run-of-the-mill spectacular; that's your common or garden 'wow'. But to make us hold our breath at a screw rattling loose in a vent, or a vacuum cleaner roaring across the floor at its own behest, or a toy monkey clanging its cymbals in the dead of night – to make unfamiliar or terrifying the clutter that we have ceased even to notice under our own feet – is near to alchemy.

Spielberg's taste for elevating the unexceptional extends to his choice of heroes. As Roy Neary, who becomes obsessed with UFOs after a dramatic sighting, Richard Dreyfuss establishes an entire repertoire of mutely bewildered or awestruck expressions. The role was intended for Jack Nicholson. 'I didn't want Rick,' Spielberg said, 'and Rick knows that.'[1] The director should fall to his knees nightly and give thanks that Nicholson was too busy directing *Goin' South*. He would very likely have made the movie an in-joke, a freakshow. Nicholson's mania, at least until *The Pledge* and *About Schmidt*, has always been comforting and vaudevillian. Dreyfuss is an ants-in-the-pants control freak, but his edginess is dulled and suburban where Nicholson's is exotic and Satanic. Dreyfuss would not look out of home at the garden centre comparing weedkillers or fondling lawnmowers; he's so anonymous that when he is called upon to deliver a series of gobsmacked reaction shots, as Roy's truck is caught in the glare of a UFO, you see how the experience awakens him – how it gives him definition. The old Roy, with his almost contemptuous boredom toward normal life, is replaced by a carefree spirit who finds inspiration in a heap of shaving foam, a mound of mashed potato. Subsequent movies – *Forrest Gump*, *Regarding Henry*, or practically anything starring Robin Williams – have taught us to dread any character who gets within spitting distance of his inner child. But, as with the UFOs' arrival, Spielberg is careful to ground Roy's metamorphosis in authentic behaviour; he knows that without that, the most dazzling display of technology will be no more than lights on a wall.

Most of the scenes featuring young Barry Guiler (Cary Guffey) offer similar lessons in the importance of a well-chosen reaction shot. Rather than instructing us in our own reactions, as those shots typically do, Spielberg uses them as insights into character and tone. It was wise to make the UFOs as seductive to Barry as they are terrifying to his mother Jillian (Melinda Dillon): the boy's appreciative smiles at what he can see off-camera, beyond the edge of the frame, are crucial in complicating the mood of his abduction. For us, as for Jillian, it's a terrifying episode, but the child's enthusiasm for his kidnappers introduces into the suspense a peculiar note of serenity.

The sequence is also important for restoring that off-screen mystery banished by *Star Wars*, which had used the edges of the frame to stimulate our greed, to make us hungry for the miles of magnificent hull that might still be waiting to pass before the camera's eye. *Close Encounters* doesn't quench our thirst for information. Even the final revelation of the extraterrestrials themselves is framed with a casual simplicity that diffuses the scene's inherent potential for grandiloquence. Complicated effects would be as redundant here as words. Spielberg keeps the camera at a discreet distance, and lets the shots play themselves out. We may feel like guests at the reunion of family members with whom we are only vaguely acquainted: there is a ripple of discomfort; we don't want to get too close. What could possibly be said to a US Air Force pilot who has been missing for over thirty years, or to the extraterrestrials in whose company he has spent those three decades? Mindful of the manipulative techniques employed on his previous film – '*Jaws* is almost like I'm directing the audience with an electric cattleprod,' he said[2] – Spielberg proved that he could be dutifully humble in the presence of immense spectacle, and serve the needs of the material, rather than the scale of the images.

This is another in the film's itinerary of unexpected reversals or inversions. Here is a work that is surely the most intimate piece of film-making ever to merit the label 'blockbuster'. Its hero is a man who goes mad and is abandoned by his family. There is a vaguely threatening military presence in the movie, as in *E.T. The Extra Terrestrial*, but no villains. 'François . . . was especially impressed by the fact that there were no bad guys in it,' remarked Truffaut's co-star, Bob Balaban.[3] And so much of the movie is about anticipation: most of the final sequence features a large group of people standing around waiting for an unspecified alien entity to communicate a message they may not be equipped to decode. *Close Encounters* is not just a film about its characters' faith, it's about the audience's faith too.

That's where Spielberg's fondness for parochial detail pays off. *Close Encounters* is one of the sturdiest fantasies ever made, precisely because – like the most enduring nightmare – it is rooted in the prosaic. This is the true closeness of the encounter.

What we witness in the movie is exactly the process of transformation that finds horror in the muffled marital tensions of *The Ice Storm*, or sexual perversity among the crisp watered lawns of *Blue Velvet*, or sophisticated forms of torture camouflaged as family rituals in Todd Solondz's films *Welcome to the Dollhouse* and *Happiness*. Those movies are dense with disgust and fascination, but Spielberg never entirely banishes from the equation a glow of affectionate wonder – the same wonder that can make a mackintosh or a petrol station seem exotic in *The Umbrellas of Cherbourg*, or invest mythic resonance in a typewriter, a bottle of milk, the ocean's restless waves, in *The 400 Blows*.

These films depict a recognizably real world rendered strange by the prolonged attention of a camera that is at once microscope and funhouse mirror. Spielberg's contribution to cinema's ongoing investigation into suburban tranquillity has been as effective, and as resolute, as the work of David Lynch. If his achievements in this area have been underestimated, that can only be because his entertainments are not by nature disruptive. Lynch plunges into depravity and disorder; Spielberg stays closer to the surface, cognizant of the ugliness disguised as normality, but never quite ready to relinquish his affection for the façade.

Close Encounters subverts suburban paraphernalia, but it also performs the same trick in reverse on the spacecraft, which are subtly anthropomorphized – domesticated even. The mothership is a brilliantly organic piece of design; it could have been yanked out of the soil, or dredged up from the ocean bed crusted with barnacles. In contrast to the streamlined flying saucers of 1950s science fiction like *The Day the Earth Stood Still*, which might have been buffed by assembly line drones in some distant intergalactic factory, it's all tendrils and roots and spikes that jut out into the darkness like needles. Another ship has a pair of electronic moon-shaped eyes, and a bank of bulbs set in a row like fluorescent teeth. The smallest of the fleet is no more than a splash of Tinkerbell light that hurries after its superior siblings like a tardy schoolchild. And of course Spielberg gives the UFOs the best line in the film – the coded musical signature that suggests erudition, warmth and wit in five sparse notes. Who knows what it means? It doesn't matter. 'I'm happy to know they said "Hello",' Spielberg remarked.[4]

It's hard to believe that a film which culminates in such a wilful absence of explanation could make it across the border now without being stopped, stripped and searched by the studio patrol unit, with its test screenings and score cards designed to weed out undesirable elements. In recent times Spielberg has given little indication that he knows how or when to end a movie. *Saving Private Ryan* is wrecked by a sentimental coda that mocks its preceding hours, while the final thirty minutes of *A.I. Artificial Intelligence* are comprised of one conclusion after another (a structural choice that will perhaps only make sense on DVD, where viewers can graduate to dispassionate editors, and choose their own ending). But at the start of his film-making career, Spielberg was as ruthless and economical a director as you could hope to find in American cinema.

Duel and *The Sugarland Express* are streamlined road movies that refuse to be distracted from a steady 60 mph. *Jaws* is a horror-comedy that's stripped down and licked clean, like human bones on a shark's supper plate. And *Close Encounters of the Third Kind* is a movie about joyful obsession that is itself joyful and obsessive. Even *1941*, for all its mistimings, is single-minded in its pursuit of the sight-gag to end all sight-gags. When it appears that Spielberg has found that elusive gag – the Ferris wheel freed from its moorings to roll along a pier – after endless shots of pratfalls, explosions, men landing in crates of eggs and dogs kitted out in naval uniforms, the whole tedious movie feels worthwhile. All at once you experience a director reaching for a goal, however modest, and grasping it. You'd like to give prints of *The Color Purple* or *Jurassic Park* or *Hook* to the man who made those movies, and let him loose on them with his secateurs.

Unlike Coppola and Martin Scorsese and Jonathan Demme, Spielberg hadn't sought the sponsorship of Roger Corman, and he didn't have the film-school background of Coppola, Scorsese, Lucas and De Palma. He had the promise of a handful of shorts, and the guts to put on a suit and stroll on to the Universal lot, where he temporarily moved into a vacant office and insinuated himself into any editing room or TV and movie set that would tolerate him. He was an uncredited production assistant on John Cassavetes' 1968 film *Faces*. In the same year, he made a wistful short, *Amblin'*. That brought him to the attention of Universal, and by the following year he had made his television debut with an episode of *Night Gallery*.

His first feature, *Duel*, was made in 1971, also for TV, though its popularity earned it international theatrical distribution. Even in the slightly extended version prepared for that release, it's still a frugal, fat-free thriller. 'If a person can tell me the idea in twenty-five words or less, it's going to make a pretty good movie,' said Spielberg in 1978, anticipating Griffin Mill in *The Player* by a good decade. 'I like ideas, especially movie ideas, that you can hold in your hand.'⁵

Here is one you could balance on the end of your pinkie: truck chases man. The fellow in question is a pitiful working stiff with the revealing name of David Mann – David for David and Goliath, Mann for everyman. Mann (Dennis Weaver) is hounded across California by an unseen adversary in a snarling, implacable truck that – like the UFOs in *Close Encounters* – is afforded the movie's most memorable non-verbal line. In this case, it's a rude blast of the horn, first heard when Mann overtakes the truck, thus setting in motion the bizarre contest for control of the highway. Few American thrillers can truthfully be described as Pinteresque, but this is one. Spielberg had admired William Friedkin's underrated film adaptation of Pinter's *The Birthday Party* (Robert Shaw's bullying performance led directly to him being cast in *Jaws*) and he cultivates in *Duel* a similar strain of claustrophobic menace that is exacerbated by the lack of available context or information. A latter day studio executive or script reader would not get to the end of Richard Matheson's screenplay without suffering a double coronary. Where is the motivation for the truck driver's campaign? Where is his back-story? Come to that, where is his face?

The film was lean, but Spielberg wanted it leaner still. When the time came to prepare the theatrical version, much of Mann's voice-over was cut. One observation that remains – 'There you are,' he tells himself as he contemplates the primitive overtones of this battle of wills, 'right back in the jungle again' – is typical of the kind of overstatement that Spielberg worked hard to temper. He also regretted the inclusion of a brief telephone conversation in which Mann's wife complains about his inability to defend her against another man's advances. Their children silently play at her feet; Mann, calling from a Laundromat, is framed within the circular window of a washing machine's open door. But that attempt to show him imprisoned by a symbol of domesticity is as needless as his wife's taunting insults, or the chatter of a radio talk-show host – 'I'm afraid of her: I've been longing to divorce her' – which corroborates the film's unhappy thesis that modern men have been emasculated by tyrannical wives.

The movie doesn't need those embellishments. Let it not be a comment on anything; let the truck symbolize nothing except menace. Give the screenwriter the day off, there is characterization enough in the casting. One close-up of Dennis Weaver – a man who looks like he's wasted a hundred humid afternoons stuck in bland, brown boardrooms – says more about the crumpled defeat of the middle-American male than a hundred pages of narration or exposition ever could.

Duel feels now almost puritanical in its devotion to concept – there is no deviation from its route. The most sensible adjustment that Spielberg made in his moderately longer 1972 cut was to begin the film not on the road but in the garage, with the camera positioned behind the steering wheel as the car backs out into the driveway. The sensation of retreating from darkness into sunlight shocks the eye, and seems to warn us of the approaching nightmare, like a visual exclamation mark.

Even Mann's pit-stops provide no opportunity for respite. When he takes lunch in a roadside diner, every ornery cowboy at the bar becomes in his paranoid eyes a potential tormentor. You experience indigestion on his behalf. When he pauses to help a busful of schoolchildren, his generosity is transformed into another demonstration of his pursuer's omnipotence. As if it were not intimidating enough that the truck is watching Mann from the end of a darkened tunnel, its headlights bursting suddenly into life like vampire eyes waking from a thousand-year sleep, it then has the audacity to do what Mann cannot, and nudge the school bus out of its rut. The tenderness of that moment, in which the truck uses its bulk for beneficent purposes, seems to make its savagery doubly terrifying. What had been a simple cat-and-mouse game is exposed as strategic psychological warfare in which dishonour as much as annihilation is the desired effect.

The driving shots, with the camera greedily gobbling up thousands of miles of hot tarmac, bring to mind *Easy Rider*, and Spielberg's movie can seem like an elaborate taunt to Hopper's hippy idealism. The road here doesn't promise anything but misery; the best you can hope for is an uneventful journey and a gas-station sandwich on the turn. And unlike the heroes of that earlier film, Mann doesn't have a triumphant soundtrack of rock 'n' roll anthems to accompany him. Radio phone-ins and advertisements for haemorrhoid cream are the closest he gets to 'Born to be Wild'.

Spielberg's cinematic debut was a long time coming, but when it finally arrived in 1974, it brought with it transparent echoes of *Duel*. *The Sugarland Express* is also structured as an ongoing chase, and in this case too the pursuers are if not unseen then relatively anonymous. A pack of cops and journalists shadow the film's protagonists, Lou Jean (Goldie Hawn) and her husband Clovis (William Atherton), who have kidnapped a highway patrolman, Officer Slide (Michael Sacks), and are determined to regain custody of their baby. Both movies are in some way responses to the trend for endless car chases that had come into favour thanks largely to the notorious chase sequences in *Bullitt* and *The French Connection*, though the commentary offered by Spielberg's films amounted to a voice in the wilderness. There was an element of resignation to his cameo in the 1980 comedy *The Blues Brothers*, in which a succession of auto wrecks is played out with all the nerve-numbed excitement of a zombie sex orgy. It was as though he had thrown up his hands and admitted: You guys won – the pile-ups are more important than the people.

Spielberg had a number of false starts before making *The Sugarland Express*. After continuing in television for a further two years following *Duel*, he flirted with various projects that almost became his movie debut. He got closest to directing the Burt Reynolds vehicle *White Lightning*, until he realized that, 'I didn't want to start my career as a hard-hat, journeyman director. I wanted to do something that was a little more personal.'⁶ That was almost *Slide*, which the out-of-work actor Joseph Walsh had written about his own gambling addiction. Spielberg worked with Walsh on the script for nine months, not writing but enthusing. 'When he didn't giggle like a little boy eating a cookie, saying "This is great", I knew something was wrong,' remarked Walsh, 'and I always took that as a gauge and somehow I looked deeper into the scene.'⁷

The collaboration looked promising until a shift in management at MGM, where Spielberg and Walsh had a deal. Walsh jumped ship when the studio insisted on casting Dean Martin and refashioning the movie in the image of the recent hit *The Sting*. Spielberg went to Universal, where he planned to make *Lucky Lady*, but became interested instead in a factually based script, *Carte Blanche*, by the young writers Matthew Robbins and Hal Barwood. With Spielberg's help it became *The Sugarland Express*.

Shortly before the picture's release, Spielberg noted, 'I haven't got any style yet . . . I'm still feeling my way along.'⁸ Yet the picture feels dazzlingly confident in its tone and purpose. Only the rather obvious and self-satisfied indictment of the media suggests a certain complacency. A memorable shot of the cavalcade departing beneath the sceptical gaze of a giant neon chicken embodies the weirdness of the whole enterprise better than any number of cutaways to reporters behaving reprehensibly.

In addition to his declaration of uncertainty, Spielberg could later be heard besieging journalists with tales of an alternative *Sugarland Express*; how he would have made the film differently, the alterations in perspective that he longed to implement. '*Sugarland* could have very easily been *The Battle of*

Algiers,'[9] he opined. As Spielberg retrospectively saw it, the picture was weakened by the relationship between the audience and the criminals that it established from the opening scene. In his imaginary alternative version, he maintains that he would have denied viewers that emotional security, and forced us instead to empathize with the police. What this fails to take into account is the inherent challenge to the audience in the film's existing structure, which tricks us into identifying with characters who are at best wrongheaded in their quest to reclaim parental responsibility.

Young film-makers in the 1970s had become freed from the obligation to play nice. A movie like *The Sugarland Express* doesn't have to declare its allegiances. The most undiscriminating Goldie Hawn fan might misread the picture as a romp, at least until the sour conclusion, but Spielberg is conscientious enough in his directing to ensure that his implicit view of the character – 'To me the real villain's Hawn; she's the heavy for me'[10] – does not escape us. It's a complex piece of characterization, and a brief but significant counterpoint in the career of an actress who rarely ventured beyond the ditsy airheads that were her stock-in-trade in films like *Cactus Flower, There's a Girl in My Soup* and *Private Benjamin*.

Lou Jean is a screw-up from the start. She implores her hesitant jailbird husband to bust out of prison just months before his release. You can see why he capitulates: her hair is like a swirl of vanilla on an ice-cream cone; when she flutters her eyelashes, you think of butterflies. But there are warnings even in the film's first minutes that something is wrong. Throughout Lou Jean's heartfelt conversation with Clovis about their son, who has been placed with foster parents, a wailing baby is heard in the background – it's like a siren warning them away from the mission on which they are about to embark. But it goes unheeded, and it becomes increasingly tough during the film's wind-in-the-hair driving sequences to share in the sense of freedom that Lou Jean and Clovis have conned themselves into feeling. The sun-bleached Texan plains longingly observed by Vilmos Zsigmond's camera become hostile and claustrophobic, like the open road in *Duel*, or the ocean in *Jaws*. It would not be unexpected for a crop-dusting plane to drop out of that cloudless blue sky and begin dusting where there ain't no crops.

Hawn is the key to the film's success. She had previously utilized her helpless persona as a come-on to the audience's protective or paternal instincts, and Spielberg cleverly toys with those expectations. It's true that Lou Jean is shielded from the realities of her situation by a succession of men, but rather than encouraging our sympathy, this only compounds the character's immaturity. This 'unemployed beautician' is so wrapped up in her cosmetic conception of motherhood – merrily picking out toys from a catalogue even as the cops are giving chase – that she can't foresee what waits at the end of the road. Her husband isn't much wiser, but he is blessed with a crucial moment of illumination, the film's most shocking scene in fact: when the cheerful but temporary demise of Wile E. Coyote in a *Road Runner* cartoon alerts Clovis to the realization that his own adventure will not have such a painless ending, or come with that guarantee of resurrection.

The camera scrutinizes Clovis as his smile drops with a clang, his face turns tombstone-cold, and his attempts at providing sound effects for the cartoon are replaced by the real soundtrack, which has become weirdly and abruptly ominous. It's a breathtaking juxtaposition of incompatible visual and aural textures, easily the equal of the 'Singin' in the Rain' sequence from *A Clockwork Orange* or the violent gunfight played out to 'Over the Rainbow' in John Woo's *Face/Off*. Further evidence that the beauty of Spielberg's cinema rests on something more resilient than spectacle; further proof that the play of emotions on a human face can beat a UFO or a giant shark every time.

It's significant that Lou Jean isn't privy to the same enlightenment as Clovis. Nor does she hear the radio bulletin in which she is denounced by her own father – 'Lou Jean, you're no good, and I always knew you was no good,' he says, providing another example of Spielberg's preference for a single revealing splinter of dialogue over an acre of back-story. Officer Slide protects her from hearing that broadcast, which again places the film's privileged knowledge exclusively in the hands of the male characters, and the audience, which knows long before Lou Jean does that the authorities' promise to let her see her baby will be broken. It's an ingenious subversion of Hawn's persona, and it seems impossible now that another actress could have brought the same invaluable baggage to the part. As usual, a character played by Hawn is mollycoddled by the men in her life, but this time it is to her detriment: the qualities that had previously made this actress cherishable and endearing contribute to Lou Jean's arrested development, and to her self-ishness in urging Clovis on to his death.

The film becomes a punishment, not only for Lou Jean's behaviour, but also for Hawn's vivacious persona, which by the final scene is in tatters. And it is punishment too for the audience that has dared to believe the movie could have turned out any other way. The star power of a Hollywood darling, formerly such a dependable commodity, is undermined, debased, reduced to dust. It had been the case that a pair of heroes like Paul Newman and Robert Redford could be redeemed from certain death by the magnificent and self-congratulatory fraudulence in the final shot of *Butch Cassidy and the Sundance Kid*. Filmgoers could leave with a spring in their step, confident in the knowledge that even death was no match for cinematic trickery or the might of the Hollywood superstar. (The same lie was still being foisted on gullible viewers in *Thelma and Louise*.)

I prefer the other version; the version in which the material is not subordinate to the star. Warren Beatty expires in a snow-storm with neither mourner nor fanfare in *McCabe and Mrs Miller*. In *Barry Lyndon*, Ryan O'Neal is humiliated, stripped of a limb, and captured mid-stumble in a mocking freeze-frame. And in *The Sugarland Express*, Goldie Hawn's schoolgirl giggles give way to a banshee howl, and a fury that compels her to destroy all traces of the son she professes to love, but who has become to her as tokenistic and functional as he is to the movie. It's not just that these endings are faithful to the material, they also actively comment on the fallibility of stardom, and the futility of our expectations. There's a dialogue with cinema there if you listen hard enough, an inherent challenge to the conventions that have reduced film-making to the level of hero-worship. Of course, it should be that too: cinema would be a poorer place without the elation that we experience in the presence of a charismatic star. But how rewarding it feels, once in a while, to see those stars gently abused: James Stewart in a wheelchair in *Rear Window*, Jack Nicholson with a bandaged nose in *Chinatown*, James Caan confined to bed in *Misery*; or else ridiculed, like Michael Douglas in *The Game* and Julia Roberts in *My Best Friend's Wedding*.

Like *Duel*, *The Sugarland Express* is a road movie that abruptly runs out of road, stranding the audience without the comfort that commonly comes upon reaching the final reel. *Duel* climaxes with an image of ostensible victory: the truck plummeting to its doom with what Stephen King described as 'the sound . . . a *Tyrannosaurus rex* would make going slowly down into a tar pit'.[11] (The roar might also be likened to the anguished protests of another kind of dinosaur: those directors – Blake Edwards, Arthur Hiller, Franklin J. Schaffner – who were about to be rendered obsolete by the new generation of Hollywood visionaries.) Spielberg underplays the triumph; the shot isn't hyperbolized, like the similar climax in *Breakdown*, which pays homage to Spielberg's film. The picture ends instead on a strangely elegiac shot of Mann basking in a fiery dusk. That golden glow returns in the final image of *The Sugarland Express*, the sunset sparkling on the surface of the river where the stolen police car has spluttered to a halt, and against which

Slide is mournfully silhouetted. The audience feels suspended; the euphoric release with which Spielberg ends *Close Encounters* or *ET* is absent.

I think that's because we know that what has really made us uncomfortable hasn't disappeared at all. The object of dread in Spielberg's work is rarely what it first appears to be. It is not the shark whom we should fear in *Jaws*, any more than it is the Japanese in *1941*, or the extraterrestrials in *Close Encounters*, or the police snipers in *The Sugarland Express*. In each of these pictures the most convincing threat, the force toward which we should feel greatest ambivalence, is human.

Spielberg's movies present one dramatic but barely perceptible reversal after another. *Jaws* is actually about the repellent vulnerability of people. The shark is only a convenient means of exposing that vulnerability. The second half of the film is about the claustrophobia of three men trapped on a boat together – or rather, one man, Chief Brody (Roy Scheider), who is clearly averse to his companions' presence. His discomfort makes you squirm. Behind his twitchy, sweat-moistened face he seems to be constantly weighing up whether or not to throw himself to the shark and be done with it.

Even before the final act Spielberg's camera is transfixed by how disgusting people can be. They scramble out of the water with no greater regard for human life than the shark that is pursuing them. An elderly man is trampled, women claw their way past children: these people are as shrill and unpleasant as the bounty hunter Quint (Robert Shaw) dragging his fingernails across a blackboard. And the film tortures and dissects them with ghoulish pleasure; each death comes with a side-order of relish. Body parts are placed on show for our delectation: a shark-attack victim's arm is lifted into shot from the mortuary table; a leg, still with its foot in sock and sneaker as though in training for an underwater marathon, drifts peacefully to the ocean floor; a severed head plays peek-a-boo in a sunken hull, one distended eyeball staring out accusingly at us as if to de-

mand, 'Is this what you wanted to see?' while the other vacant
eye-socket hints at the cost of our voyeurism.

Even when there are no corpses to be broken like bread before the camera, Spielberg finds symbolic substitutes to keep
our tastebuds lubricated: the oversized glass of red wine that
Brody greedily pours himself; the slab of meat that's used for
bait; the illustrations of injuries sustained in shark attacks,
flicked through with tantalizing speed. Then there are the images of fishermen viewed through the lattice of their own nets,
or Quint's boat shot through the open mouth of a shark's skeletal jaws, or the beachfront fenceposts that strongly suggest a
row of incisors jutting out of the sand.

What chance of survival do the feeble human characters
have when their very environment has been infiltrated by such
predatory *mise-en-scène*, or turned upside down by a distorted
perspective? The film begins with an image of disorientation:
the camera observes a midnight skinnydipper from below, as
though she's floating in the night sky, kicking her legs against
gravity. The cameraman is like a schoolboy dropping dimes on
the dancefloor to get within viewing distance of women's underwear. But that voyeuristic thrill is quickly subverted by our
realization that we have been assigned the role of shark.

The subjective camera is the purest instrument of torture at
a film-maker's disposal. It is the means by which the audience is
most comprehensively and viscerally implicated in the on-
screen action. And now it is you, as the viewer, who is about to
punish this swimmer for her night of innocent hedonism. That
heartbeat on the soundtrack – is it yours or hers? You're getting
closer: the moonlight looks hazy through the water; you can almost feel her legs between your teeth; the heartbeat is quicken-
ing. What has she done to you? Nothing. She's just food: food
for a shark; food for a camera. What's your agenda? Well, your
agenda is pleasure. This is cinema – remember?

That first death is so violent, so needlessly protracted, that
you have to ask what is at stake here. People are killed all the

time in movies, and we gasp through a stifled yawn, or a mouthful of popcorn. This one is different. I think part of the horror comes from the film's double dose of disgust at the fallibility of human beings. It's not only the victim of the attack that the camera seems to despise: there is her boyfriend too, who is lying unconscious on the beach, oblivious to the bloodbath in the water. He's every bit as useless as we are, marooned in our cinema seats, murderers one moment and dumb spectators the next. The movie seems to mock us – to say, 'You did this' but also 'How could you let this happen?' Or, as that accusing eyeball asks, 'Is this what you wanted to see?'

Jaws is the kind of entertainment that has come to be described as a 'rollercoaster movie' – a commonplace endorsement but in this case particularly pertinent. Excitement and trepidation aren't the only feelings provoked by the rollercoaster ride: there is nausea too. And it seems the strongest of ironies that a director whose greatest work is characterized by a struggle to reconcile the wonder of human experience with its bleakness should get his first big hit with a picture that seems to despise everything in the world except the shrill kick of a well-timed effect.

Which is not to denigrate the importance of well-timed effects. *Jaws* has plenty of them. Everyone remembers the visual distortion technique that makes Brody appear to be floating toward the camera even as the background is receding. Spielberg had poached that from *Vertigo*, and had already given it a test-run in *The Sugarland Express*, to convey a sniper's viewpoint. What impresses me more in *Jaws* is the cutting rhythm in that same scene of Brody on the beach gazing out to sea. Where he could have used straightforward edits, or a slow zoom, to bring us into Brody's face, Spielberg instead structures the shot-sequence as a series of disorientating jumps – not quite jump-cuts in the Godardian sense, but as near as mainstream cinema has dared to get. The camera is watching Brody; someone walks past, blocking our view of him; when we see Brody again, he is a little closer. Another figure walks in front of the camera, then Brody is closer still. The seamless flow of shots has been disrupted; we have been disrupted. In the shark sequences, John Williams' score mimics a panicked heartbeat. And throughout the film, Spielberg's camera is also engaged in the business of mimicry, finding striking visual equivalents to the physical sensation of fright.

The reputation of *Jaws* as the seminal blockbuster, as we know that term today, is beyond dispute. This was the start of the event movie; this was where the marketing of films blurred into military strategy. And anyone who has weathered long summers with nothing for comfort but a *Twister* or a *Men in Black 2* (both of which were executive-produced by Spielberg) – or, for that matter, *Jaws 2*, the toothless 1978 sequel that Spielberg briefly considered directing – will look on that season in 1975 with envy. It is such a skilful movie, and such a patient one. In the boat scenes, Spielberg is revealed as a film-maker in receipt of one of this art form's rarest gifts: the courage to wait. He knows how to bide his time – just to keep the camera still, just to brood – like no director since Henri-Georges Clouzot, whose *Wages of Fear* was a punishing forerunner of *Duel* and *Jaws*.

But he hasn't yet learned how to take his feelings and transform them into dramatic material. In *Jaws*, Spielberg's terror of other people is sublimated into violence. He once confessed, 'I'm a little frightened of working with a "movie star". Other than movie stars I have helped to create . . .'[12] And between directing Joan Crawford in his first TV assignment in 1969 and Tom Cruise in *Minority Report* twenty-three years later, he had managed to avoid it. Spielberg effectively made the careers of Scheider and Dreyfuss when he cast them in *Jaws*, and there is, in the interplay between those two Joe Nobodies and the movie's only 'name' actor, Robert Shaw, some of the tension that the director evidently feels about working with performers who may be bigger or better than the movie.

Shaw's Quint is more fearsome than the shark. The shark is at least obeying natural urges: Quint's urges, you suspect, are anything but natural. His eyes, like the shark's, seem to twinkle with morbid thoughts. Experience has hardened him; he's all scar tissue. (If his monologue about the shark attack on the crew of the torpedoed USS *Indianapolis* has some of the lullaby chill of Kurtz's wartime reminiscences in *Apocalypse Now*, that's no coincidence – both scripts passed through John Milius's typewriter at some point.)

We hear Quint before we see him – the sound of his nails on the blackboard is as abrasive an introduction as the orchestral hyperventilation that announces the shark's presence. And even in death, Quint is uglier and more unruly: bitten in half, he screams and flails around, spewing blood, whereas the shark at least has the good grace to explode in long-shot (another example of how messy and repugnant human beings can be). Quint too must be destroyed, he's the sort of antisocial element that cannot be allowed to roam free at the end of a mainstream entertainment. The remainder of the film after his death is disappointingly jaunty. Without Quint's boozy-breathed seediness the sense of jeopardy seems quaint and academic. The shark is sleek, slick and hungry for meat. You were never quite certain what Quint was hungry for, but you could be sure it was something unsavoury.

Neat answers to the same questions are in shorter supply in *Close Encounters*. The phobia of human beings, and family in particular, is never resolved, but is instead absorbed into the film's fabric. Because the prevailing tone of the picture is one of intergalactic benevolence, it becomes easy to forget that this is the story of a man who subjects his wife and children to such extremes of emotional torture that they are forced to desert him. In the course of the movie, the home becomes a place of insecurity and danger: machines turn against their masters; Roy sits in the bathroom crying, while his children express their discontentment by slamming doors. Admittedly, Spielberg has stacked the odds against them. When we first see Roy and his family, they are huddled in the far right-hand side of a cluttered frame, where the youngest child is smashing a doll against the bars of the playpen. It's a kind of hell. What better escape than to fabricate an alien rescue fantasy? It's the ultimate excuse for not coming home on time – for not coming home at all.

In 1978, Spielberg said, 'I haven't made my *It's a Wonderful Life*. I haven't done that yet. I will some day.'[13] What he was aspiring to was obviously a work that would secure international approbation and affection, and be guaranteed endless TV reruns. But it is not hard to see *Close Encounters* as the nearest he has got to the strange trade-offs of compromise and happiness that run through Capra's movie. *It's a Wonderful Life* is an unusual kind of pick-me-up; it's on such intimate terms with death and despair that until the magical fillip of its final moments it seems possible that the title will transpire to be no more than a sick joke. *Close Encounters* doesn't rely so much on chance; it's structured as a crescendo, and the final ascension of the UFO fleet gives you the sensation that you too are rising from your seat – it's a pure emotional high.

But the departing UFO leaves in its wake a question-mark not confined to the matter of Roy's destination. He has turned his back on the human race, a species toward which he felt little affection and even less affinity. His voyage is therefore a kind of symbolic suicide. He gets what was denied to George Bailey in Capra's film: a release from all obligation to others, topped off with self-abnegation in a blast of celestial light. The miracle of *Close Encounters* is that this conclusion is successfully smuggled in under cover of optimism; that audiences still manage to file out of the exits wearing grins as big and bright as UFO searchlights; and that even as I recall the mothership's departure, the sadness of the sequence remains undiminished by its splendour.

Making *Badlands* (1973): Martin Sheen (Kit) and Terrence Malick.
(© Warner Bros)

Days of Heaven (1978): Linda Manz. (© Paramount Pictures)

4. Terrence Malick

Hand your watch to the usher on your way into a Terrence Malick movie. Time doesn't really figure here. It's never quite clear how long these lovers-on-the-lam have been driving, or that couple have been courting, or that dying man has got left to live. This uncertainty is forged by Malick's narrative ellipses and drawn-out dissolves, and by his lingering shots of scarred skies piled high with unsteady towers of clouds, shots that seem to say: let's take as long as we need here; let's look at this sky for ever if that's what we feel compelled to do.

Those same narrative ellipses and drawn-out dissolves, and years spent in thrall to nature, extend beyond Malick's films and into his life. When his third film, *The Thin Red Line*, opened in the US at the close of 1998, a full twenty years had elapsed since the release of his last feature, and though no one knew how he had spent that time, it seemed entirely plausible on the evidence of his movies that he had been waiting for the perfect sunset or counting blades of grass. It wasn't the longest gap between directing assignments, even among his peers; George Lucas waited twenty-two years between directing *Star Wars* and *The Phantom Menace*, though he filled that time conspicuously by producing the intervening *Star Wars* instalments, the *Indiana Jones* trilogy, and features directed by friends (Paul Schrader, Francis Ford Coppola, Ron Howard).

But Malick left no tracks, no fingerprints. It was rumoured that his old friend Martin Sheen had enlisted him to usher Sheen's son Emilio Estevez through his directorial debut, *Wisdom*, in 1986. Then there were the reverent whispers about Malick's ambitious *Q, or The Beginning of the World*; this picture-that-never-was remains one of those tantalizing unmade movies, like Stanley Kubrick's *Napoleon* or Robert Altman's *Ragtime*, which plays on an endless loop in the film buff's parallel universe.

The intensity of the speculation and adoration that rose up around Malick in the long years leading to *The Thin Red Line* is a testament to the potent spell cast by his previous features, *Badlands* in 1973 and *Days of Heaven* in 1978. And it suits the Malick mythology more than adequately that he just seemed to walk on set and pull that magic out of thin air. His collaborators testify to a spontaneous streak. Jack Fisk served as production or art designer on each of Malick's pictures; he also took the same role on the early films of Brian De Palma and David Lynch, and together with his wife Sissy Spacek helped finance Lynch's gruelling 1977 debut *Eraserhead*. Fisk remembers that Malick was 'eager to change things. He'd see something in the yard and say, "Let's put it in the bedroom." That's one thing I learned from him: spontaneity.'[1]

'The shoot went on forever because the crew kept quitting,' recalls Spacek, who stars in *Badlands* as Holly, the baton-twirling South Dakota schoolgirl who elopes with her father's killer, Kit (Martin Sheen). 'They were completely brutalized; they'd be setting up one shot over here, then Terry would look over in the other direction where the moon was rising up and he'd go, "Let's shoot over there!" I have these memories of everyone tearing off across the desert in pursuit of one sunset or another.'[2] As effectively as it is integrated into the movie, the central segment of *Badlands*, when Kit and Holly hide out in their idyllic woodland sanctuary, does indeed exude that impromptu air, as though Malick had stumbled upon the magnificent treehouse one day and decided to tailor his film to accommodate it. The general mood and rhythm of the movie closely mimics its protagonists, who drift along about as purposefully as tumbleweed, regarding with numbed incomprehension the acts of brutality that they witness or commit.

In an art form that often seems devoted to tricking the audience into feeling empathy or indignation, both *Badlands* and *Days of Heaven* are odd films out. They positively resist all temptations for catharsis, drowning out potential moments of overt passion with noise or silence, while affording emphasis to peripheral elements: a lone bird skirting the horizon, the play of sunlight on a riverbank, the knotted nodules on a branch. In conventional narrative terms, it's poison: motive is sacrificed for mood, and story arcs are forced into the background or abandoned altogether. But paradoxically this distance implicates us in a more intimate sensory relationship with the characters and their world. We may not understand their motives, or be equipped to précis their lives, but we feel that we have passed through their environment, smelling the air, touching, tasting. When *Days of Heaven* was released, the publicity department must have been at a loss for promotional ideas. But the hopeful, grasping tag-line which they came up with for the poster – 'Your eyes . . . your ears . . . your senses . . . will be overwhelmed' – was as close as anyone could expect to get to the film's essence in under ten words.

More than any other film since *The Big Trail* or *The Searchers*, *Badlands* and *Days of Heaven* integrated landscape into American film-making, showing how it could affect, influence and comment upon the action. In *Badlands*, the characters are inextricably linked with the land. The cluttered paradise of the film's first half properly evokes the sense of menace in Kit and Holly's garden of Eden, while the flat, forbidding landscapes that dwarf them in the second act are as implacable as their own actions. *Badlands* was shot by a trio of cinematographers, including Tak Fujimoto who would collaborate two years later with Jonathan Demme on *Caged Heat*, and would thereafter be director of photography on all but two of Demme's films. *Days of Heaven* too was shot by more than one cinematographer – Nestor Almendros, who won an Oscar for his work on the film, left the long production to honour his commitment to François Truffaut's *The Man Who Loved Women*, passing his duties on to Haskell Wexler, who had supervised the shooting of *American Graffiti*. (Almendros claimed that Wexler shot for nineteen days to his fifty-three; Wexler, disgruntled at his credit for 'additional photography', is said to have taken a stopwatch to a screening of the film to prove that he had shot over half the footage.) Meanwhile, George Tipton's score for *Badlands* – since used and abused by various TV commercials, just as Ennio Morricone's darker-toned compositions for *Days of Heaven* would be (in, among others, a Disneyland campaign) – is a thing of fragile wonder. It sounds like cherry blossom riding a breeze.

The primary tool of cinema has long been subjectivity, encouraging the audience to experience every rise and fall of the main character's emotions. So those films that eschew hysterical identification in favour of objective scrutiny are liable to be treated with some suspicion. So it is with *Badlands*. If it is filed in the 'Thriller' section of your local video shop, that can only be because the sheer volume of titles forces them to be classified according to superficial similarities (and because there is no 'Lyrical Cinematography' or 'Emotional Dislocation' shelf at Blockbuster). If it is a thriller, then it's one marked by a conspicuous absence of thrills: this road movie offers richer, less pedestrian pleasures. One of Malick's most impressive qualities is the democracy of his perspective – an inherent acknowledgement that while a particular film is focused on one story, it is not the only story in the universe. This runs counter to the prevalent sensibility of film-making, which decrees that uniqueness and value will automatically be lavished upon whatever happens to catch the camera's eye, and that the story being unfurled is not just the only one that matters, but the only one which exists (split-screen experiments like Warhol's *Chelsea Girls* or Mike Figgis's *Timecode* notwithstanding). Robert Altman's use of interweaving narrative strands and overlapping dialogue also challenges this preconception, as does the crossbreeding between real people and fictional characters in *Nashville*, and in his later films like *Health* and *The Player*.

For Malick, context is more crucial than clarity. The essence of his film-making is arguably embodied in an observation near the end of *Days of Heaven*, spoken by the child narrator Linda (Linda Manz) as she notices strangers on the riverbank from the distant vantage point of a boat: 'You couldn't see what they were doing,' she notes in passing. 'They were probably calling for help, or burying somebody.' The implication is that the story that Malick has told us is only one out of an infinite number of tales that he might instead have chosen to divulge. The boat, and the movie, drifts calmly on, leaving us to contemplate the undisclosed yarns unfolding just outside the frame.

It might be that this democratic approach has a journalistic basis, though it feels above all compassionately philosophical. Malick has experience in both fields. Before he made *Badlands*, he had primarily worked as a journalist (on *Life* and *Newsweek* among others) and a philosophy teacher, and as he tells it his detour into movies was at best casual – 'They seemed no less improbable a career than anything else,' he said.[3] In 1969, he studied at the American Film Institute in Los Angeles and made a short, *Lanton Mills*, before notching up some assignments rewriting other people's screenplays – a script doctor before the phrase was common currency. (Many of the most influential screenwriters of the 1970s – Robert Towne, John Milius, William Goldman, James Toback – were doing the same.) Malick did a few days' work on *Drive, He Said*, Jack Nicholson's 1971 debut as a director; he also scripted the original version of *Dirty Harry*, with Irvin Kershner attached to direct, and Marlon Brando cast in the role that would eventually go to Clint Eastwood. He rewrote the melancholic western *Pocket Money* and the trucker comedy *Deadhead Miles*, by which time he had already pieced together *Badlands*, based on the real-life case of the 1950s murderer Charles Starkweather and his girlfriend Caril Fugate.

Death is everywhere in *Badlands*, coolly absorbed into the *mise-en-scène* from the moment when Kit, a garbage collector, discovers a dead cat on his rounds and dares a colleague to eat it. Kit's relationship with death is childlike, as is Holly's, who despite expressing sadness when her catfish dies, or when her father shoots her dog as punishment for her relationship with Kit, appears unfazed as Kit's victims mount up. Death has no context or consequences for Kit, as symbolized by his gentle callousness when, for no apparent reason, he stands upon a dead cow. By the time Kit starts killing people, Malick has prepared us for the drabness of death: how it blends into the background while the rest of life carries on; how it isn't necessarily announced by an orchestral crescendo or a lightning bolt. When Kit shoots his friend Cato in the belly, the man just rises to his feet and carries on walking, struggling to his bed, where he quietly expires while Kit and Holly inspect his collection of junk in an adjoining room.

Somehow the camera neither sentimentalizes his death, nor admonishes his killer. It assumes the same blankness as Cato, who simply accepts his fate and waits for the life to drain out of him, and as Kit, who does what he feels he needs to do and then steps back, unable to acknowledge, let alone process, the moral repercussions. Any gesture Kit does make in the direction of comprehending mortality – announcing that he wants a girl to scream his name when he dies, or assembling a pile of rocks to mark the spot where the police have apprehended him – are consistent with his admiration for James Dean, rather than with any emotional sophistication.

This is film-star behaviour, taught in movie theatres, and it defines Kit. In fact, his tendency to affect iconic poses strikes you only when the camera catches him sleeping, curled up and momentarily unburdened of his self-consciousness, which comes without a redemptive undercurrent of self-awareness. Kit is fuzzy and indistinct, a puppet of the various contradictory values which he has accumulated – James Dean's surly, narcissistic heroism, oddly combined with a conservatism which surfaces when Kit says 'Listen to your parents and teachers . . . Don't treat them as enemies' in one of several non-committal farewell messages that he records to ensure his longed-for posterity. 'The movies have kept up a myth that suffering makes you deep,' explained Malick. 'It inclines you to say deep things . . . It teaches you lessons you never forget. People who've suffered go around in movies with long, thoughtful faces, as though everything had caved in just yesterday. It's not that way in real life, though, not always. Suffering can make you shallow and just the opposite of vulnerable, dense.'[4]

Those words sound like a pre-emptive taunt to Michael Mann, who in films like *Heat* and *The Insider* has made a career out of depicting pain and brooding introspection as being integral to masculinity. Kit, on the other hand, could be carried away on the breeze. Even Martin Sheen's physical appearance suggests something superficial and manufactured, a façade to disguise the lack of identity. His hair looks too big for his head, and his head looks too big for that slender body shrink-wrapped in denim.

In some ways, Kit is an indictment of how society had begun to fashion itself in the image of popular culture, so that viewers took movies as anthropological documents, lessons in how to behave, what to say, what to feel. If we are disappointed at being left unseduced by *Badlands*, our empathy for its characters neither requested nor required, then perhaps we are merely experiencing the uneasiness of finding ourselves without the home comforts of narrative cinema. *Badlands* is a sad and beautiful picture, but it isn't an explicitly moving one, at least until the final shot, which delivers us beyond the clouds that we have hitherto only seen crowded on the distant horizon. Malick keeps the emotional lives of his characters carefully hidden, just as they keep them hidden from one another; to reveal what they themselves will not reveal would require fraudulence and subterfuge. Consequently, Kit and Holly are constantly held at arm's length, not because Malick doesn't understand or respect them, but because he does. Compare *Badlands* with a film like *River's Edge* or *kids*, where the director intrudes on his characters' privacy to satisfy the audience's desire to be informed, guided or scandalized, and the extent of Malick's restraint becomes apparent. Of course, any camera is an instrument of manipulation, however unwitting; by zeroing in on one subject, one story, it distorts reality. But Malick, like Altman, uses the camera wherever possible as a tool of observation.

In *Badlands* and *Days of Heaven*, there are significant disparities between what we can see and what we can hear – or at least they seem like disparities to those of us lulled by years of voice-overs that repair ambiguities, rather than creating them. *Days of Heaven* relates the story of Abby (Brooke Adams) and Bill (Richard Gere), migrant workers who become involved with the wealthy, dying owner of the Texas farmland where they toil during the harvest. It is narrated, or rather commented on, by Bill's kid sister Linda, who processes the story as any twelve-year-old might: omitting the details which she finds uninteresting, or to which she was not privy, while speculating on others and dwelling on matters that no conventional script would have accommodated. A naturally inquisitive viewer might wonder how long Abby has been romantically involved with the farmer (Sam Shepard) before he expresses his love for her – after all, they have barely shared more than a few shots before their al fresco wedding. But Malick isn't concerned with assembling a chronology. Basic facts are given short shrift,

while ample room is made for, say, Linda's admission that she
likes to 'roll in the fields, talk to the wheat patches'. Fundamentally this is because the film itself is unspooling out of
Linda's mind. But it also indicates that anything with only one
answer or interpretation doesn't register on Malick's radar: he
works in fluid tones, building a cumulative wealth of expres-
sionistic detail that no amount of narrative exposition could
match.

The stories in Malick's work are rarely to be found in the
script. Look at the casting. Both *Badlands* and *Days of Heaven*
are steered by young girls with inscrutable faces: Sissy Spacek
permits little emotion to pass across that freckled, milk-white
skin; Linda Manz, hard and boyish, looks bruised and bored
to the bone, until something catches her eye and she crinkles
with excitement, or breaks into a celebratory cartwheel. Jim
Caviezel in *The Thin Red Line* could be a big brother to Spacek
and Manz; even in repose his face seems to ask a thousand
questions. Malick has chosen these actors as carefully as he has
selected each word of dialogue, each camera angle. Their faces
contribute as much to our understanding of character as any
line they speak. Indeed, it is best to watch *Badlands* without
noting what Holly says so much as how she says it. She guides
us through the movie in a steady, meticulous tone, as though
preparing a class assignment entitled 'What I did on my holi-
days'. Sometimes an impatient sarcasm creeps in, as when she
confides in us that 'at times I wished [Kit] would fall in the river
and drown so I could watch'. Mostly, in contrast to the film itself, she never departs from the stark facts, the barest observations, and some brief flourishes of movie-speak ('Little did I
realize that what began in the alleys and backways of this quiet
town would end in the badlands of Montana') delivered in a
monotone voice that stifles all possibility of excitement.

When faced with the accusation that Holly is unfeeling or
insensitive, and that even the killing of her father had no effect
upon her, Malick's response was illuminating. 'She might have

cried buckets of tears,' he said, 'but she wouldn't think of telling *you* about it. It would not be proper. You should always feel there are large parts of her experience she's not including because she has a strong, if misplaced, sense of propriety.'[5] This demonstrates the picture's absolute fidelity to Holly, just as *Days of Heaven* refused to deviate from Linda's interpretation. But more problematically it challenges our fundamental faith in storytelling; that is, the belief that we are being furnished with all the information necessary to arrive at a moral judgement about the characters. It is bold enough that Malick denies us specific scenes which other directors might have exploited for their emotional power: when Holly witnesses her father killing her dog, or confesses to Kit her desire to rid her life of 'hellbent types' like him, the details are relayed to us through her distancing narration, just to ensure that we don't get swept along by the heat of the moment. It's a similar deployment of voice-over that we find in Kubrick's *Barry Lyndon*, where surprise, suspense and even the hero's own free will are persistently thwarted by a narrator who warns us in advance of every trick that fate has in store.

But to obscure significant details about the characters themselves, and their emotional responses to situations, is an altogether more radical technique that challenges the audience's unquestioning (and, to be fair, not unreasonable) assumption that they will automatically find themselves in receipt of every scrap of relevant knowledge. The suggestion that Malick has concealed parts of Holly's personality puts the privilege, or the burden depending on whether you like your movies predigested or not, on the audience, who must complete this jigsaw without possessing all the pieces. There may not be much stylistic connection between Malick's work and earlier arthouse successes like *Last Year at Marienbad* or *L'Avventura*, but viewers could find in all three, to varying degrees, unsolvable conundrums, unanswerable questions and unyielding characters.

From the very first scene of *Days of Heaven*, in which Bill murders a man at a steel-mill in early twentieth-century Chicago, we are made implicitly aware that certain information will be denied to us. Much of the film's dialogue sounds distant, as though we're eavesdropping on workers in the next field, but in that opening confrontation all speech is overwhelmed by clanging, squealing machinery, so we have no context in which to read the scene. Of course, by the time the film has finished, whatever sparked the disagreement has become irrelevant. Bill's unruly temper, which will later drag the three adult characters to either doom or despair, is the only important element here, and Malick, in his wisdom, strips away all other superfluous elements from the first shot onwards.

While he removes those 'active' elements of cause and effect upon which conventional storytelling depends, he transfers significance elsewhere. The wheat itself has a physical presence, whispering its unintelligible warnings on the soundtrack as Linda wades through the fields. Nature in general is the film's most dominant character, and it is fitting that the production itself famously paid such deference to the natural order. Not only did Nestor Almendros increasingly rely on exclusively natural light sources, but Malick would sometimes only shoot during the shimmering 'magic hour' at the close of the day (though as Almendros pointed out, 'the term "magic hour" is an optimistic euphemism . . . [because] the time between sunset and total darkness is only about twenty minutes').[6] There is an oblique lesson contained in the film about obeying natural orders, and when this is contravened, a plague of locusts descends upon the fields in an act of divine retribution. It also seems that the film itself is careful not to incur any celestial wrath. The camera falls in love with every grain of wheat and wisp of cloud, and it can only be the fact that Richard Gere was not at that point a fully-fledged star with commercial clout which led him to accept a role in which fields and sunsets and grubby-faced peasants got the lion's share of close-ups, not him.

While most films strive to sweep us along in the action, *Days of Heaven* keeps accentuating our detachment by pulling back to survey a scene of pastoral beauty in which we have no investment; in which we rarely even recognize the characters chasing pheasants, or larking in the pond, or grappling together in an oafish wrestling match. (Never has the term 'extras' been so inappropriate – those unsung supporting players are not employed here to fill out the edges of the frame, as in the films of David Lean or Richard Attenborough: Malick is easily as enamoured of them as he is of Adams or Gere.) But perhaps some viewers were moved to ask, quite pertinently, what they were gaining from the removal of the traditional narrative formula – what was being put in its place?

The answer is that Malick delivers us closer to the spiritual centre of these people, and this place, by removing the artificial constructs that movies impose to give the false impression of momentum. Malick isn't especially taken with what is occurring at the notional 'centre' of the story, because he knows that the centre itself is a fallacy. He is drawn to the margins, which is how he succeeds in making films without any physical centre at all. You could describe *Days of Heaven*, as I have done above, as the tale of a pair of lovers who (in a plot-line borrowed from Henry James) conspire to exploit a dying man, but you wouldn't be very close to capturing the film's spirit, which is rooted in what is happening around these characters, rather than to them.

In many ways, Malick's style of film-making is indicative of the most positive trend in 1970s cinema, a trend inherited from the European art-house directors admired by these young Americans. With cinema geared so relentlessly toward the principles of excess, indulgence, and gratification, the prospect of deprivation – or at least a certain narrative and emotional frugality – must have been anathema to some viewers. But Malick, like Lucas in *THX 1138*, demonstrated that a film that fully sates its audience's appetite is one certain to have no external life once the end credits have rolled. Just as Lucas has his desperate hero simply outlast his pursuers, and Coppola in *The Conversation* ends what had promised to be a murder mystery with the physical disintegration of the investigator figure, so Malick allows *Days of Heaven* to trail off into the distance, just like its itinerant narrator, refusing to enforce upon it an artificial sense of summation. He gives us work to do: he encourages us to complete the film in our heads, to fill in the holes ourselves, and that's why time has not diminished a single frame. (Unlike Paramount, which destroyed many millions of Malick's frames when a clear-out of surplus prints of the Tom Cruise vehicle *Days of Thunder* led to the accidental destruction of some of the last remaining 70mm prints of *Days of Heaven*.)

It is possible after seeing *Badlands* and *Days of Heaven* to look again at the preconceived relationship between director and audience. Of course the director can give the viewer only what is necessary. Of course he can deprive us of anything he chooses. And in doing so he can put the movie in our hands, to make of it what we will. As much as the 1970s was a period of intense freedom and discovery for film-makers, audiences too found themselves trusted for the first time with movies that demanded a degree of home assembly. While the received wisdom that this trend in American cinema screeched to a halt the second that 1979 became 1980 is at best a misrepresentation, it is true that those viewers who pined for Malick's visionary approach to cinema had to look elsewhere for their fix – to Iran, for example, or China – after *Days of Heaven*, or else steel themselves for a lengthy wait.

Of course, all the waiting in the world can be justified when the end result is as profound and complex as *The Thin Red Line*. But then that's another movie, another decade, and another story.

Brian De Palma.

Carrie (1976): Amy Irving as Sue Snell. (© United Artists)

5. Brian De Palma

What a perverse exercise it would be to discuss Brian De Palma without mentioning Alfred Hitchcock – like thinking about Leni Riefenstahl but banishing from your mind her beady-eyed sponsor with the cow's lick hair and cigar-ash moustache. It can be said that the De Palma–Hitchcock relationship exerts similar pressure in the viewer. How could it not?

De Palma's 1975 film *Obsession*, co-written with Paul Schrader, would not have existed without *Vertigo*, and he's not about to let that fact escape us. If the two films were not already joined at the script, there would be the relentlessly circling cameras, the air of romantic fatalism, and the music of Bernard Herrmann (who scored *Vertigo*) to tip us off. Then there is the hidden corpse in De Palma's 1973 *Sisters* which harks back to the grisly stowaway in *Rope*. And his quickfire montage of static shots to deliver us suddenly closer to a disfigured corpse in *The Fury* (1978) – the visual equivalent of a stutter, or a double-take – had already been employed by Hitchcock in *The Birds* to ambush us with the graphic sight of a dead farmer, his eye sockets scooped out like Halloween pumpkins. Hitchcock said, 'The staccato jumps are about catching the breath. Gasp. Gasp. Yes.'[1] The shots come so swiftly that there's no time to look away, no chance to analyse the whisper of trauma rippling through you – only to feel it.

De Palma is the son of a surgeon – 'I've seen my father amputate legs and open people up,' he has boasted.[2] But like the references to Hitchcock, it's easy to let that biographical insight overwhelm your reading of De Palma's work. It would not take too much deliberation to see this director's cherished split-screen technique as the ultimate cinematic incision – the bisection of the conventional film frame. And I detect in *Sisters* and *The Fury* an exalted terror of the operating table and of insanity. But let's not blame on the father the sins of the son. And let's try, at least, to leave Hitchcock out of this.

Like Riefenstahl, De Palma could claim to have been an impressionable innocent swept along by the charismatic influence of a famous master. But remove from both directors the baggage of their celebrity mentors and you are still left with exacting film-makers whose exquisite skill and eye for detail are not just clinical but cinematic, in the sense that it is used to remind you where you are – in a cinema. There in the dark you are prone, vulnerable, susceptible to pleasure – or pain. When Margot Kidder places two vivid-red capsules on the edge of the sink in a pristine white bathroom in *Sisters*, there is something breathtaking in the simple contrast of colours, in the way the tiny dots of red disrupt and sully the vast expanse of white like damn'd spots of blood resisting Lady Macbeth's disinfectant and scouring pad. We don't even know at this point that those pills are all that stand between Kidder and a severe psychotic episode that will end in the apartment's white walls being splashed and smeared with blood – but we have been quietly forewarned by those little red specks. What we respond to is the desecration of that formal purity by a rogue element, and the insinuation of chaos and carnage. The tension that flourishes in the long minutes between the audience registering that delicate shift in key, that intimation of impending horror, and the film unleashing the tumultuous, symphonic rush that has begun to build, might accurately be termed essence of Brian De Palma.

It's present in *Carrie* (1976), in the unbearably protracted prom sequence, which exploits the same suspension of time that is spoken of by survivors of car wrecks. Everything seems to hang in the air, each moment passing with that serene lethargy with which a feather succumbs to gravity. *Carrie* is one of De Palma's weakest films for being structured entirely around that climax. Nothing in the picture makes sense until it is viewed in the shadow of that sequence. But it is also the purest example of this director's capacity to tease, to frustrate and exploit our primitive greed for what happens next.

Every scene in *Carrie* points toward the apocalyptic finale, in which the bullied schoolgirl Carrie White (played by Sissy Spacek) is rudely and spectacularly baptised in pig's blood (her very name, like the gleaming walls of that apartment in *Sisters*, invites a terrible violation). As the bucket of blood wobbles on the scaffold above the stage where Carrie is being crowned prom queen, De Palma does everything he can to prolong our agony, like a sadistic executioner toying with the guillotine blade. Slow-motion would be enough on its own – that would make us wriggle and squirm. But he wants us to suffer physically, to feel the weight of each shot, and the passing of each second, until we are urging that bucket to tumble, if only to release us from this torture – just as we have willed the runaway pram in Eisenstein's *Battleship Potemkin* to crash to a halt.

It's a pleasurable pain. I can feel it in my fingers just thinking about it – it's an itchiness. And that's what can be so exhilarating about the first time you see a Brian De Palma film, if it's *Sisters* or *Phantom of the Paradise* (1974) or *Carrie*: the movies hit you *right there*. They make contact with you, and the shock is as tangible, if not as profound, as the elation you feel at the end of *Close Encounters of the Third Kind*, or the exhaustion in your limbs in the closing passages of the first two *Godfather* movies. De Palma has been slighted because of a perceived emptiness behind those shock effects, and that visual dazzle. But those things are organically connected with who he is as a director. David Fincher has described film-making as an art form that 'encompasses everything, from tricking people into investing in it, to putting on the show, to trying to distil down moments in time . . . It's four-dimensional chess, it's strategy, and it's being painfully honest, and unbelievably deceitful, and everything in between.'[3]

The giddiness inherent in that description is at the heart of De Palma's work. It's worth remembering that Fincher is a kindred spirit: it's there in the visual gimmickry of his 1999 film *Fight Club*, and in the interplay between CCTV footage and subjective camerawork in *Panic Room*, which might well have been implemented using old Brian De Palma movies as instruction manuals. In fact, the pure desire of the film-maker to terrorize the audience, not to mention the audience's eagerness to be relieved of its sense of comfort and well-being for two hours, feels so startling in *Panic Room* because these pleasures have become undervalued in the years since De Palma's pioneering suspense work in the 1970s and early 1980s. The newest traces of innovation in the modern suspense movie have been found in the features of M. Night Shyamalan, but his early films – *The Sixth Sense* and *Unbreakable* – are grave and dutiful masquerades. He's so ashamed of the material's pulpiness, and so desperate to evoke profundity, that he dresses his movies as high art, and slows the action to the speed of a funeral procession – a funeral procession in rush hour.

Conversely, De Palma and Fincher don't disparage the highs that can come from a perfectly pinpointed 'Boo!', whether it takes the form of a sudden thump in the face, like the hand lunging from the grave in *Carrie*, or a regime of slow, tantalizing torture, like the prom night that seems to last a semester.

Before the miraculous breakthrough of *Sisters*, De Palma had made six features that would not look incongruous in a latter-day student festival, save for the fashions, the hairstyles, and the presence in three of them of an energized, whippet-thin Robert De Niro fresh out of the Actors' Studio. Those pictures suggest the Nouvelle Vague relocated to off-off-Broadway. They are jamboree bags of technical wizardry – film speed becomes as pliable as putty, jump-cuts and title cards and films-within-films (a De Palma specialty) abound. It may be irrelevant that De Palma was raised in the same corner of Philadelphia from which Richard Lester originated, or it could have been something in the water.

Nothing in those features suggested the sustain or expertise of *Sisters*. They are largely stylistic experiments predicated upon visual or structural polarities: *Murder à la Mod* (1966) repeatedly replays the same murder mystery in varying styles (soap opera, suspense, silent movie), and *Dionysus in '69* (1970) captures a performance of Euripides' *The Bacchae* rendered for its entirety in a split-screen format that separates audience and actors. (It was completed before *Woodstock*, on which Martin Scorsese served as supervising editor, and which utilizes the same technique.) The three features starring De Niro – *The Wedding Party* (De Palma's 1964 debut, unreleased until five years later), *Greetings* (1968) and *Hi, Mom!* (1970) – are the most irreverent, the last film wearing its revue mentality proudly in a self-consciously scandalous sequence featuring a black theatre troupe that performs in white-face and terrorizes its middle-class audience. De Palma became a figurehead of young, radical, independent film-making. He toured his work around the university circuit, and encouraged students to make films off their own backs. Terrence Malick was among those who heard the gospel according to Brian De Palma after a screening of *Greetings*; he later credited that experience with inspiring him to become a director.[4]

Greetings and its semi-sequel *Hi, Mom!* led directly to De Palma landing the job of directing *Get to Know Your Rabbit* for Warner Bros. The studios were too high on the fumes trailed by *Easy Rider* to recognize that the mavericks they were hiring would be unlikely to resort to formula. Casualties of this crossover between graduates hungry for a big break and executives looking to turn a fluke hit into a sure thing began mounting up; De Palma and George Lucas were two of the more conspicuous cases. Warner Bros removed De Palma from *Get to Know Your Rabbit*, an anti-establishment allegory about an aspiring tap-dancing magician, and tacked on its own ending. Around the same time, he underwent a kind of rebirth. 'I wanted to do a whole film,' he said, 'instead of these little pastiches that were basically just a whole bunch of short scenes tied together.'[5]

When I read that quote, I feel an involuntary sigh of relief pass through my body. How easily that resolution might not have occurred. How plausible that alternative universe seems, where De Palma goes on to make *Fuzz* (the Burt Reynolds–Raquel Welch thriller that he dropped out of at the last moment) rather than *Phantom of the Paradise*, while Robert Altman decides to stick to his steady pay-cheque and slog it out on mediocre television shows, and Steven Spielberg makes *Lucky Lady* instead of *The Sugarland Express*.

Sisters is where this story really starts. It's a thrilling film, tightly controlled throughout its first half, where horror gradually penetrates the atmosphere of numbed banality like raindrops trickling through a leaky roof. And then suddenly, terribly, the entire ceiling gives way and you are knee-deep in the stuff. The disadvantage of this effect is that nothing else can hope to surpass that initial shock when the sky caves in, when anarchy descends. De Palma's solution to this is to go for broke, to throw in every vaguely cuckoo idea he can pull off, and some he can't, with the result that the movie's latter half transforms the pent-up tensions of its agonising first act into demented farce.

The movie is, like its inferior sibling *The Fury*, partly about seeing. The creepy credit sequence lingers for a painfully long time on one shot of a foetus staring straight at us, the camera's protracted attention investing in its black, uncomprehending eyes an unnerving malevolence. The beginning of the film proper hinges on one of De Palma's characteristic double bluffs: we think we are watching a blind woman undressing in front of a male stranger, but the joke is on us – the scene actually forms part of a *Candid Camera*-type TV show called *Peeping Toms*. De Palma described *Sisters* as 'very much the story of the voyeur getting it . . . It's like an ice-pick in the voyeur's eye.'[6] Except that the voyeur who is destined to receive disproportionate comeuppance is not really Grace Collier (Jennifer Salt), the reporter who witnesses a murder and embarks upon an investigation in which her own perception, her own mind, is penetrated and violated. Or rather, she's not the only one being punished for looking: it's us too.

That trick opening immediately establishes tone and purpose. Inserting the TV frame into the cinema screen is one of De Palma's numerous distancing devices to make us aware of the act of looking even as we are engaging in it. His desire to seduce us, and then chide us for our surrender, is almost Brechtian. For all its flippancy, his 1979 comedy *Home Movies* is crammed with compositions designed to heighten artificiality, or accentuate voyeuristic undercurrents. Shots of the teenage film-maker Denis (Keith Gordon) witnessing his father's infidelities from the vantage point of a tree outside his office window invite such treatment. But an emotional exchange between Denis and his mother cannot pass without De Palma relocating that too in its own internal frame within the film frame, in this case shooting the entire scene through its reflection in a mirror. The frame in De Palma's films is always subject to divisions and fractures, within which can occur dissolves, flashbacks, alternate perspectives; it may be the most faithful imitation of the human thought process. Conversely, we have incorporated televisual and cinematic language into our own patterns of thought – we are not just media-literate, we're media-organic too.

De Palma's cinema is a reaction to that confused dynamic,

where the media has taught us fresh styles of thinking rather than fresh thoughts. To any mildly ambitious film-maker working in the 1970s, the encroaching influence of television was something to be challenged and resisted. Popular movies would eventually become subject in the early 1980s to a kind of homogenization in which the various components – scripts, stars, set design – levelled out into a televisual blandness. But in the 1970s, cinema was serving up spectacles with which the television networks could not dream of competing and De Palma's genre of choice only advertised the resolutely cinematic nature of his vision. '[Horror] is one of the few forms that hasn't been invaded by television,' he explained in 1980. 'The stations have picked up the situation comedies and the political stories and all the other forms you used to go to the movies to see. But they've avoided the horror and suspense genre because these works lose their scariness when they're broken up by commercials . . . [Horror is] the closest thing we have today to pure cinema.'[7]

The screen in De Palma's movies keeps splintering into frames within frames, while characters in *Home Movies* such as Denis and his film teacher The Maestro (Kirk Douglas) interpret reality in exclusively cinematic terms ('You're an extra in your own life,' The Maestro tells Denis). That film's animated credit sequence features a startling image that chimes fiercely with De Palma's obsessions – a house transformed into a giant projector, so that the images flow from the windows, from the very building itself, and on to a cinema screen. The human mind and the editing suite have come to resemble one another; the rhythms of thought are by now interchangeable with the cinematic grammar of close-ups and cut-aways, emotional flashbacks and rousing soundtracks. Admiring the night sky, The Blue Danube comes unbidden to your ears; a stroll through Rome in a snazzy pair of sunglasses makes Marcello Mastroiannis out of most of us; a deserted highway is an open invitation to momentarily become Mad Max.

The gimmick of the false start – an opening scene that does not appear to be part of the formal narrative – enables De Palma to further scrutinize the intimacy between life and cinema, by forcing us to actively analyse what we are watching. *Carrie* and *Dressed to Kill* (1980) begin with heightened softcore reveries in which the camera focuses on the naked body of a woman who is clearly lost in the movie in her mind, before the façade is disrupted by blood or violence; *Blow Out* (1981) and *Body Double* (1984) both lure the audience into what transpires to be a movie-within-a-movie. Even a more sober, nongenre work like *Casualties of War* (1989) is bookended by a prologue and epilogue that render equivocal the film's tone and form. Then there are the film parodies, or the other films-within-films, that form such a central part of *Murder à la Mod*, *Hi, Mom!* and *Home Movies*. On the rare occasion that a De Palma movie does open on a note of realism rather than illusion, the seasoned viewer is likely to remain sceptical for the initial ten or fifteen minutes, expecting the hero to wake up, the curtain to be yanked back. Even when he's on his best behaviour, De Palma has always got us lulled into a false state of insecurity.

In the cold light of analysis, the fact that these movies are plainly fun is sometimes forgotten. Perhaps the evident precision of De Palma's methods detracts from this. 'For Francis and Marty, their movies are almost created in the editing,' he has said. 'For me, it's just finishing the design.'[8] But then the best jokes are all in the timing. I can see how close *Sisters* or *The Fury* might come to an icy, Kubrickian rigour, but this is thwarted by the presence of zanier tendencies. De Palma is two kinds of student: he's the med-school nerd greeting the icky, gooey business of human biology with a straight face; but there is also evidence to suggest that he has just stumbled out of the Cambridge Footlights or a *Saturday Night Live* brainstorming session. I can't dismiss as mere coincidence the fact that both *The Fury* and Monty Python's *The Meaning of Life* build to climactic and graphic shots of a man exploding in a fountain of blood and bone and gristle. De Palma shares with those British surrealists a taste for the comedy of excess.

In a body of work where gags and shock effects are endlessly reflected back on themselves, it can't be coincidental that De Palma would go on to make a film called *Blow Out* – not just a riff on that movie's chief inspiration, *Blow Up*, but also the English-language title of Marco Ferreri's *La Grande Bouffe*. This gastronomical shock-comedy inspired that key scene in *The Meaning of Life*, and pretty much embodies the anarchic, taboo-busting sensibility to which De Palma was increasingly drawn throughout the 1960s and 1970s.

In a De Palma film, anarchy is constantly lingering in the corners of the frame, threatening to disrupt the carefully choreographed shots, the symmetry of the divided screen. The threat of its eruption is the whole point of the long split-screen sequence in *Phantom of the Paradise* in which the Juicy Fruits, a band of gormless Beach Boys clones, perform on the right of the frame while on the left an audibly ticking bomb is stowed in a prop car that is then wheeled on stage, eventually entering screen right. De Palma noted that 'you can look at your watch – tick, tick, tick – and know there's no intercutting',[9] and indeed the scene has that uniquely charged urgency that you may feel from watching live TV broadcasts of real disasters. There is another layer of trickery too: the scenes of disparate action eventually converge and anarchy is suddenly dispelled by a peaceful sense of completion and clarity, as when the bomb explodes, razing the artificial barrier that divides the screen. Or in *Sisters* when the police arrive at the killer's apartment after a prolonged sequence in which we have seen that their tardiness has enabled the scene of the crime to be comprehensively cleaned, and the corpse hidden. In these episodes we feel the simultaneous presence of the horrific and the humdrum, the close proximity of order and chaos; the ticking bomb within the candyland pop song, the slaughter behind the anonymous apartment door.

Those anarchic tendencies are given full rein in De Palma's 1960s films, which is what makes those pictures inherently inferior. The separate disciplines of suspense and slapstick become mutually nutritious in De Palma's best work; the comedy exacerbates and intensifies the suspense and horror. I think that's because the humour is used to whet our appetites, to show us how far he's willing to go. When the horror kicks in, we can't be certain that he'll know when to stop, or how. The humour doesn't dissipate either: the buzz can come in a shriek being halted in your throat by a laugh, or vice versa. The comic scenes in *Carrie*, for instance, have a bawdy, leering kinkiness. We can't be sure that the camera's intentions are honourable when it converts a raucous shower-room scene into a slow-motion tribute to naked teenage netball players everywhere, or when it patrols a line of miscreant female students as they sweat it out doing push-ups in detention while a rubbery synthesizer contributes a sleazy porno symphony in lieu of commentary.

Those creepy, surveillance-style camera movements that slowly ping-pong from left to right and back again might echo the methodical rigour with which the camera surveys the traffic jam in Godard's *Weekend*, or the supermarket checkouts in the same director's *Tout Va Bien*. But in *Carrie*, there is seediness mingled in with the style, something scalding, something naughty, bubbling away behind that implacable lens.

In most De Palma films there is that almost epiphanic point at which the director's apparently contradictory qualities fully and richly converge. In *Phantom of the Paradise* it comes during the heartbreaking scene when the Phantom (William Finley) performs in the studio, squeezing his strangulated voice out of a set of torn and tangled vocal chords while Swan (Paul Williams) manipulates the controls to tease out the tender voice that is hidden within the howls of pain. As the camera admires the wires and cables, the knobs and dials, there is a physical and metaphorical fusion of pop culture and movie classicism, and of flesh and technology, that makes the film, and the viewer, suddenly elated: you know you are witnessing the complete, unencumbered realization of an artistic concept, and that all the playful, trashy gags and allusions have been pointing toward this moment. In *The Fury* it happens when Gillian is transported into a man's memory by squeezing his hand, and De Palma replaces the background with back-projection that simultaneously inserts Gillian into the memory and renders her dislocated from it.

These are audacious effects, but it is De Palma's unique comic imagination that allows them to take flight. Without that wild streak, you can end up with a film-maker as prosaic as William Friedkin, who doesn't have the verve or ambition to free a picture like *The Exorcist* from its cumbersome moorings and let it roam in the viewer's imagination, as well as on the screen.

On its own, De Palma's anarchic humour can obliterate all sense of purpose. It needs something to fight against, and the rigid conventions of genre, in De Palma's case horror or suspense, provide that necessary conflict. Without it, you end up with pictures that are ineffectual or madcap, like *Get to Know Your Rabbit* and *Home Movies*. It isn't that those films reveal a side of De Palma that is fraudulent, or which should be suppressed. But only when it is harnessed to other traditions – to the grandiose schlock of *Phantom of the Paradise* or the plush horror of *Carrie* – does his antsy, impudent sensibility start to make sense. Even then, it can occasionally falter. There is the suspicion in *The Fury* that Kirk Douglas – called upon to break down over his son's disappearance one moment, then clown around in a comical, Inspector Clouseau-style disguise the next – hasn't been let in on the gag. The balance of tones isn't convincing and Douglas, who has to carry most of the film's shifts between comedy and portentousness, becomes the joke. But for the most part, De Palma's irreverent flashes acknowledge the absurdity of movie conventions in the same instant that he encourages us to surrender to them. The films tease us about the hoary old gimmicks of the movies, while simultaneously jolting them into life again.

In *Phantom of the Paradise*, this even becomes part of the movie's fabric. The film takes *The Phantom of the Opera* and *Faust* and dolls them up in inches of glam-rock slap – not to sneak outdated material past the audience in a groovy disguise, but to emphasize the timelessness of those source texts, the longevity of their insights and resonances. The film's college-revue mentality co-exists happily with its classical overtones. The former allows for a creation like the preening performer Beef (Gerritt Graham), who wears Shirley Temple ringlets and an Elvis Presley sneer, and whose demeanour is not radically altered by his eventual electrocution; while the latter necessitates and fosters a genuinely aristocratic sense of evil in the form of the sinister Svengali, Swan.

What distinguishes *Phantom of the Paradise* from a broader crowd-pleaser like *The Rocky Horror Picture Show* is that it isn't just commenting on cinema and pop culture, it is implicating itself in them. Where *Rocky Horror* has a tinny, rinky-dink feel, *Phantom of the Paradise* is suitably operatic in its execution. Jack Fisk's extravagant sets (decorated by his wife, Sissy Spacek, the future star of *Carrie*) include the Swan Records office, where black vinyl corridors spiral steeply upwards, and Swan's desk, embedded within a vulgar, oversized gold disc. 'I'd think of the most outlandish thing I could,' recalls Fisk, 'and he'd say "A little more, please. A little weirder."'[10] The same criteria might have been applied to the casting of the pocket-sized singer-songwriter Paul Williams as the exploited Phantom's mentor and tormentor – after meeting him, De Palma re-imagined Swan as 'this Napoleon of rock'.[11] Williams resembles Peter Lorre in a Susan George wig, and his reedy, insinuating voice would surely have landed him the role of chief doctor if there had ever been a *Carry On Asylum*. He was made to peep through keyholes, and crack up at the basest horrors, just like De Palma, and us.

But even the simple acts of seeing and watching are in these films complicated beyond all recognition. The whole of *Obsession* hinges on what the businessman Michael Courtland (Cliff

Robertson) thinks he is seeing. Pursuing a car in which he believes his wife (Genevieve Bujold) and daughter to be travelling with their kidnappers, he is distraught when it crashes and explodes – or as distraught as Robertson, the man with the iron mask, can ever be. He does not know, as we do, that you should never trust anything in the movies unless it happens right before your eyes, with no cut-aways or long shots. In both *Sisters* and *The Fury*, De Palma confuses the identification process by placing us within the mind of a character who is already, via hypnosis or telepathy, inhabiting the mind of someone else. In *Sisters*, Grace imagines herself into the experience of the Siamese twins, Danielle and Dominique (played by Margot Kidder) at the point of their separation, while in *The Fury* it is the telekinetic Gillian (Amy Irving) who is plugged into someone else's sensations.

This disorientating hall-of-mirrors effect incorporates a quartet of perspectives – the camera, the viewer, and two characters – which takes to its natural conclusion the gothic tradition of narrators addressing stories within stories to an audience within the audience. It's there too in *Phantom of the Paradise*, as Swan caresses Phoenix (Jessica Harper) in his mirrored boudoir, while the jealous Phantom looks on through the glass ceiling – his own voyeurism in turn spied upon by Swan, who is using a security camera to watch the Phantom watching him. De Palma's manipulation and layering of assorted perspectives calls into doubt the validity of what we are 'seeing' at any given moment.

In *Sisters*, Grace witnesses a murder, and when there appears to be no corroborating evidence, she implores the police to trust her recollection. 'I saw it!' she cries. 'Saw it happen! Actually saw it happen!' But exactly what has she seen? Her perspective has already been exposed as subtly biased. As a crusading journalist battling racism and police injustice, she witnesses an African-American man in the opposite apartment being stabbed, and filters what she has 'seen' through her own socio-political agenda. 'A white woman kills her black lover,' she fumes, 'and those racist pigs couldn't give a damn.' But we have seen what she has not: that the murderer was delusional, not racist. Grace's entire investigation hinges on the search for that corpse – essentially the search for a single, definitive truth – but she never finds it. The film denies her the privileged information that it gives us, which is what makes the closing shot so richly witty, as Grace's accomplice (Charles Durning), posing as a telephone engineer, straddles a telegraph pole and keeps watch over the sofa in which he is convinced that the body is stored. We know that his suspicions are correct; we have seen the body being bundled in there. But by withholding that un-equivocal resolution, De Palma keeps the film from finishing. A title proclaiming 'The End' might appear over that last shot of Durning, but we are not foolish enough to believe those words. The picture continues unspooling in our minds, long after it has finished unspooling on screen.

Beginnings and endings are traditionally placatory in cin-ema, easing an audience into and then back out of an unfamil-iar world, confirming the circularity of the narrative, and of life. In De Palma's work it's not so simple. His movies don't begin in any conventional sense. That beginning-within-a-beginning that we witness in *Sisters* is for the viewer a misstep, a wobble, that forces us to reassess what we are watching and how we are watching it. *Obsession* starts with a slide show in which the words 'And they lived happily ever after' are pro-jected on to the screen-within-the-screen. The rest of the movie is dedicated to making a nonsense of that phrase.

And if these films rarely begin in any conventional sense, so they rarely end at all; the audience doesn't get anything as lux-urious, or as fabricated, as closure. De Palma has become noto-rious for signing off with a visual exclamation mark – the cemetery nightmare in *Carrie*, John Cassavetes being 'deto-nated' in *The Fury*, the surprise murder (another nightmare) in *Dressed to Kill*. The intention is to send the audience out into the night with a fresh supply of unresolved fear and discomfort. In *Sisters*, that effect is achieved without the cathartic pay-off that a shock ending would bring. The superficial mystery of Dominique's whereabouts has been solved, and Daniele has overcome the ostensible villain (William Finley, part of that early De Palma repertory company that also includes Salt, Durning and Graham). Indeed, her victory is announced when she symbolically opens her eyes while kissing him. But Grace's own investigation has been curtailed, leaving her effectively blind to the full picture, and it is possible to experience the same note of agitation that might be felt after the unexplained calm which allows the credits of *The Birds* to finally roll: yes, the movie has ended, but without the customary sense of completion and finality on which our satisfaction depends.

The elliptical closing note on which the film ends, with the camera tilted suggestively downwards as though observing the tableau from some cosmic vantage point (as in the parting shots of *Carrie* and *Dressed to Kill*), preserves its mysteries in our mind, and leaves us with the suggestion that the story might still be unfolding out there, in the night, in the dark. As long as the comforting borders of a happy, or at least finite, ending have not contained that narrative then it still has the potential to impinge on our consciousness, for its horrors to be in some way loosed on us. In a conventional thriller like *Fatal Attraction*, the threat must be vanquished in order for equilibrium to be restored, and the audience calmed. But De Palma knows that this must never happen; it would mean that the game is over, the spell broken.

That explains why the end of a De Palma movie is often such a rich source of ambivalence and speculation. The questions thrown up by the twist in *Obsession* – in which Michael discovers that his wife's double, with whom he has fallen in love, is actually his long-lost daughter – are arguably more intriguing and provocative than anything in the preceding ninety minutes. And yet the shot with which De Palma bids us farewell is a brazen taunt to our curiosity: Robertson and Bujold, as his daughter, locked in an embrace while the camera circles them in a piece of visual grammar normally reserved for lovers. As the screen spins, so too does the viewer's head. Has the father's sexual attraction to the daughter terminated at the realization of their relationship to one another? If so, how will he process the feelings of guilt and shame attached to his initial desire for her? How will he ever be able to trust his eyes again? More to the point, how will we trust ours?

In these moments, a crucial transformation is effected. The director who measures out his films shot-by-storyboarded-shot with no margin for spontaneity becomes joint signatory with the prankster who loves to slay an audience with a punchline, or the gaping absence of one.

Making *The Long Goodbye* (1973): Robert Altman directs Nina Van Pallandt (as Eileen Wade) and Elliott Gould (Philip Marlowe). (© United Artists)

McCabe and Mrs Miller (1971): Julie Christie as Constance Miller.
(© Warner Bros)

6. Robert Altman

No modern film-maker has done more for the advancement of special effects in cinema than Robert Altman. With *2001: A Space Odyssey*, Stanley Kubrick increased the screen's capacity for vastness more dramatically than anyone since D. W. Griffith. George Lucas tickled our eyes with laser beams. Steven Spielberg parted the heavens to usher into the night sky a convoy of twinkling spacecraft, and opened the earth to admit a stampede of dinosaurs. James Cameron liquefied physical matter in *Terminator 2: Judgment Day*; John Lasseter and his Pixar cohorts made reality itself malleable in the *Toy Story* films, while the Wachowski Brothers in the *Matrix* trilogy and Ang Lee in *Crouching Tiger, Hidden Dragon* fought the laws of physics and won.

None of these pioneers has got anything on Robert Altman.

Our natural tendency to equate special effects with the visible technology demanded by fantastical or futuristic visions has caused his particular innovations to be undervalued. But no one has challenged and revolutionized the way in which we watch and listen to movies like Altman. Nor has anyone fought so hard to liberate cinema from the influence of literature, theatre and television. In his hands it has become an autonomous art form, and audiences have undergone a corresponding emancipation. He doesn't ever forget that cinema itself was the original special effect.

Altman released fourteen films between 1970 and 1979. Of those, there are only two – *Images* from 1972 and *Quintet* from 1979 – which I would not willingly watch again. That's some strike rate. How did he find the time to make them so good? How did he find the time to make them at all?

Of the remaining twelve, another two – *McCabe and Mrs Miller* (1971) and *Nashville* (1975) – are masterworks. A further three – *The Long Goodbye* (1973), *Thieves Like Us* and *California Split* (both 1974) – are as near as dammit. The other films from this period are *M*A*S*H* (1970), *Brewster McCloud* (1970), *Buffalo Bill and the Indians* (1976), *3 Women* (1977), *A Wedding* (1978), *A Perfect Couple* and *Health* (both 1979). Even these less rewarding pictures prove that Altman on an off-day still makes most other film-makers look like savages scratching storyboards on the walls of their caves.

That *M*A*S*H* was his breakthrough movie had as much to do with synchronicity as quality. Altman had spent the preceding twenty years writing scripts, making largely undistinguished features and forging a career in television on series like *Bonanza* and *Alfred Hitchcock Presents*. He abandoned that medium out of frustration in 1964, and after a few more features he found himself eighteenth or so on the list to direct Ring Lardner, Jr.'s Korean War-based comedy *M*A*S*H* after the likes of Stanley Kubrick, Sidney Lumet and George Roy Hill had passed on it.

M*A*S*H is best viewed now as a statement of intent. The first lines of dialogue spoken in the picture are overlapping. It sounds so simple – just like the concept of cinema sounds simple unless you happened to be in the audience at one of the Lumière Brothers' first screenings, cowering in terror under your seat or running screaming from the room.

Two actors are talking at the same time; you can't separate one voice from the other. It's all right to admit that you feel confused. Imagine if you opened a novel and the first two lines had been deliberately typed over one another: you wouldn't really know what to make of it; you might take it back to the bookshop. But the feeling you get from Altman's movies is that it doesn't matter if you miss a line here or there, or if your attention wanders toward some trivial detail in a far corner of the frame. Perhaps I have misheard a line in *M*A*S*H*, or been distracted away from whatever Donald Sutherland or Elliott Gould is doing in a particular scene. Altman's cinema rests on the generous principle that the material is created in the hands of the actors, and the movie is completed in the eye of the viewer. He uses long lenses, slow zooms and tiny microphones to ambush his performers – to catch them accidentally being natural. 'Always assume that everything is going to be kept [on film],' advised Paul Dooley, co-writer of *Health*, and a regular fixture in Altman's movies in the late 1970s.[1] The zoom, in particular, prevents an actor from switching off. Whereas the common method of shooting alerts a performer to the moment when he or she is in close-up, Altman prefers to render the process less mechanical for both actor and audience. We may not always be certain of a scene's intended emphasis, and it's a safe bet that the performers on screen aren't either.

In the most elegantly composed of Altman's pictures, this looseness can be the source of the purest pleasures. In a film like *Brewster McCloud*, there is no such thing as a trivial detail. The movie is comprised entirely of absurdist skits and defined by its appetite for loopy, half-finished scenes and cock-a-hoop gags that even the camera seems scarcely to register. A crow pecks at Altman's name during the opening credits; the sound of a police siren is layered over the image of a plodding tortoise; an ornithologist's lecture about crests and plumages accompanies a rain-drenched funeral scene in which the mourners have turned out in gaily-coloured mackintoshes, wielding garish umbrellas. (Perhaps Altman's 1980 film *Popeye* tasted stale because he had already made it several times over; all along he had been decorating the frame like a comic-strip panel from *Mad* magazine.) When you see a modern film that adopts the same kind of style – Spike Jonze's *Being John Malkovich*, say, or Otar Iosseliani's *Farewell, Home Sweet Home* – it can make you realize just how bored you have become with directors who lead you to the trough and force you to eat. The arrangement of the film frame in Altman's movie encourages the eye to roam, just as the multi-layered sound design extends the same invitation to the ear.

Brewster McCloud is ostensibly a whodunnit with a garnish of satire and allegory. But Altman shows as much interest in plot as he later would in *Gosford Park*, a murder mystery in which even the closest relatives of the victim cannot conceal their boredom at the whole sorry affair, or wait to attend to their social engagements. Some of the most pleasing moments in *Brewster McCloud* occur when Altman is signposting a similar contempt for narrative demands. A car-chase ends with the police vehicle simply coming to rest in a pond, before the cop (Michael Murphy) commits suicide from behind the wheel. As if this were not enough to remind us that we are not watching *Bullitt*, the whole thing happens largely in long-shot, with the foreground occupied by a group of extras posing for a photograph. Sometimes Altman won't even adhere to basic formalist conventions. *Nashville* begins with an advertisement for itself; *M*A*S*H* ends with a Brechtian announcement regarding the film we have just watched; *Brewster McCloud* actually 'starts' twice because the on-screen band botch the opening music, while it closes with the cast being introduced by name as they parade across the screen in circus garb, stepping over the prone body of the Icarus-like hero.

In the wrong conditions, the charm of Altman's anarchic spontaneity doesn't always win out over the material. This is most obvious in *M*A*S*H*, where the undercurrent of hostility is at odds with the picture's informal approach. In order to appreciate the film in any sense other than an academic one, it becomes necessary to subscribe to Altman's view that the strangely spiteful hi-jinks and cultivated zaniness of the film's anti-heroes are actually funny. And I can't. The blitheness of the camera in the face of those opportunities for hysteria provided by the war genre is something to be treasured. But a similar perspective is adopted in *Catch-22* and *Three Kings*, in *Pretty Village, Pretty Flame* and *Kippur*, without a corresponding cost to compassion. It's true that *M*A*S*H* provided an important counter-cultural voice in early 1970s cinema, both as a foghorn-blast of irreverent protest in the face of Vietnam (a conflict that is implicit in the movie, but never mentioned), and as a signal that the days of the callous, rigid heroism of John Wayne – still the biggest male box-office star in 1971 – were numbered. But the alternative, as proposed by *M*A*S*H*, doesn't seem any less elitist or discriminatory.

If you can't chuckle along with the attempts by Hawkeye (Donald Sutherland) and Trapper John (Elliott Gould) to intimidate anyone who doesn't share their idea of a good time – whether it's Major O'Houlihan (Sally Kellerman), who objects to Hawkeye's sleazy sexual innuendoes, or the prissy Major Burns (Robert Duvall) – then you can feel as excluded by the movie as the targets of the gags are from the atmosphere of frat-house tomfoolery. Scenes such as the broadcast over the PA system of the lovemaking between O'Houlihan and Burns play now like unhappy harbingers of a genre that would effectively paralyse American cinema in the late 1970s and early 1980s – the infantile, through-the-keyhole sex comedy, from *Porky's* and *Revenge of the Nerds* downwards. Of course, this could be a minority view: it's the sort of scene glossy men's magazines regularly single out with retrospective reverence.

But to laugh at the picture now seems to me to require an act of calculated regression; a throwing-off of the kind of comic sophistication at play in later Altman movies like *Nashville* or *Gosford Park*. The paranoid suggestion peddled by Hawkeye and Trapper John, that anyone who isn't with them is against them, turns up again in a diluted form in some of Altman's other films. In *California Split*, an ageing transvestite becomes the butt of a protracted and rather excruciating gag, ridiculed for the amusement of a quartet of 'normal' heterosexual men and women. In *A Wedding*, the gay characters are treated with a cavalier cruelty that seems to enforce the same outdated social structures contested by the rest of the film. And in *Health*, the possibility that a woman might have started life in a different gender is beyond the comprehension of the movie. In the gruff, cigar-chomping manner of that woman, played by Glenda Jackson, there is a request to the audience to share in the appalled laughter of the other characters.

Film-makers and screenwriters should be relieved of the pressure to tend to their creations like loving parents, lest the screen be populated entirely by virtuous men and women enslaved to learning curves and story arcs. But the misanthropy of the pen or the camera is a different matter, and it is a minor problem in Altman's work that he isn't always content to pass insidious judgements on the least favoured of his characters: he wants us to collude in his casual misanthropy.

Later in *Health*, there is a scene in which the characters are gathered in a hotel bar. One man cheerfully confesses to being gay, while the women air their casual complaints about sex. James Garner, a light-heartedly macho actor best known from the TV series *The Rockford Files*, surveys the scene and remarks, 'I feel like the oddball here.' The film seems to be suggesting that such a prospect is unthinkable; that something has gone very wrong when a man as handsome and as confident in his heterosexuality as Garner can feel like a freak.

I think there's a streak of moral conservatism in Altman's work that is consistently at odds with his jubilantly liberal filmmaking style. If the only evidence that you had to go on was *Nashville*, then this claim would be laughed out of any court in the land. That film has its own noxious imp, the country-and-western singer Haven Hamilton (Henry Gibson), through whom most of the conservatism is filtered. 'You get your hair cut,' Haven snaps at a vaguely hippyish pianist, 'You don't belong in Nashville.' On the contrary, the picture goes to extraordinary lengths not only to demonstrate that it is Haven who is close to being obsolete in the modern cultural landscape, but also to rejoice in that fact. When you become conscious of Altman sneering through the lens in parts of *A Wedding* and *Health*, it can feel as though Haven Hamilton himself is directing the picture.

I wonder if people aren't occasionally more than Altman can take. The disfigurement motif in *The Long Goodbye* – a mummified figure in a hospital bed, an injured woman who squawks through the layers of gauze on her face – would suggest so. Those images make me squirm, and I can feel the camera recoiling from them too. Like Spielberg, Altman immerses himself in the frenzy of the crowd, only to identify most passionately with those among his characters who choose isolation or escape over assimilation. The celibate loner Brewster (Bud Cort) in *Brewster McCloud* sees his dreams of flying crash to the ground after he has lost his virginity – intimate human contact has depleted his uniqueness and resilience. In *The Long Goodbye*, the jovial nonchalance with which Philip Marlowe (Elliott Gould) greets the world ('It's OK with me,' he shrugs repeatedly) leaves him vulnerable and friendless by the end of the picture, when even his cat has deserted him. *Thieves Like Us* ends with Keechie (Shelley Duvall), who is soon to bear the child of her late boyfriend, climbing the train station steps and becoming lost in the crowd – the eerie switch to slow-motion making her fate, and the film's attitude toward it, seem ambiguous. In *California Split*, the compulsive gambler Bill (George Segal) quietly retreats for ever from the limelight before his buddy Charlie (Gould again) has even finished totting up their $82,000 jackpot. The tentative lovers in *A Perfect Couple* are each struggling to find independence from sprawling and oppressive families, surrogate or biological. And both the title characters in *McCabe and Mrs Miller* nervously guard their own individual sanctuaries, never quite able to achieve unconditional intimacy. The closest they come is when they make love – an act that is transformed into a monetary transaction by the brothel madam Constance Miller's insistence that payment be deposited on the dressing table before flesh touches flesh.

Even that potentially erotic scene is subverted in an act of brilliant blasphemy against Hollywood. You simply don't get Warren Beatty and Julie Christie in the same film, the same shot, the same bed, and then cut away before their lips even meet. But Altman does. And the absence of the scene says as much about the movie as anything that we actually see. A love scene would have violated the romance of isolation; it would have provided a physical union in a movie full of rickety uncrossed bridges and walkways, each one a symbol for the emotional connections that the film's characters are unable to make. Constance is in her room with her books and her music box; McCabe is banging on the door, demanding to be allowed in. I'm almost embarrassed to commit it to paper, for fear of making it sound too literal. The truth is that it's a funny, moving, heartbreaking image that effortlessly encapsulates the movie's theme. 'I never knew anyone in my life who spent so much time behind a locked door,' grumbles McCabe, incapable of seeing that he is as firmly barricaded behind his own defences as the woman he lacks the wherewithal to woo. He's another of those Altman misfits who – like Marlowe in *The Long Goodbye*, Charlie in *California Split* and Millie (Shelley Duvall) in *3 Women* – talk a mile a minute, but take hours to uncover the simplest truth. You have to ask what all that chatter is concealing.

McCabe and Mrs Miller is Altman's most devastating evocation of the loneliness that lies at the heart of most of his work, buried beneath the noise – the incessant overlapping banter on top of sound effects on top of music. John McCabe is an entrepreneur who establishes a whorehouse in the Pacific Northwest mining settlement of Presbyterian Church in 1902. He's a shambles, a vain and foolhardy clown dressed in burdensome furs on which you can practically smell every bar and brothel he's passed through on his journey. His own brothel is a shambles too, at least until Constance Miller rolls into town and demands to show him how to make it a success.

The picture is coarse-grained; the film stock is peppered with dirt, as though it was dragged into town tied to the tail of McCabe's horse. Here is a movie that will frustrate restorers, not to mention the DVD generation, obsessed as it is with crispness and cleanliness of image. Your eyes can feel the very texture of the film itself in every scene, the way your fingers might caress the stiff parchment of an ancient scripture, or the gnarled leather of a gunfighter's boots. The dialogue is correspondingly profane and earthy – there is talk of a 'turd in your pocket', a 'tit in the wringer', of 'screwing with the wind whistling up your kaiser'. That's when you can hear the dialogue. 'The sound was fucked,' said Altman's editor, Lou Lombardo, 'but he never changed it. I think he accomplished what he wanted to do with sound in *M*A*S*H* – where it was audible but it was overlapped. He did it well. But on *McCabe*, it was recorded in there – a dirty track, a muddy track. It was like trying to get an out of focus picture in focus.'[2]

And yet this movie, this filthy-looking, barely audible movie, is a thing of immense beauty and piercing eroticism. The scene of the prostitutes piling into the tub together is palpably hot and sticky, like Ingres' painting *The Turkish Bath* sprung to steamy life. The shots of Constance alone in her room with just an opium pipe and a music box for company are profoundly affecting; the camera pulls out of a close-up on her neck, and retreats through the flame of a lamp, to reveal her reclining on her bed, softly caressed by the light in the midst of her nocturnal sanctuary. She looks like she's floating out to sea.

Then there is that much decried sound design: mumbled, slurred, prone to the distorting effects of inclement weather.

Miraculously, each individual layer of noise – the dialogue, the background bustle, Leonard Cohen's compositions – seems to be emanating from the same source. Through the plangent strains of Cohen's opening lament, you can make out the wind whistling between guitar strings strummed by frozen fingers determined to play on through the chill; the rain seems to pitter-pat in the gaps between the notes. The music isn't layered over the images so much as soaked into them, and it may be surprising for audiences raised on the spurious association of songs and images to find these elements organically intertwined. Cohen isn't just a voice: he's the unseen balladeer who accompanies the characters in their loneliest moments, providing counsel and sanctuary.

Voices trickle in from all corners throughout the movie, none of them entirely audible, just as nothing in the film is ever completely visible. But then what are we supposed to be looking at, or listening to? You have to train yourself not to ask that question. The movie's yours: free your mind; renounce your old Hollywood ways.

The camera zooms in through the drinkers in a seedy bar, toward a man plucking at his violin. Then it veers over to McCabe, before finally returning to the violinist as the focus of the shot. When something conventionally dramatic does occur – a woman attacking a man with a knife – it is likely to be treated as an aside, cut together in elliptical shots that suggest a fond detachment. Emphasis comes when you least expect it, like the sharp zoom on to McCabe's grinning face, a gold tooth flashing in the dark like a bright idea.

Celebrity and beauty are given equally short shrift. Our first glimpse of Julie Christie comes without the lingering soft-focus and orchestral bloom that a lifetime of Hollywood movies have taught us is the only way to introduce a star. Here, the camera hardly registers her presence: she's in a doorway, she looks up, walks away; the door is shut behind her. We don't see her again for another ten or fifteen minutes. Such a humble entrance: if you didn't know who she was, you would have written her off as a fetching bit-player. Somehow the possibility that radiance and beauty of that magnitude might be hiding behind a clapboard shack – might, in fact, be hiding anywhere – is uplifting. It's also another minor but telling affront to the accepted hierarchy of mainstream cinema.

When Constance arrives in Presbyterian Church in the drizzle and the mud, there is something irrepressibly classy about her. She might cuss and spit like a sailor; we might sympathize with McCabe's apprehensiveness as he watches her wolfing down her fried eggs. (His expression suggests that he fears he will be next on her plate.) And it may be that by the end of the picture Altman will have won his battle against Hollywood, as Warren Beatty silently dies on his belly in the snow, the ultimate symbol of impotence and defeat for a man whose face is his fortune. But whenever Christie is in shot, star power blasts through the defences that have been erected against it. When she arrives in town, we might be watching Marie Antoinette clocking in for her shift at the milking stool.

Altman's disrespect for the fluctuating hierarchy of stardom again finds a willing ally in Christie, who contributes a brief cameo to *Nashville* playing herself. 'Ain't she the one who got off the train in the snow?' snorts Delbert (Ned Beatty), alluding to *Dr Zhivago*. Earlier in the film, Delbert has been embarrassed by his own failure to recognize Elliott Gould. 'I just shook the man's hand like he was someone off the street!' he cringes. The scepticism of the singer Connie White (Karen Black) best identifies our expectations of what a superstar should be, and points up Altman's distaste for that entire culture of glamour, when she casts an unforgiving eye over Christie and scoffs, 'Come on! She can't even brush her hair!'

The scene has the sharp kick of a severe breach of etiquette. It's the sight of Altman eating soup with his fish knife: he has insulted the notion of celebrity, and in the same instant razed the divisions between film and reality by having fictional characters conversing with real actors, a practice that would reach a euphoric peak in his 1991 film *The Player*. Altman has a wonderfully restless, resourceful quality that leads him to draw at liberty from wherever he chooses, regardless of protocol. When you see the ease with which he integrates real characters into fictional narratives – Charlie Parker in *Kansas City*, Ivor Novello in *Gosford Park*, the talk-show host Dick Cavett playing himself in *Health* – you can only mourn again the fact that he never got to make his mooted film of E. L. Doctorow's *Ragtime*, a novel that exploits its knowing, prickly humour from precisely those situations where fact meets fiction.

Altman's anti-star tendency is also manifested in something as fundamental as his keen eye for an idiosyncratic face. His camera falls in love with people who resemble parodies of bad yearbook photographs. And magically he persuades us to fall in love with them too. Another director would have identified the gormless, goggle-eyed beauty of Shelley Duvall, but I don't think anyone else could have promoted her so adoringly, or recognized her capacity to play so many variations on the role of ditz. Her delusional chatterbox Millie in *3 Women* feels strongly like a climax to her work for Altman. Millie has the dislocated serenity that Duvall brings to her small role as a nervous prostitute in *McCabe and Mrs Miller*, and the skittishness that she had in *Brewster McCloud* (where she was Brewster's corruptor, with long, crunchy eyelashes like tarantula legs), and the febrile vulnerability of Keechie, the lovestruck teenager and unwitting moll in *Thieves Like Us*. Those actors who have built a body of work with Altman become with each new role for him more like musicians toying around with old tunes. There's a revealing continuity in Keith Carradine's performances, from his cameo as the luckless cowboy – all buckteeth, pointy hat and daddy-longlegs limbs – in *McCabe and Mrs Miller*, to the tender but muddleheaded crook Bowie in *Thieves Like Us*. And then how frightful to see that seductive naivety deployed for manipulative purposes in his role in

Nashville as Tom, the folksy singer who gets through women like underwear. Though it's himself he's really in love with: Altman uses the sight of rotating tape reels as shorthand to prepare us for another shot of Tom in bed with a different woman – the guy can't get through sex without one of his own songs on the stereo.

Duvall and Carradine, and Elliott Gould – whose tightly-wound curls make it seem like he's let slip a wisecrack before he has even opened his mouth – were never used as sympathetically by any other director. (Carradine was luckiest in his films for Altman's erstwhile assistant and sometime co-writer, Alan Rudolph, the best being a slight variation on Tom in the 1984 *Choose Me*.) But there is a whole other league of Altman players who seem suited to his pictures, and his alone; you fear for them in the jungles of Hollywood. It is a pleasant surprise to see Henry Gibson turn up in Paul Thomas Anderson's *Magnolia*, and the homage is fitting: this is, after all, a multi-character narrative that owes everything to vintage Altman, even if it is realized with the kind of intense directorial manipulation that is the antithesis of the freewheeling *Nashville*. And Gibson's carnivorously carnal fop in *Magnolia* was clearly a close relative of his earlier characters – perhaps a queer twin brother disowned by Haven Hamilton, or a cousin of the venal Dr Verringer from *The Long Goodbye*. (It's a measure of Gibson's natural creepiness that even behind a voluptuous bosom and an inch of slap in *Health*, he's still not quite as unnerving as when he's plain old Haven in full neckerchief-and-sequinned-jumpsuit get-up.)

There were other faces among Altman's children for whom you feared: Rene Auberjonois, whose tasks for Altman included slowly turning into a bird, feather by feather, in *Brewster McCloud*; or Bud Cort, an innocent adrift in the chaos of *M*A*S*H*, who was promoted to the lead in *Brewster McCloud* before winning a starring role in Hal Ashby's *Harold and Maude*. Cort resembles a hundred-year-old baby; he looks like he fell in the fountain of youth. The shock of seeing him

muscular and near-naked in *Brewster McCloud* only compounds your suspicion that he was grown in a petri dish, not a
womb.

And what would Paul Dooley have done without Robert
Altman? His charisma needs space to develop on screen – lots
of space. When you first set eyes on him as Alex in *A Perfect
Couple*, you instinctively hold on to your wallet. In the first
scene, when he's wisecracking so relentlessly that he fails even
to notice the indifference of his companion, I felt a physical
slump. So this is the guy we're going to be following throughout the entire film? Great. As if his crummy jokes weren't
enough ('My father was Greek, which would ordinarily make
me half-Greek. But my mother was Greek too'), he gets a scene
early on in the picture where he has to force a goodnight kiss
on the unwilling lips of Sheila (Marta Heflin). But Altman gives
us time in his company, and thirty minutes into the movie I had
scribbled in my notepad 'I like this guy – he's so weird', followed by three exclamation marks to adequately convey my
surprise. You'll see Dooley crop up now in minor parts: he's a
cop in Christopher Nolan's *Insomnia*, and his presence in *Runaway Bride* and *Happy, Texas* reminds you how Altman might
have turned those cautious endorsements of small-town eccentricity into full-scale celebrations.

While there may not be much call now for Altman's former
collaborators, there are younger Altmans with their own en-
sembles. Paul Thomas Anderson has an unofficial repertory company, as does Christopher Guest, whose semi-improvisatory
work in pictures like *Best in Show* and *Waiting for Guffman*
shares crucial DNA with the films of Altman and Mike Leigh.
You might look at actors like Gibson, Dooley or Cort and
think, That's no face fit to put before a camera. Which is one of
the things that makes Altman's casts such a feast for the eyes –
the notion of movie stars is there to be denigrated. In the case
of *McCabe and Mrs Miller*, even the most glamorous goddess
ends up alone, getting strung-out on opium and dreaming, per-

haps, of a time when the final reel ended with a discreet kiss, and an even more discreet fade-out.

It wasn't only superstars that found their way into Altman's crosshairs. *McCabe and Mrs Miller* is the first of his regular assaults on genre. It's a western with rusty spurs and a three-legged horse. The hero's a fool who isn't half as tough as the woman he desires but can't give himself to. When the villain shows up, he comes armed with a business deal. And when that has no effect, the assassin arrives for a stark, clinical fight to the death. Admittedly it wasn't quite as confounding as Peter Fonda's own lovely, languorous anti-western, *The Hired Hand*, which also opened in 1971 and shared with Altman's film a cinematographer (Vilmos Zsigmond), the demotion of the frontier hero, and a blasé rebuttal of the genre code. But the point had been made – top-dollar superstars could expect to receive no quarter.

Fans of Altman's work have come to anticipate the undignified slump that immediately succeeds a soaring triumph, and in the way of these things *McCabe and Mrs Miller* was followed in 1972 by the portentous psychological thriller *Images*, about a woman (Susannah York) unable to distinguish between reality and hallucinations. John Williams' doomy score competes with a symphony of sounds by Stomu Yamash'ta – disembodied groans, wind chimes, unidentified clangs – and accidentally illuminates the picture's own struggle between Bergmanesque sobriety and the high-camp horror of Hammer. Despite some coldly beautiful photography – again by Zsigmond – and one bona fide shock, in which the identity of York's seducer suddenly alters mid-kiss, *Images* is wrecked by a single glaring fault in its conception. In *Repulsion* and *Rosemary's Baby*, a woman's mind and body hang in the balance. In *Under the Sand*, we have an overwhelming emotional investment in the widow whose sanity is crumbling. In *The Butcher Boy*, the exaggerated reality provides gradual and revealing access into a child's damaged brain. But at no point in *Images* does it matter in the slightest which one of York's alternate lives is actually real; nothing is at stake.

Altman wasn't about to give up on the attempt to make his own *Persona*, as evidenced by *3 Women*, which five years later played out similar fantasies of sexual threat, identity crisis and distorted reality. But at least in that film, Altman had the good sense to filter his pretensions through performers of some vision. Shelley Duvall as Millie, the Desert Springs carer whose self-image is violently divorced from reality, brings a stinging sense of desolation to a fractured woman who has become her own Barbie doll. She's lost in her awful role-playing games as the belle of the ball, the perfect hostess. When the film itself fractures halfway through – in the manner of David Lynch's *Lost Highway* and *Mulholland Drive* – and psychological suspense intrudes on what previously had been a pastel-coloured replay of a Mike Leigh horror-comedy of suburban embarrassment, the switch in tone doesn't jolt you out of the picture. When you watch *Images*, it seems that the shock tactics and the trashy gimmicks came first, and the characters second. In *3 Women*, the theft of Millie's personality by her formerly ineffectual chum Pinkie (Sissy Spacek) feels like the most natural thing in the world. You couldn't imagine anyone more ripe for possession than this poor winsome creature whose self-absorption is like an all-over scab.

But there remains something unconvincing in the latter stages of *3 Women*, when the picture becomes an advertisement for symbolic sisterhood, that reinforces just how inflexible Altman can be when he makes one of those concerted departures from the funkiness of his ensemble pieces. You would never guess that a film like *Quintet*, for instance, had been made by the same man who positively swooned at the sight of human beings going about their mundane chores in *Thieves Like Us*, or who gulped down the boozy bar-room chit-chat in *California Split* as though it were Tennyson. In the sound of George Segal and Elliott Gould trying to name the seven dwarves, you could hear a director who knew how to keep his actors alive on the screen, and the audience energized in their seats.

In *Quintet*, that's gone, along with everything else. It may be one of the most inert films ever made. I don't think Paul Newman is an actor suited to Altman. He felt bashful and tentative in *Buffalo Bill and the Indians*, like a parent who has arrived too early to collect his daughter from the disco. But that film had a liveliness unconnected to him. *Quintet*, which revolves around a futuristic board game, the rules of which we neither know nor want to, gives the eye a choice between icy landscapes and Newman's deep-frozen face. The ear doesn't even get that much variety: if you can't brave the dialogue – fit as it is for one of Woody Allen's parodies of Chekhov ('Yes,' says one character sombrely, 'we must be careful with a man who hunts seals where there are no seals') – then the only alternative is the sound of a pack of wild dogs fighting over precious scraps of meat, or possibly the last remaining VHS copy of *Nashville*.

What disappeared from Altman's work in the late 1970s was the clarity and fluidity that had characterized his films from the first part of the decade. *McCabe and Mrs Miller*, *The Long Goodbye* and *Thieves Like Us* remained faithful to their respective genres even as they dismantled them. Still, it would be difficult now to comprehend the outrage with which the casting of Elliott Gould as Raymond Chandler's private dick Philip Marlowe was greeted. This was really Humphrey Bogart's role, and the dishevelled, apathetic Gould was about the farthest thing from Bogart this side of Rin-Tin-Tin. He might have been cast to attract disapproval. Even the animals in *The Long Goodbye* disrespect him: a pooch refuses to be dislodged from the centre of the road by his car horn, a Doberman tries to savage him, and he is upstaged in one shot by a pair of dogs insolently fucking in the background.

In the film's opening minutes, he is reduced to playing elaborate tricks on his cat to disguise the fact that he's all out of its favourite chow. Could you imagine Bogart stooping to that? If that cat had complained, he might have snapped its wee neck between his thumb and forefinger.

In a film that takes the form of one extended kiss-off, one long goodbye, to the inherited clichés of the hardboiled crime genre, Gould is an apposite figurehead. When Marlowe is grilled by a cop, he sniffs, 'Is this where I'm supposed to say, "What's this all about?"?' The picture is informed by an equivalent knowingness. It turns everything inside-out. The emphasis is placed not on motivation, as we have come to expect from the detective genre, but on the dreadfulness of human behaviour as an end in itself. It's almost irrelevant that the suspected murderer turns out to be guilty; by the time that revelation arrives, we have been sickened enough. A gangster breaks a Coca-Cola bottle in his mistress's face seconds after boasting of his tenderness. The teensy-weensy Dr Verringer intimidates the writer Roger Wade (Sterling Hayden), an ogre twice his size, with a sound slap in the face. These disorientating reversals erupt out of the woozy, late-night LA calm that seems so comforting in the movie's opening moments, as Marlowe wanders the aisles of a 24-hour Thrift-E-Mart at 3 a.m., his somnambulant coolness looking like a defence against the vagaries of modern life, rather than the handicap that it will transpire to be.

The ceaseless repetition of the title song insulates us within the world of the movie, but what feels novel to begin with soon evokes claustrophobia. Music is a primary means of storytelling in Altman's work. In *Nashville*, the seamlessness with which the film cuts from country and western to gospel, bluegrass to rock 'n' roll, reflects the cross-section of characters, and the film's sense of limitless possibilities. But in *The Long Goodbye*, we are trapped, like Marlowe, in a city that's tuned to one melancholy ballad, with no possibility of switching stations.

With the exception of the bitterly ironic blast of 'Hooray for

Hollywood' with which the movie opens and closes, 'The Long Goodbye' is the only composition that is permitted on to the soundtrack. We hear it everywhere, in countless incarnations – as a smoky torch song or smoothed out into supermarket Muzak; pounded on a sorrowful piano in a deserted bar, or ringing out in the chime of a doorbell. It's played on sitars, and it's expanded into a freeform jazz workout. But there is no escaping it.

Thieves Like Us offers its own commentary in the form of the radio adventure serials to which the characters in 1930s Mississippi tune in. One of the film's most lyrical scenes plainly quantifies the downtime after dinner, when a household is listening to 'The Shadow' ('Who knows what evil lurks in the heart of men?'). A mother is washing up at the sink; her young daughter is admiring herself in the mirror as she parades in her sister's clothes; the youngest child fools around with matches. There is warmth and respectfulness in the way Altman simply catalogues ordinary life, illuminating those episodes that would not normally attract the camera's attention, let alone grace the cutting-room floor – those passages that don't make the grade as narrative.

When I watch the film, I'm struck by how much takes place off-screen. Which is to say that an entire movie could be made of the parts Altman doesn't show, or only half-reveals. The death of one of the film's main characters isn't even depicted. Instead, the young hood Bowie learns of it during a radio broadcast in which the temperamental reception distorts every alternate sentence. Only one of the gang's numerous bank robberies makes it to the screen, photographed with a high-angle camera that surveys the heist with the stubborn detachment of a CCTV system. Even Bowie's death is hidden from us, perhaps in defiance of the graphic shootings at the end of *Bonnie and Clyde*, but also because the camera is more interested in Keechie, whose distress is emphasized with a rare use of slow-motion. Until that scene, anyone anticipating a re-run of Arthur

Penn's film will have had to make do with the sound of fire-
crackers – a kind of surrogate gunfire that foreshadows Bowie's
demise without the film needing to stoop to any spurious shoot-
outs.

Here was a case of a film that categorically failed to deliver
on the promises of its genre, and one of which you feel certain
Roger Corman would not have approved. But I would take its
modest insights over the barnstorming tendencies of exploitation cinema any day. You want action cinema? Take the scene
where Bowie and Keechie are getting to know one another:
they're sitting on the porch as night draws in; they are listening
to the wireless and talking just enough to disguise the fact that
they don't know what to say to one another. She's dragging on
a cigarette and swigging from a Coke. He asks her hopefully,
'Did you ever shoot a .45?' Their rocking chairs are performing
a duet of squeaks and creaks; a dog is barking in the distance.
You can feel their twitchiness, and their pleased-as-punch excitement, along the back of your neck. Altman knows not to
rush this: he teases out the magical suspense of romance and
desire, so that when Bowie and Keechie are finally in bed together, it feels in some way substantiated – we have seen how
they got there, and we believe in it. This isn't just a liaison created in the editing suite. He pulls off the same trick in *A Perfect
Couple*, a much less distinguished picture but one in which the
eventual bed scene is even more hard-earned, coming as it does
an hour into the film, after Sheila has knocked Alex unconscious with an iron poker, and he has wrestled with one of her
prospective suitors. Love in Altman's films doesn't fall out of
the clouds. It's struggled with, or squandered.

Whereas *McCabe and Mrs Miller*, *The Long Goodbye* and
Thieves Like Us challenged the conventions of existing texts,
California Split and *Nashville* patented an untested form,
drawing from the simple subject of human interaction a newly
expansive species of anthropological comedy. Altman came
across *California Split* after it had slipped through the fingers of

its original director, Steven Spielberg, who had worked with the writer Joseph Walsh on the script back in the days when it was titled *Slide*. *California Split* has an air of informality, but it's driven by a momentum that only seems casual; like Jeff Goldblum's tricycle in *Nashville*, it might look 'long, low and laid-back in the front' but it carries a hidden kick. The picture has just two main characters – Charlie and Bill, compulsive gamblers who head to the roulette and blackjack tables of Reno in search of sufficient funds to placate Bill's bookie. There isn't any more to the picture than that, but Altman's control over what looks like deceptively baggy material marshals you toward an unexpectedly moving and downbeat ending, just as it would on a larger scale in *Nashville*. And the playing of Gould and Segal is exquisite. It's a movie of crisply funny moments undercut by a lingering despair, of silver linings dogged by clouds.

In one scene, Charlie is cornered by a mugger immediately after a big win, but refuses to surrender his bounty, instead persuading the crook to take half the prize without complaint. It's a measure of the film's skew-whiff charm that scenes like this retain a salty realism despite their absurdity. I think you can believe that Elliott Gould has no internal censor – ideas and observations form on his lips, not in his brain, and they're out before he knows it himself. Behind his languid delivery lies the crackling comic ingenuity of a skid row stand-up. When the camera patrols the gamblers at a poker table, Gould turns Charlie's observations about each player into a kind of lolling, Bukowski-esque poetry. 'Lyndon Johnson's definitely his hero . . . That kid's seen *The Cincinnati Kid* too many times . . . One-time cha-cha dancer . . .' A stack of chips before an empty chair prompts a mention of Claude Rains from *The Invisible Man*. Gould never lets up; he's all interior monologue. In that respect, he is the ideal spokesperson for Altman's world, where anything is possible as long as you just keep talking. When Gould requests $100 credit on the one-armed bandits, or forlornly calls for the pit boss after a final tally of two cherries on the fruit machine fails to yield a pay-out, he's like the poster child for sad sacks everywhere. 'I feel like a winner,' he bleats, 'but I know I look like a loser.' No matter how low he sinks, the sparkle in his eyes never dims.

Spielberg was grudging in his praise for *California Split*. It's easy to imagine that the climax, in which Altman works against the grain of suspense, would infuriate a director like Spielberg, who regards any distance between the audience and the action as potentially hazardous. But Altman keeps his cool, and ours, during that long stretch in Reno. Just when the chance presents itself for a triumphant flourish, he pulls back, alerting us to Bill's moment of solitary contemplation. 'Steven would have built that last scene, that gambling scene, into one gigantic orgasm,' said Walsh, 'climaxing the last forty pages of the script until you were on the edge of your seat. He would never have filmed it as loose [as Altman] . . . But Steven knows it is a really special film. Yes, he might have made more money, but he didn't know if he could have made a better film.'[3]

Nashville has a comparable looseness to *California Split*, only on a bigger scale. And here too the mood grows overcast before you have time to run for cover. There's a scene in *California Split* when Bill's bookie is making increasingly aggressive threats, and George Segal's face seems to crumble under the strain of genuine panic. That's when you stop laughing, and scramble to pinpoint the moment at which the mood turned mortuary-cold. In *Nashville*, that feeling of disorientation is palpable but always slightly out of range, like the low hum of machinery in the next room, or the screams from an adjacent apartment block.

Altman had been asked by United Artists to make a musical with Tom Jones: he declined, but proposed instead an alternative music-based project, and to this end dispatched Joan Tewkesbury, his co-writer on *Thieves Like Us*, to Nashville with the suggestion that she compile a diary of her experiences there, and one stipulation – that the story should end with the death of one of the characters.

The finished feature retains that air of informality; the camera leads you through Nashville, and lets you draw your own conclusions. Only in the character of Opal (Geraldine Chaplin), the droning reporter who claims to be from the BBC, do you detect the diarist at your elbow, steering your responses. Mostly the characters drift into view so casually that you are steeped in them before you realize their significance in the broader picture. Barbara Jean (Ronee Blakley) is a country-and-western diva systematically falling apart behind her armfuls of bouquets while her snake-eyed rival Connie White (Karen Black) steps into the spotlight whenever she is frail or hospitalized. Albuquerque (Barbara Harris) is a cute white-trash runaway hounded by her husband (Bert Ramsen), who memorably and inappropriately describes her as 'an ordinary-looking lady'. Linnea Reese (Lily Tomlin) is a gospel singer whose gone-to-seed husband Delbert is helping to arrange a political rally for the presidential candidate Hal Philip Walker, who, even as his voice booms out of the PA system, remains as mysterious and sinister as the unseen trucker in *Duel*.

Then there are the freaky faces in the crowd: Goldblum as 'the Tricycle Man', who cruises around town performing impromptu magic tricks in bars and in restaurants; Shelley Duvall as a Californian airhead in a floppy hat and a range of wacky hairdos; Scott Glenn in a tight-fitting army uniform and a tight-fitting face. The camera seems cheerfully distracted by them, and it's only with slowly dawning regret that you realize some or all of these funky minor fruitcakes are being established as potential killers in preparation for the climactic assassination.

The film has more generous surprises in store than trying to tip us off to the killer's identity. Someone like Wade (Robert Doqui) can seem incidental to the narrative until he delivers the movie's most sharply resounding line to Sueleen Gay (Gwen Welles), a tone-deaf amateur singer who has just been cajoled into a striptease. 'They're gonna kill you in this town, girl,' he hisses, and all at once he seems like the most profound voice in the movie, just as Albuquerque will when she takes to the stage in the final scene after having been lurking in the wings for the entire movie. There is no such thing here as a main character or even a primary narrative, which means that the picture can play differently each time you look at it. Points of emphasis shift, new connotations are revealed. Even Haven Hamilton can unexpectedly appear in a flattering light. The film encourages you to deride him: not only does he belt out pompously reactionary anthems like '200 Years', but his eyes tell you he means every chest-thumping word; he has the hardened stare of a born persecutor, and a tyrant's tongue as stinging and sadistic as a cat-o'-nine-tails. Goodness knows we have enough reasons to despise him. But when Barbara Jean is shot, Haven clutches his own bloody arm and tells the audience, 'This isn't Dallas, this is Nashville! Show 'em what we're made of!' And suddenly you realize that you've witnessed a character, a movie and your own set of prejudices change before your disbelieving eyes.

Nashville is a vast picture, which makes it all the more remarkable that it is comprised entirely of intimate moments. The elderly Mr Green (Keenan Wynn) learns of his wife's death just as Barbara Jean is being cheered and celebrated on her departure from hospital. It's a touch typical of Altman's aversion to the unobstructed soliloquy, or the manufactured movie moment. He knows that life doesn't clear out so you can savour your moments of heartbreak in peace. You don't get a spotlight and a sympathetic string section when you're feeling glum.

In a Robert Altman movie, private space blurs into public territory. Those moments in *Nashville* that should be intimate happen mostly in front of a faceless, baying crowd that is like a proxy cinema audience. Tom's on-stage dedication is prized by three of his former conquests, each woman wrongly believing from her place in the throng that his affections are directed toward her alone. Barbara Jean's nervous breakdown also occurs before an audience, which only increases our tension and embarrassment: not only are we watching a woman warped by dementia, but we are doing so through the eyes of another audience – and a hostile one at that. Altman lets the scene run and run, until we are praying for Barbara Jean to pass out just so that her delirious monologue might be halted. It isn't just the agony of her breakdown that makes us shift in our seats, it's the contempt of the audience, who in their jeering are expressing at least part of the same discomfort that we are feeling.

Sueleen's humiliation is also not only observed but insti-gated by an on-screen audience that makes us doubly aware of watching, and of our own voyeurism. When she gets her big break, the price of the trade-off she makes in exchange for the crowd's approval is heightened by our complicity in her ordeal. We laughed at her off-key singing only minutes earlier; now suddenly her torment has intensified, and our mocking laughter has lodged in the throat. The movie has a way of creeping up on you, of ambushing your preconceptions about characters – such as Delbert, who has essentially elected himself Sueleen's pimp for the evening, or Linnea, who has become the latest woman to get a personal audience with Tom for one night only, only to do so without diminishing her integrity one jot. The final scene, on stage at the Parthenon, is another moment of in-timacy forged in the eye of a hurricane. Albuquerque finds her-self in the right place at the right time, and picks up the microphone to perform an ecstatic version of 'It Don't Worry Me' that promises to spiral on for ever. As she scatters petals across the stage, her voice wanders up and down the register like an orphan looking for a home, and it should be noted that the song never actually ends. (Albuquerque's determination is so persuasive that you can believe she's still standing on that stage in Nashville, singing herself hoarse.) Instead, the sound fades out, and the camera tilts upwards to the sky in its own expression of contemplation – or exhaustion.

Altman's experiments with visual and aural textures repre-sent his lasting contribution to cinema, and already his influ-ence is keenly felt. It can seem today that many film-makers want only to stretch the lens beyond its natural capacity – to shoot the biggest battle, the largest crowd scenes, to plunge deeper into space. Now that computer effects have begun to make feasible these objectives, there is a concern that cinema will lose sight of intimacy, or rather that it will forget how to render such a resolutely uncinematic state in visual terms. But the work of Edward Yang, strongly reminiscent of Altman's ensemble pieces, tempers these anxieties. In pictures like *A One and a Two* and *A Confucian Confusion*, Yang has demonstrated that he can dextrously organize multiple narratives without extending his directorial instructions to the audience's emotions.

At the root of the noise and the restlessness in Altman's pictures lurks a tangible fear of silence and, by extension, death. The most common exit in his movies is by water: the cowboy blasted into the frozen river in *McCabe and Mrs Miller*; Roger Wade marching out into the Pacific Ocean, never to return, in *The Long Goodbye*; the swimming pool that is central to *3 Women*, and in which Pinky almost dies; another pool, this time in *Health*, where a man who appears to have drowned is exposed as a shameless publicity hound harbouring a concealed oxygen tank; and much later, in *Short Cuts*, the vacationing friends who are beguiled by a girl's corpse that they discover on a fishing trip. It is hard not to see this recurrent motif as an expression of dread and fascination at those spaces that cannot be penetrated by the tools of Altman's trade. His multi-tracked sound system is useless underwater; his roving cameras can unearth no ambiguities in a cadaver.

Fear of death in Altman's work is inextricably linked with fear of silence. These are movies that revolutionized film sound more than anything since the emergence of talkies. In the 1970s, dialogue was at last freed from its customary talking-heads format, just as the talkies had removed the need for explanatory intertitles. Altman rescued the spoken word on film from its laborious shot/reverse-shot pattern, and threaded dialogue throughout the movie's fabric, rather than assigning it to whoever happened to be on screen at any given time. External commentary forms a significant part of the soundtrack in a typical Altman movie, from the instructional poker videos in *California Split*, to the radio broadcasts in *Thieves Like Us*, to the songs in *McCabe and Mrs Miller* and *Nashville*, as well as the political speeches that permeate the latter film.

Altman's characters keep talking because they have come to dread the impending silence that would force them to confront themselves. When Charlie begs Bill for $200 in *California Split*, it takes only Bill's hard, unblinking stare to knock Charlie all the way back down to zero – he scuttles away without a cent, humbled into submission by Bill's silence. Like McCabe, words are all Charlie has. When McCabe tries too late to make a deal with the assassin Butler, he is confronted with the terrifying realization that his words are useless. 'This here deal can be made,' pleads McCabe. 'Not with me,' says Butler grimly. In that moment, McCabe must face what he has managed to fend off even in his darkest hours spent talking to himself: silence. And that silence leads to an acknowledgement of mortality – the most daunting silence of them all.

Only the deeply compassionate portrayal of Linnea's relationship with her deaf children in *Nashville* indicates acceptance of a world not governed by words, microphones and overlapping commentaries. The children's elation and enthusiasm provides one of the few flashes of unequivocal hope in the picture: Linnea's determination to defend them against the pity of strangers ('Oh, how awful!' cries Opal when she learns that the children are deaf) and the indifference of a father who cannot even be bothered to learn sign language is intensely moving. This is one of the rare instances in cinema when disabled characters are dignified without sentimentality or condescension. It's also valuable in another sense. For the first time in Altman's work, silence – a state in which this director's greatest innovation has no currency – has become synonymous with salvation, not annihilation.

Making *Barry Lyndon* (1975): Stanley Kubrick directs Ryan O'Neal (as Redmond Barry) and Pat Roach (Toole). (© Warner Bros)

Barry Lyndon: Redmond Barry (Ryan O'Neal) and the Chevalier de Balibari (Patrick Magee). (© Warner Bros)

7. Stanley Kubrick

While Robert Altman probes the corners of the frame, savouring every eccentric mannerism of each neglected bit-player, Stanley Kubrick commandeers an expedition in the opposite direction. Altman sniffs out the individual within the chaotic mass or yawning landscape. Kubrick will take that individual and lose him in the mass, abandon him in the landscape. His films remind us how small we are, and how human.

By 1980, Altman had made more films, and more truly great films, than Kubrick would manage in his entire forty-six-year movie career. But in the year that *Easy Rider* was released, Altman, who was forty-four, had yet to make even a moderate impression on cinema. Kubrick, on the other hand, was already a titan at forty-one, revered as much for the fastidiousness of his methods as for what those methods sporadically produced. He had followed the unhappy compromises of *Spartacus* by re-locating to Britain in 1961. Penelope Houston observed that 'he has kept himself apart from all worlds, appearing neither as an expatriate American director, nor as a resident British film-maker. From *Lolita* on, his films have been set in Kubrick country.'[1]

No national cinema that counts among its practitioners the

likes of Fritz Lang and Claus Detlev Sierck (aka Douglas Sirk), or the Vienna-born Edgar G. Ulmer, Billy Wilder and Fred Zinnemann, can claim geographical purity. So the whereabouts of the Brooklyn-born Kubrick's film sets and living quarters seems largely irrelevant. This was, after all, a decade in which non-Americans made two of the most influential and lauded American pictures. Would *One Flew Over the Cuckoo's Nest* have withdrawn so vehemently from hysteria and sensationalism without the humane guiding hand of Milos Forman? A different kind of enquiry can be levelled at *Chinatown*. We know now that the screenwriter, Robert Towne, smarted at the oppressive cruelty that Roman Polanski imposed on his narrative's denouement. But without Polanski's sense of doom and desolation, would that movie have emerged from history as anything more than a well-dressed B-movie? It has left an odour hanging about the American thriller, something like the smell in a back bedroom from which a corpse has been recently removed.

There are movies from which American cinema is still trying to recover – *The Birth of a Nation, Sunset Boulevard, Blue Velvet*. And for its dazzling audacity in staring evil right in the face, like a child determined to bare his pupils to the dull glare of a total eclipse, *Chinatown* should take its place in that list. It is tempting to label the picture refreshing. And it *is* refreshing – that much becomes obvious when contrasted with the sappy compromises of *L.A. Confidential*, a film that invites comparisons with *Chinatown* at its peril. But let's plump instead for bracing. It's the kind of picture that makes you want to be alive in a hundred years' time, just to see what an as-yet-unborn generation of cinemagoers will make of the ghosts that it awakens.

Polanski, the European in America, and Kubrick, the American in Europe: both scrutinized the nature of the anti-hero who dominated 1970s cinema. Towne may have created the stylish, well-turned-out private eye Jake Gittes on paper, but it is hard to believe that any director other than Polanski could have amplified his vulnerability with so little regard for the comfort of the audience, or the niceties of genre. When Jake is abused on screen, it is an affront to us: he represents our eyes, our means of beating a path through the thicket of the movie's immorality; and when he is rendered impotent we suffer the consequences. Just as it is significant that Martin Scorsese cast himself as a ghoul in his own movie *Taxi Driver*, so it seems impossible now that anyone else could have slit Jack Nicholson's nose with quite the sadistic aplomb that Polanski mustered in his cameo in *Chinatown*. If Kubrick had forced himself to act, he might have continued in his film *Barry Lyndon* the tradition of director-as-tormentor by awarding himself the voice-over duties of the withering narrator whose every pronouncement, no matter how trivial, stymies the hero's lunges at independence.

In the 1970s 'Kubrick country' only became more impregnable when Warner Bros guaranteed its ongoing financial commitment to the director's work. The studio's generosity might have been a cause for subsequent regret – on a par with the artistic decline that coincided with George Lucas's commercial success – if during this period Kubrick had not released one of his two masterpieces (*Barry Lyndon*) and begun shooting the other (*The Shining*).

The first shot of his first picture of the 1970s, *A Clockwork Orange* (1971), takes the form of a protracted withdrawal. The camera presents us with the face of Alex (Malcolm McDowell). It might be portraiture, only we can see him breathing. Our primary point of focus in any close-up – the eyes – is immediately distorted by the presence on one eye of ostentatiously false lashes. The symmetry of the shot is therefore disrupted from the moment it has begun. Everything that follows will feel off-key, against nature somehow, as though in deference to the title, which refers to a human being whose capacity for free will has been eradicated. Faces are constantly distorted in sickening close-up: the clown masks, with their obscene Pinocchio noses, worn by Alex and his droogs; the gurning face of their victim,

Mr Alexander (Patrick Magee), into whose mouth they stuff a ping-pong ball; and Alex, eyelids hoisted open during his course of aversion therapy.

These corruptions have been foreshadowed by that first shot, and the way the camera dollies backwards along the aisle of the Korova Milk Bar – a movement that feels as wrong-headed, as rude, as the petrified female mannequins that serve as footrests and furniture, or from whose breasts drugged milk is disgorged.

The nature of cinema is implicitly challenged in that camera's tentative manoeuvre. Everything about this art form from the motion of the projector onwards promotes forward momentum, and anything that upsets that flow can create an air of uncertainty or foreboding. Our natural inclination as viewers is to gravitate toward the image on screen. Film vocabulary flatters us in this respect with conventions such as the zoom shot and the close-up. In Altman's work, we see (and hear) more than other film-makers have ever revealed before; if we were any closer to the action, we would need to be credited as extras. The contrast with Kubrick is dazzling. Most of the camera movements in 1975's *Barry Lyndon*, his only other work of the 1970s, are staged, like that opening shot in *A Clockwork Orange*, as cautious retreats. As you watch the picture, you can experience the sensation of slowly and relentlessly falling backwards.

Kubrick had originally planned to follow *2001: A Space Odyssey* not with an adaptation of Anthony Burgess's futuristic parable, but with *Napoleon*. 'I start from the premise that there has never been a great historical film,' he said with characteristic boldness, blithely dismissing Abel Gance's 1927 *Napoleon* in the process. 'I don't think anyone has ever successfully solved the problem of dealing in an interesting way with the historical information that has to be conveyed, and at the same time getting a sense of reality about the daily life of the characters.'[2]

His diagnosis of the shortcomings of period cinema was astute, but the film-makers of the late 1960s and 1970s had already begun to address them. Along with Penn's *Bonnie and Clyde*, Altman's *McCabe and Mrs Miller* and *Thieves Like Us*, and Malick's *Days of Heaven*, Kubrick provided in *Barry Lyndon* a coruscating example of how to render a historical narrative without recourse to the fusty clichés of tour-guide film-making – where emotional authenticity is overshadowed by admiring shots of heirlooms-on-loan and country manors rented by the day. In *McCabe and Mrs Miller*, when Altman showed two barflies discussing facial hair, that inconsequential scene felt like a minor revelation. No film-maker had so strongly suggested that people in the past behaved just as we do – that they might also talk about their hairdos, or the latest fashions. More than twenty years later, in Mike Leigh's *Topsy-Turvy*, it still seemed peculiar to see a character slouch idly on a bed with no regard for the regulation posture of the period genre. After all, the conventional idea of history is best epitomized by a line in *Maverick* in which a character refers to the 'Old West', as though the West was always Old, even in the days when it was young.

The performers in *Barry Lyndon* couldn't be mistaken for the trussed-up clotheshorses of a Merchant–Ivory costume drama. Just as you could imagine Bowie and Keechie in *Thieves Like Us* reincarnated in some later era as daydreaming mallrats or couch potatoes, so the characters here have an external life not restricted to their period trappings. When a man leans in to kiss the wife who means no more to him than his paintings and carpets, the gesture still smarts – a loveless kiss is a loveless kiss in any period.

Kubrick's *Napoleon* might never have gone into battle – the budget required was more than could realistically be provided by the major studios, each of which was well into its post-*Easy Rider* backlash against the spendthrift 1960s, and scarcely distracted from this frugality by the dismal takings of recent

Napoleon movies. But lessons learned in that film's preparation evidently enriched *Barry Lyndon*, which in its evocation of eighteenth-century life makes good on its director's assertion that the epic and the prosaic must be afforded equal attention.

The film's key line comes just before the British army is advancing on its French adversaries. 'Though this encounter was not recorded in history books,' purrs the narrator (Michael Hordern), 'it was memorable enough for those who took part.' In that throwaway observation lies the essence of the picture's skilful negotiation between the vastness of historical hindsight and the frailty of immediacy – it's a reminder, as if Kubrick's anthropological approach required one, that the distance in centuries between our lives and those of the characters is not reflected in any corresponding emotional polarity. From the film's conception, Kubrick keeps the audience at one remove, even going so far as to shift the narration from the title character – from whose perspective Thackeray's source novel was written – to an unseen and sardonic commentator who alerts us to the significance of events that we can barely discern. The opening scene is a duel in which the figures are no more than blemishes on a landscape; it is the narrator who informs us that one of those men is the hero's father. Likewise, the narrator also has to assure us that Lady Lyndon (Marisa Berenson) has fallen in love with the effete Irish scallywag Redmond Barry (Ryan O'Neal) because without that information we could not have guessed that such passion was even within the range of these bored and intractable people.

Hiring O'Neal to play Barry must count as Kubrick's wickedest game of rib-the-Hollywood-heartthrob – at least until he cast Tom Cruise in the lead and out to sea in *Eyes Wide Shut*. (Kubrick had interviewed Steve Martin, his original choice for the Cruise role, back in 1979, when Martin's sole contribution to cinema had been *The Jerk*. How astonishing that Kubrick glimpsed so early the emotional tensions in this gangly buffoon which would not be exploited by other directors – Lawrence Kasdan, David Mamet – for more than a decade.) O'Neal was never the most riveting of screen presences, his popularity deriving largely from a vacant befuddlement that could be adapted to screwball comedy (*What's Up, Doc?*), innocuous tearjerker (*Love Story*) and not much else in between. He had found his fortune playing little-boy-lost. But there was something pampered about him too that was pertinent to Barry, who in one scene sits mutely at the dinner table while his cousin and mother argue about where he should be sent to escape the scandal of a duel in which he has apparently killed his opponent.

Throughout the rest of the picture, he displays no greater involvement in his own fate. Invited to rummage in his cousin's cleavage to retrieve a ribbon, he has to be given a helping hand by his seducer. When highwaymen rob him shortly after he has fled his home, he looks born to the role of victim. 'Mightn't I be allowed to keep my horse?' he meekly enquires, not quite grasping the etiquette of this particular transaction. Later, he will find himself in a duel with his own stepson, Lord Bullingdon (Leon Vitali), and will again drastically misinterpret the requirements of the situation, this time with dire consequences.

With the appearance of Bullingdon, the film, and Barry's life, acquire a sense of impending doom. As viewers, the mere sound of the name Bullingdon is like a promise of the conflict of which we have been starved. Barry has drifted from one episode to another as casually as he has assumed stolen regimentals to disguise himself as an officer, or slipped into the elaborate dandyish costume of his sponsor, the Chevalier de Balibari (Patrick Magee). He wants now to secure himself the title and collateral that his lowly upbringing and itinerant early adulthood have denied him, and to this end he marries the newly widowed Lady Lyndon. But this liaison brings him into close proximity with her son, Lord Bullingdon. Even as a child, Bullingdon is an affront to Barry. The boy's face is impassive – but this is impassivity as defiance. From the moment we see

Bullingdon, we know he's trouble, thrillingly so. His prim coat is the colour of blood on a guillotine blade. When he grows up, his lips have swollen, presumably from all the years of biting on them as Barry thrashes him – another unconvincing lunge in the general direction of discipline, from which Barry emerges much the weaker party.

Barry's downfall at the hands of Bullingdon is a fitting comeuppance for his lack of identity. We are never quite certain who Barry might be; he's the original man-who-isn't-there. And the price he pays is to return home at the end of the film in possession of less than he started out with; he's half a leg and a considerable amount of pride poorer. In many ways, Barry is the perfect protagonist for the 1970s, a decade that tolerated like no other before it the fallible, the anti-heroes, the knights in tarnished armour. Clint Eastwood still spent much of the decade sleepwalking uninjured through storms of gunfire, while Burt Reynolds drove cars on two wheels under collapsing chimney stacks, and barely ruffled his moustache. But actors like Jack Nicholson and Robert De Niro provided an authentic alternative to the bombast of mainstream action heroes. It's easy to see how Barry fits in with these lost or lacking souls. The unconventional climate of 1970s cinema lent itself to character studies that were not necessarily dedicated to seducing the audience – Travis Bickle in *Taxi Driver* providing the most extreme proof that audiences were willing to spend two hours in the company of someone whom they would cross the road at a demolition derby just to avoid.

Kubrick had a phrase for this breed of film: he called it a 'Who Do You Root For Movie'.[3] *A Clockwork Orange* doesn't fall into that category: there is no one to root for but Alex, since all the other characters are ciphers, and the only element with any vitality is the magnificent set design, which suggests a series of showhomes for depraved emperors. *Barry Lyndon* is more complicated. There is no one to root for here. And the camera seems initially to be holding us back from the action,

even as we long to sink our fingers into the painterly landscapes. But that detachment only makes the disruption of etiquette, when it comes, more shocking and resonant. Lord
Bullingdon attacks Barry; Lady Lyndon attempts to poison herself; violent arguments break out between relatives and staff.
The polite veneer that has cracked and splintered under the
pressure of Barry and Lady Lyndon's deathly marriage can no
longer be maintained.

It's not just in these more demonstrative scenes that the
film's thrilling physical vitality comes through. Those scenes
festooned with candles, and shot with custom-made lenses to
render more faithfully the candlelight, give the picture an un-
usually visceral charge. This is not a sterile situation, but one in
which the actors' very breaths affect the movement of light on
their faces, as the flames around them flicker and dance.

Both *Barry Lyndon* and *A Clockwork Orange* are experiments in manipulating form to contradict content. One works,
the other doesn't. *Barry Lyndon* uses the camera's objectivity
strategically, to draw us into a narrative that appears at first so
remote as to be imperceptible to the eye, or the heart – until we
realize that remoteness has been used to snare us. Not everyone
was convinced. 'I like *Barry Lyndon*,' said Steven Spielberg,
'but for me it was like going through the Prado without lunch.'[4]
On the other hand, *A Clockwork Orange* enthusiastically solic-
its our identification with its protagonist, only for the painstaking rigour of its methods to jar uneasily with its incitements to
freedom and spontaneity. That film warns, in its dispassionate
way, of the abhorrent corruptions that take hold when man is
denied fundamental liberty. But the movie itself has no stake in
that commodity: there is no emotional sense of what precisely
is being sacrificed in Alex's abnegation, only an intellectual one.

Barry Lyndon offers a more intense demonstration of the
same idea. Here is a man whose actions are rendered futile
from the moment he is born by the presence of an omniscient
and scornful narrator, whose very timbre undermines Barry's

autonomy. In maintaining control of the narration in *A Clock-work Orange*, Alex retains his own destiny and identity, which rather diminishes the threat posed to him by the reconditioning process that robs him of free will. Oddly, *Barry Lyndon* is a more forcefully convincing version of *A Clockwork Orange* than *A Clockwork Orange* ever manages to be. Here the oppressive force of economic status narrows the possibilities in Barry's destiny, and as viewers we experience first-hand the horror of a life lived by predestination.

The final irony is that *Barry Lyndon* has gained a reputation for being listless and forbidding, when in fact it offers the sustained and torturous spectacle of one man's gradual downfall, while *A Clockwork Orange*, one of the chilliest films ever made, was withdrawn from distribution in Britain by Kubrick after a spate of copycat attacks. No one was ever going to imitate Barry, of course. With his dogged pursuit of undeserved riches, his willing capitulation to situations that confirm his own impotence, and his despair in the face of destiny, he is too much our worst nightmare already.

8. Woody Allen

In 1977, with the help of his co-writer Marshall Brickman and his editor Ralph Rosenblum, Woody Allen invented Woody Allen. The character proved so resonant that its creator would never be required to trade it in for a jazzier model. Although he augmented or modified it over the decades, the essence of that persona could not be negotiated, which is a testament to the protective properties inherent in his peculiar breed of ingrained resignation.

The friction in the persona was initially rather seductive. There was Allen's awkwardness with modern life – with the machines that revolt against him in *Bananas* and *Sleeper*, or the spectre of all things Californian or televisual (in Allen's universe the two things are synonymous) in *Annie Hall*. But flashes of disarming sexual confidence punctuated that ineptitude or bewilderment. Of the male box-office stars of the 1970s, only Robert Redford displayed convincing signs of tenderness, though there was some reprieve in the form of Warren Beatty, a man not afraid to appear vain as well as sexy (*Shampoo*) or to confront his own vulnerability and mortality (*McCabe and Mrs Miller, The Parallax View*).

But Allen – who had almost worked with Beatty on the 1965 comedy *What's New, Pussycat?*, until Beatty objected to

Sleeper (1973): Woody Allen as Miles Monroe. (© United Artists)

the shift in Allen's script away from his character and on to Allen's own – takes that vulnerability even further. His screen persona offers a pure tonic to the marinated macho values of 1970s cinema. Locked inside that half-pint body is an insatiable genie at whose feet schoolgirls (Mariel Hemingway in *Manhattan*) and intellectuals (Carol Kane in *Annie Hall*, Diane Keaton in *Manhattan*) will unironically fall. He is defined by his contradictions. It isn't enough for him to oppose the impenetrable machismo of an Eastwood or a Reynolds; he must prove himself unique among other intelligent middle-class white males. The Woody Allen we see on screen may be an intellectual, but he's one who is not too snooty to appreciate a good ball-game or a hot centrefold. In *Annie Hall*, his character eschews a roomful of professors and journalists in order to watch the Knicks on TV. When his wife implores him to join the party, he tries to tempt her into making love, but his advances are greeted with a horrified, and very telling, riposte: 'There are people out there from the *New Yorker* magazine!'

In that brief scene, Allen has established himself as an intellectual for the people, a man who would rather have sex or watch sports than exchange dinner-party chit-chat with the Upper East Side elite. The on-screen Allen will even choose sex over the *New Yorker*, one of the off-screen Allen's former employers. Elsewhere in the same film, he weeds out and humiliates a pretentious university lecturer in a cinema queue. In *Manhattan*, he contests a pompous partygoer's appraisal of satire ('Really biting satire is always better than physical force,' the fellow suggests. 'Bricks and baseball bats are better with Nazis,' counters Allen). As far back as *Bananas*, he was alternating references to literature, politics and sex, or kneading them into the same gag: the prowl along the newsagent's shelf that reveals the *National Review* pegged up alongside *Casual Nudist* and *Fling*, or the attempt to sandwich a copy of *Orgasm* between *Time* and *Newsweek*. However disingenuous these protests seem, it is hard not to be touched by Allen's desire to be regarded as both salacious child and erudite adult – a gifted prodigy possessed of preternatural intelligence, yet devoid of the will to deploy it as a weapon.

Of course, the difficulty for the prodigy comes when he is called upon to match as an adult those achievements that earned him acclaim as a youth. The remarkable thing about Allen is not that he managed to accomplish it – the task long ago dropped off the foot of his 'to do' list – but that no one has come close to patenting a persona that might render redundant this old Woody Allen. There is no dearth of evidence pertaining to his legacy. Open a recent cinema and TV listings guide and you will find something or someone that could not have evolved as fully without him. It might be a sitcom – *Seinfeld* or *The Simpsons* or *Malcom in the Middle* – or any number of stand-up performers; it could be one of the glittering, too-rare comedies by Whit Stillman, or the latest adaptation of a Nick Hornby novel, where the flawed heroes are just a pair of spectacles and a New York accent away from being Woody Allen. There may not be much to celebrate in the misanthropy of Todd Solondz or Neil LaBute, both of whom have crafted acidic black comedies that echo Allen at his least forgiving.

But comedies like Wes Anderson's *The Royal Tenenbaums* and Tim Burton's *Ed Wood* resemble extravagant frescoes that might have been adapted from one of Allen's absent-minded doodles. Anderson and Burton specialize in precious, precocious characters insulated in their own domains, much like Allen's creations, which have as tenuous a relationship to reality as his New York does to that real city. But those film-makers take the stylistic risks that Allen has rarely attempted since *Annie Hall* in 1977, and they can also be mindful of their characters' absurdities or shortcomings in a way that Allen no longer is. He can't entertain the possibility that the cloistered cosiness of family life in *Everyone Says I Love You* is borderline delusional, whereas *The Royal Tenenbaums* is fraught with revulsion at the horrors of the homestead.

If no one else has actually applied for the job of being Woody Allen, there have been other writer–director–actors who have, on occasion, made better films in the same milieu. Albert Brooks is the chief contender. His 1985 yuppie satire *Lost in America* has the goofiness of Allen's best work, and the good sense not only to harness it to modern concerns, but also to situate it within a vast social and cinematic landscape that is the antithesis of Allen's suffocating, Manhattan-centric chamber pieces. Conversely, whenever Allen has entertained modern themes – in two of his worst films, *Celebrity* and *Small Time Crooks*, which both address the perils of fame – the result has been pompous and hateful. The viewer is left with the impression of a curmudgeon who has outlived his usefulness even as a voice of dissent.

And yet Allen remains deeply implicated in the collective consciousness, where our emotional investment preserves him from the damage done by the erratic quality of his later pictures. Few film-makers create and maintain such an intimate bond with the audience, chiefly because most other directors aren't also actors who make themselves physically available to the camera, but also because Allen crafted a film vocabulary that would flounder without the express collusion of the audience. He needed us. There was no room for manoeuvre. If you didn't buy into Allen himself, then you didn't buy into his movies, which were an extension of that persona, with its flibbertigibbet digressions and scatterbrained allusions.

It was a vocabulary that could not have been constructed without the influence of Buster Keaton and the Marx Brothers, Richard Lester and Sid Caesar (for whom Allen was a gag writer), and kooky 1960s TV shows like *Rowan and Martin's Laugh-In*. Where Allen came into his own in the 1970s was in using this montage of forebears as a backdrop to the promotion of his persona, which in a non-humorous context might have found its ideal home in the Ingmar Bergman films which Allen adores. To those who know Allen only from his rather timid and confused 1990s output, it might seem unlikely that his work ever had a daredevil kick to it. But *Annie Hall* was a breakthrough, and not only in commercial terms. Allen's first collaboration of eight with the noted cinematographer Gordon Willis, who had been responsible for the stately gloom of the *Godfather* pictures, was in every way a profound leap forward for him, and for cinema. Suddenly a stark confessional tone was present in the comedy. The gags came with a rattling rat-tat-tat rhythm unheard since Preston Sturges, but, intriguingly, the humour never quite dispelled the pain of the material: like Scorsese's *New York, New York*, released the same year, *Annie Hall* is dark, despairing stuff dolled up in the natty threads of a cherished genre.

And like the big-band numbers in Scorsese's film, the humour in *Annie Hall* seems to heighten rather than conceal the ugliness and anxiety within. This is comedy, but of a uniquely prickly kind. Allen's skits on Jewish family life have their roots in Neil Simon's warm-hearted and soft-headed observational comedy, but in Simon's writing laughter is commonly a balm for whatever quandary or despair the characters find themselves in. (An exception is his script for *The Heartbreak Kid*, though that film's unsparing cruelty is more obviously attributable to its director Elaine May.) In *Annie Hall*, there is no such loophole: the movie is a downer through and through. Allen may never have approximated the savagery of Lenny Bruce or Richard Pryor, but in the fiercest work of all three comics there is a refusal to differentiate between material fit for comedy, drama or confessional – it all gets dumped in the same cauldron.

Annie Hall was very nearly not the movie it transpired to be. Or rather, *Annie Hall* was buried somewhere inside a picture that was nudging three hours and titled *Anhedonia* (named for the condition that prevents the sufferer from experiencing happiness). It just took some getting at. In the original cut, the relationship between the stand-up comic Alvy Singer (Allen) and his girlfriend Annie (Diane Keaton) was not the focus. By all accounts, there *was* no focus, which suggests that without judicious pruning the movie would have taken its place among Allen's earlier, nuttier comedies – the films from which *Annie Hall* now represents such a striking departure.

In the five features that he made before *Annie Hall*, Allen had grown steadily more sophisticated as a director. His initial advancement in that period was confined to the task of making the movies leaner and funnier, without necessarily enriching them as works of cinema. Those first three films – the spoof documentary *Take the Money and Run* (1969), the anarchic, vaguely countercultural *Bananas* (1971) and the sketch compendium *Everything You Always Wanted to Know About Sex But Were Afraid to Ask* (1972) – are marked by a deference to the joke as an end in itself. It's a hangover from his days as a stand-up comedian, and from one of his earliest film exercises, the 1966 *What's Up, Tiger Lily?*, a Japanese thriller for which Allen was hired by AIP, home of Roger Corman, to dub a new voice-track.

There is in those early pictures little consideration for the role played by framing or pacing in the detonation of a punchline, while the concerted wackiness frequently impedes the flow of humour. In *Bananas*, the Eisenstein-like montage of a political assassination, carved into close-ups of a trigger, a gun-barrel, and the victim's eyes, interrupts what has been an otherwise inspired restaging of history in the form of a TV sports broadcast. In other places, the camera will linger expectantly, in the aftermath of a joke, on the face of an actor (sometimes Allen himself) who seems unsure of what's expected of him. Nothing in those early pictures matters so much as the audience's laughter, and the positioning of Allen himself at the centre of that approbation.

Parts of *Everything You Always Wanted to Know . . .* have remained intact. Gene Wilder's performance as a doctor who falls in love with a sheep is pleasantly sedate, and eventually quite moving, more so for coming in the middle of a relentless, bawdy comedy, and from an actor who at that point in his career was renowned (and perhaps dreaded) for the shrill hysteria that he had contributed to Mel Brooks' *The Producers*. Other elements of that picture are valuable for less heartening reasons. The opening episode, in which Allen plays a court jester attempting to seduce the Queen (Lynn Redgrave), provides depressing proof that the misogyny which surfaced in *Mighty Aphrodite* and *Celebrity* was actually there all along, festering just below the surface. Hostility toward women, and toward sex, has rarely been expressed as vehemently as in the moment when Allen attacks Redgrave's chastity belt with a battering ram.

Only with his next films, *Sleeper* (1973) and *Love and Death* (1975), did he begin to realize that the single-mindedness of his technique was sealing off other options: once the gags in his earlier films had been heard, the movies themselves were effectively dead; they had no external worth after the laughter had faded. *Sleeper*, on the other hand, is refreshing on a number of counts. Chiefly, it is the first Woody Allen film that could not have been rendered in any other art form but cinema. Whereas those earlier pictures have now found their rightful place programmed into the graveyard slots of TV stations across the world, the vastness and formal purity of the images in *Sleeper* justify the larger frame. It may not now be Woody Allen's finest film, but it is certainly Joel Schumacher's. The man who would later bring new shame to the word 'hack' with movies like *Batman and Robin* and *8mm* here excels in his previous capacity as costume designer, supplying a wardrobe of crisp and economic clarity – all tuxedos and smocks and ballgowns – that complements Dale Hennesy's antiseptic production design, where futuristic vehicles with glowing, bubble-shaped cockpits patrol serene rural landscapes.

Although the premise of *Sleeper* – in which Miles Monroe (Allen) wakes from an anaesthetic to find himself in a totalitarian future – is fundamentally incidental to the comedy, it is encouraging to see Allen as a director at last taking into account the effect that the film will have on the eye as well as the funny bone. The movie looks cheap, but it looks great. The Orgasmatron, a machine in which lovers can find instantaneous sexual gratification without the hoopla of foreplay, or indeed sex, is all the more amusing for its resemblance to an authentic item of spaced-out 1970s furniture. The robotic butlers look like downhearted entertainers at a children's party; baking foil is much in evidence.

Allen pitches the science-fiction tone of dislocated calm just-so. He was always a good mimic. To appreciate this you need only peruse the joyful literary parodies that he wrote in the early 1970s for the *New Yorker* and the *New Republic*, sending up everything from penny dreadfuls to Joycean esoterica and jazz-era memoirs. In *Sleeper* and *Love and Death*, he is for the first time as careful with the camera as he always was with the pen. The camera in *Sleeper* enlarges the comedy; there's none of the tricksy, eager-to-please novelty angles with which the simplest exchanges are rendered in *Bananas*, while even the least sophisticated bouts of slapstick – such as the chase sequence involving an inflatable, rocket-powered suit – are regarded with a near-deadpan objectivity, which expunges all those traces of self-conscious zaniness left over from the 1960s. Sometimes, the clarity of a joke can be funnier than the joke itself. One scene is centred on a crop of oversized fruit for no other reason than to enable Allen to set up the banana-skin gag to end all banana-skin gags. Your willing surrender to this shameless contrivance can in itself be more pleasurable than the pay-off – giving in to the movie is like being tickled.

The emergence of a cinematic aesthetic in *Sleeper* and the Russian literature parody *Love and Death* sharpens Allen's comic instincts. Now he's immersed in the crafting of an entire opera, not just the high notes, and you can feel how he is energized as a film-maker by that assumption of responsibility. It's

no coincidence that these were the first films in which he cast
Diane Keaton, his then-partner, and his co-star in both his stage
hit *Play It Again, Sam* and Herbert Ross's staid 1972 film version. Allen has never been better than when Keaton was at his
side – she's the straight man who isn't. Where less wilful and
charismatic performers might have settled into the role of foil
alongside Allen's passive-aggressive comic persona, Keaton's
personality demands more than just feed-lines. Her presence
makes Allen work harder, and not just as a performer (though
their double-act has a fizzy, competitive streak, with Allen's jit-
teriness jarring pleasurably with Keaton's distracted benevolence). You can see him scrambling to give her the material she
deserves.

Everything comes together on *Love and Death*. Allen has a
new-found flexibility and confidence here. If you want to see a
director proud to cast his camera over the fruits of his location
scout's labour, look at this movie, where the Budapest landscapes actively enhance the context of the humour. It begins to
be another kind of joke that these parochial, anachronistic
wisecracks are set against this imposing rural magnificence.
Many of the exchanges would on their own merit a giggle.
'Your skin is so beautiful,' a suitor tells Keaton. 'I know,' she
purrs, 'and it covers my whole body.' The relocation of these
gags, which would have happily suited any one of Allen's previous pictures or magazine articles, to a historical context provides a new resonance that would have been absent in a
latter-day setting. It's schoolyard impertinence on a par with
the cheerful defacement of a *War and Peace* dust-jacket. But
with style.

Any discussion of *Sleeper* or *Love and Death* risks descending into a simple transcription of the screenplay, so dependent
is their effectiveness on precisely weighted epigrams and one-
liners. But there are visual flourishes in Allen's 1970s features
that he has attempted all too infrequently in his subsequent
work. One scene in *Bananas* – a dream in which two men

borne aloft on crucifixes compete for a parking space in a New York back-street – suggested that within the sensibility of the sketch writer was a devilish imp itching to burst free. You could feel that image's primal, shocking undertones even as you were laughing; there was something almost blasphemous about it, oddly soothed by its cheery dream logic, that brought to mind the last supper tableau peopled by beggars in Buñuel's *Viridiana*. Allen had dredged up an image that was too hot for him or the film to handle, and you wondered if he knew what he had found. There is some of that frisson in *Love and Death*, in Allen's prosaic encounters with the Grim Reaper, or in the dream sequence in which waiters are disgorged from a score of coffins standing upright in a field. Anxiety is translated into absurdity or slapstick, but the faint whiff of existential dread is still discernible.

If Allen had begun to realize the possibilities of cinema with these two films, he had not yet developed his own distinctive language. In the first half of the 1970s, Mel Brooks had also found success in the realm of parody with comedies that were as informed and affectionate – if not as witty – as Allen's. *Love and Death* borrowed images from *Battleship Potemkin* and *Persona*, but Brooks' finest work, the 1974 horror parody *Young Frankenstein*, employed the actual sets used in James Whale's *Frankenstein* movies, and was suffused with a fan's tender, uncomplicated passion for his target of choice (unlike other Brooks parodies like the comic western *Blazing Saddles* and the Hitchcock spoof *High Anxiety*, both of which could be described as love letters written in poisoned ink).

The point of divergence between those directors is instructive. Brooks immersed himself in another parody, the 1976 *Silent Movie*, which was exactly what it said on the tin, barring a single word spoken, in the film's most succulent gag, by Marcel Marceau. But Allen turned, if not back to the drawing board, then toward the editing suite, where his collaboration with Ralph Rosenblum in teasing a coherent film from the three hours of *Annie Hall* material created a new species of film comedy, a new species of film. The original cut of *Annie Hall* was riddled with fantasy sequences – one set in Nazi headquarters, another in the Garden of Eden, an *Invasion of the Body Snatchers*-style digression in which Alvy and Annie go to Los Angeles and are almost replaced by pods, and a tour of the seven layers of Hell (an idea that would later be dusted off for *Deconstructing Harry*). 'It was clear to Woody and me that the film started moving whenever present-tense material with [Alvy] and [Annie] dominated the screen,' said Rosenblum, 'so we began cutting in the direction of that relationship.'[1]

That almost makes the film sound linear, but few straight lines are drawn in such a dizzying array of media. The French New Wave had taught film-makers that even the basic verisimilitude of a scene – the flow of time and action, even the flow of a line reading – could be fractured or disrupted by a random jump-cut, an intertitle, the wobble of a hand-held camera. Without that epiphany, and the effect it had on directors like Richard Lester and Lindsay Anderson, Allen might not have rebelled so spectacularly against the conventions of film language.

It is easy to take for granted the eclectic textures of *Annie Hall*, which is a measure of how liberating and influential the film has been. But look again: this movie has so many ideas, and so many notions about how to animate those ideas, that it's almost too much for the eye and ear to contain. Even marshalled into a rudimentary list, the breadth of the film's styles and techniques is astonishing: there are flashbacks and straight-to-camera addresses, sometimes within an otherwise realistic scene; stand-up excerpts and animation; split-screen; fantasy sequences; characters crossing different time frames, so that, for instance, Alvy and Annie mingle with their youthful incarnations; and subtitles divulging the characters' intimate thoughts, in contrast to what they are actually saying. In addition, Allen makes judicious use of Alvy's voice-over, sometimes to confide in us, and at other points to coach himself through an arduous experience, such as when he is given a personal audience with a crummy and outdated Vegas entertainer – a character designed to illustrate, as if we could not have guessed from the radical nature of the film's form, that Allen is anything but old-school.

The inbuilt challenge to an audience's expectations actually begins when *Annie Hall* has been on screen for barely a second. The white-on-black titles to which audiences at Woody Allen movies have become accustomed actually began with *Sleeper*, but the opening credits of *Annie Hall* are more subtly alarming: it's the stark absence of music, the way the movie withholds that fundamental element on which we unwittingly depend, that prepares us for the tone of vague discomfort that is the picture's speciality. Movie audiences have come to anticipate that musical cue as readily as theatregoers at a Broadway musical expect an overture; its absence feels like a kind of violation. How are we supposed to become settled in our cinema seats without that induction into the picture? The answer is that we're not. Allen secures our curiosity, but not our complacency. It's an edge-of-the-seat movie, for an unusual reason: the tension comes not from our apprehension at finding out what happens next, but from a suspicion that we are witnessing more than it is proper to see.

It can be hard to square that feeling with the unblemished cleanliness of Gordon Willis's photography, which adoringly renders every perfectly symmetrical crease of every dry-cleaned duvet cover. *Annie Hall* might share with Allen's stand-up routines and early movies a jovial frankness about sex, but there's no possibility that anyone could actually fuck in one of those beds – no chance of a wet patch, let alone a debate about whose turn it is to sleep in it.

Compare the subject matter to Mike Nichols' *The Graduate* and *Carnal Knowledge*, or the dialogue to Hal Ashby's *The Last Detail*, and *Annie Hall* can appear rather coy. But one of Allen's cleverest tricks was to introduce difficult material into film comedy without scaring off a mainstream audience. He saw that those viewers who took their dates along to coo over *The Goodbye Girl* in the same year could also be painlessly tutored to read a similar narrative conveyed in a contrasting idiom. The picture isn't confrontational, but it buzzes with that same edgy excitement that you get from hearing a couple arguing in an adjacent room. It's not exactly voyeuristic either, since the scenes are frequently presented with the complicity of the protagonists. When Alvy conducts an impromptu vox pop about the sexual habits of passers-by, the enthusiasm of that complicity is part of the gag. But not for nothing does Allen frame one scene of Alvy and Annie in bed together within the second frame of a bedroom doorway. In that moment we have intruded on them. We are houseguests passing their room on our way to fetch a glass of water and, finding the door ajar, we sneak a peek to discover if our hosts' problems are the same as ours.

The notoriously self-critical Allen has slighted the tone of the movie – '*Annie Hall* to me was a very middle-class picture,' he said, 'and that's why I think people liked it. It was the reinforcement of the middle-class values.'[2] He may, of course, be reacting as much to the four Academy Awards bestowed upon the film (including Best Picture and Best Director) as to the content of the movie itself: far better to have your work snubbed than rewarded by the very value system that you profess to despise. Parts of the picture do err on the side of politeness or conservatism. The flashbacks to Alvy's childhood are like offcuts from Neil Simon's *Brighton Beach Memoirs*, while the typical Woody Allen snobbery toward pop culture, directed here against the vacuous rock journalist played by Shelley Duvall, is disappointing given his willingness to explore new modes of cinematic expression.

But at its best, *Annie Hall* doesn't concern itself with the audience's contentment. In the movie's most disquieting scene, a class of schoolchildren, who resemble the cast of Charles M.

Schultz's *Peanuts* cartoon strip, reveal arbitrary details of their future selves, weirdly delivered in the present tense. One girl says, 'I'm into leather,' while an innocuous-looking classmate admits, 'I was a heroin addict, now I'm a methadone addict' – the blitheness of his delivery and demeanour lending his words a tragic lilt. Even as they disclose these supernatural flashes of foresight, the children are unaware of what they are saying; they are mere vessels for these lines, unknowing messengers of their own fates, perversely detached from any involvement in themselves.

The intended humour in this scene comes specifically from the contrast between the children's faces and the prosaic or re-pellent nature of the words placed on those young lips. But the scene depends for its effectiveness on such a dramatic distortion of time, context and pathos that nothing in it is recognizable any longer as comedy. If you can laugh during that scene – if you can watch it from anywhere but between splayed fingers – then you must be a well-adjusted soul for whom dread and anxiety are exotic and unfamiliar emotions. In which case, *Annie Hall* must seem to you an especially implausible slice of science-fiction fantasy.

There was disappointingly little of that emotional unease in his next two films, *Interiors* (1978) and *Manhattan* (1979). Al-though the former is a stilted and sombre homage to Bergman (with nods to Chekhov and Strindberg), and the latter is a shimmering metropolitan comedy that again rests partly on a dysfunctional relationship between Allen and Keaton, they are almost of a piece. Both are visually sumptuous, and hinge on odd polarities: the colour is all but drained from *Interiors* (the cast appear to have frostbite), while in *Manhattan* the mono-chrome images throb with a vibrant, healthy glow. And Allen has a lively eye for performers, as ever; having lifted Duvall and Jeff Goldblum from Robert Altman's unofficial repertory com-pany for *Annie Hall*, he cast Michael Murphy, another Altman regular, in *Manhattan*.

Despite these pictures' artistic accomplishments, and their evident sincerity in evoking two worlds beloved of Allen, there is something academic in the execution. As experiments in style and tone go, they are pleasing to the eye but unrewarding to the heart. There's nothing to wrestle with. *Interiors* is like a dress rehearsal in which the actors, having been struck by the realization that they are better than the script they are performing, have resolved to cover for its shortcomings with ponderous line readings endorsed by their director. You hear that dialogue, that delivery, and you wonder how the man who had in print so cruelly spoofed Chekhov ('I . . . must go on. Yes, night is falling . . . falling rapidly. So rapidly, and I still have all those chickpeas to rearrange.') could have allowed writing of such painful austerity to sneak below his radar.[3]

Manhattan is easier to warm to than either *Annie Hall* or *Interiors*, which is perhaps what makes me so suspicious of it – and I speak as a person who some years ago hung a *Manhattan* movie poster in the hallway, and has yet to remove it to make way for *Cannibal Holocaust*. But then it is the sort of image you can put up in your home, and the sort of film you can advertise your fondness for, without unbalancing the colour scheme, without frightening the party guests. It is no fault of Allen's that the ghosts in Anthony Minghella's film *Truly, Madly, Deeply* during a sojourn to the material world waver between watching *Manhattan* and *Fitzcarraldo*, before finally settling on the former. But the decision of those cosy middle-class apparitions to settle down for a tearful afternoon in front of that movie reinforces the extent to which Allen's film mashes its hard-earned lessons into easy romance.

The George Gershwin score transforms every moment in which it is used into a triumph, which would be witty if the picture pointed up the disparity between the splendour of what we can hear, and the petty trade-offs of these pampered metropolitan worrywarts. I don't know what is being celebrated in the movie's final scene except the willing rehearsal of that old movie convention, the race to declare an almost-squandered love. But there is no glory or redemption in the efforts of Isaac (Allen) to persuade his teenage ex-girlfriend Tracy (Mariel Hemingway) to return to him; this is another example of the casual vindictiveness that runs through his character, and which Allen, bound up in soliciting the audience's sympathies, cannot afford to acknowledge. We are witnessing Isaac's last-ditch attempt to smother the woman he loves for the sake of his own vanity. But the camera and the surging score try to dupe us into swallowing this as a moment of victory, when in fact it is just another instance of Isaac bulldozing the feelings of those around him. Earlier in the film, we can't comprehend why Isaac's contradictory account of a near-hit-and-run accident involving his ex-wife's lover (to his ex-wife, he denies that he floored the gas; to a potential girlfriend, he boasts about it) goes unchallenged by the film. Or rather, we can, but the idea that the movie has been designed to flatter its characters even more than its audience is too great a comedown after the candour that made *Annie Hall* such a difficult film, and such an important one. In this instance, as in so many others in his subsequent movies, the integrity of the picture has been sacrificed for the sake of Allen's persona. It's a poor trade-off.

Manhattan and *Interiors* are beautiful movies. It's not just the posters that would look swell in the hallway: any framed still from either film would give your living room that touch of class that you know it's crying out for. But *Annie Hall* is something else. This is the kind of movie that belongs in the attic, in the same trunk as those well-thumbed love letters and painful mementoes – irreplaceable, but not something with which you can bear to be confronted every day of your life.

Jonathan Demme.

Caged Heat (1974): Barbara Steele as Superintendent McQueen. (© New
World Pictures)

9. Jonathan Demme

It would be true to say that in the films of Jonathan Demme the camera loves people, if that didn't imply that the director was divorced from his lens. In Demme's work, there is no such distinction. From the first frame of his first movie, his irrepressible visual style – gently barmy and buzzing with busy-bee exuberance – is so consistent with the compassion dished out to his characters that the movies play like expressions of undiluted joy.

He turns the crummy and the humdrum into art, but you'll never catch him doing it – you can't see the process. The eye is titillated by his compositions, yet there is nothing rigidly composed about them. The prosaic settings (second-hand car lots, grungy roadside diners, supermarkets, junkyards) are elevated by a casual lyricism, but you will search in vain for a lofty or patronizing shot. Every detail of costume or set design, no matter how droll or diverting, is faithful to the characters' inner lives – the candy-striped wall against which an attempted insurrection is staged in the prison movie *Caged Heat*, or Roy Scheider's eerie white suit in *Last Embrace*, or the rows of threadbare tyres leading along the driveway toward the mobile home in *Melvin and Howard*. Throughout this there exists a functioning narrative sensibility, but it hasn't squeezed out the humanistic elements; it's organic. Jonathan Demme loves people; he can't help it.

He learned his trade under Roger Corman, and wrote and produced a handful of exploitation features for him (among them *Angels Hard as They Come* in 1971 and *The Hot Box* in 1972) before being commissioned in 1974 to write and direct *Caged Heat*, a tardy addition to the women-in-prison cycle that Corman's company New World had begun at the dawn of the decade with *The Big Doll's House*. Unlike most of Corman's protégés, Demme has never relinquished the essence of that apprenticeship. As late as 1988, he crafted an affectionate tribute to all things kitsch and Cormanesque in *Married to the Mob*, while his exploitation roots brought an edginess to the expert comic thrillers *Something Wild* and *The Silence of the Lambs*. It wasn't only that he didn't stop celebrating those roots: they simply never ceased to be pertinent. Roger Corman is forever present in a Jonathan Demme picture, sometimes in body – in his cameos in *Swing Shift*, *The Silence of the Lambs* and *Philadelphia* – and always in spirit, in the films' fondness for eccentricity, the uncomplicated delight with which pleasure is greeted, and the enthusiasm with which it is served up.

Whereas Corman seems now like a youthful passion destined to be outgrown by Scorsese and Coppola, it is clear that Demme was snugly suited to bashing out exploitation quickies on tight schedules with budgets many times smaller than the shoeshine allowance on a Hollywood blockbuster. It was no hardship: it played into his idea of the kind of director he wanted to be, a real Raoul Walsh, fingers itching, ready for action. He and his Cormanville colleagues Joe Viola, director of Demme's early scripts, and George Armitage, who later made *Grosse Pointe Blank* and the Demme-produced *Miami Blues*, had a mantra: 'Just give us an assignment and we'll make something of it. We're professionals!'[1]

Demme directed *Caged Heat* at the age of thirty. It feels odd to write that; it sounds so old now, in a culture where you should hang up your riding crop and loudhailer if you haven't maxed out your parents' credit cards to make a widely acclaimed début feature by the time you've passed your driving test. I think Demme's early films benefit from this comparatively late start. They subscribe to formula, but you can feel the life in them: he's been around, he's used his hungry magpie eyes to hoard images and experiences, and he has the artful grace to know how to integrate them into the frame. 'I've been lucky enough to have been invited into a lot of different houses,' he has said, 'and I guess I developed an eye for kitsch.'[2] Not just an eye, a heart too.

Caged Heat starts with a long shot of a motel forecourt crowded with palm trees. It's only there as a backdrop to a chase scene, but in a matter of seconds you feel that Demme adores this place, and he wants you to cast aside your prejudices and adore it too. Even once the picture retreats into the women's prison that is its chief location, there's still a prevailing sunniness about it. It's as though Demme and his cinematographer Tak Fujimoto are seeing everything for the first time, just as we are, and they can't believe how exotic and vibrant it is either. The oddness of the images speaks to us, often literally – the 'No Laughing' notice in the exercise yard is a dare to audience and inmates alike, and the disregard with which it should be treated is signalled by the spinach-spattered 'No Food Throwing' sign in the canteen. The legend 'Kiss Me Quick' painted on the seat of one prisoner's shorts is like a come-on to those audience members who have paid to see the film deliver on its genre's promises, a task that Demme performs with aplomb. How convenient that any woman in solitary confinement is required also to be naked; what a happy accident that the prisoner accused of theft should have forgotten to put on her bra that morning, so that she might be more comprehensively exposed when her shirt is ripped open in the hunt for stolen cigarettes.

Much of the delight in any exploitation film arises from the

ingenuity with which the standard genre elements are incorporated. It isn't that the audience wants to see something original,
but that it requires familiar elements to be deployed in idiosyncratic, even devious ways, whether it's the nude scenes in *Caged
Heat* or the sadistic violence in 1976's *Fighting Mad*. These are
films from which audiences know exactly what to expect; the
mixture of 'action, nudity and a little social comment'[3] that
Demme identified in the exploitation genre might be administered in varying degrees, but it will always be present, often in-
congruously so – such as in a brief love scene in *Fighting Mad*
which clearly exists only to reveal a comforting glimpse of bare
flesh before the violence kicks off.

It's a misrepresentation to claim, as the magazine *Film Comment* did, that in his early movies Demme was 'an overly sophisticated director contemptuously slumming among lesser
genres'[4] when in fact he embraces the demands of those genres,
adding a dash of his own devilry to the potion. When Roy
Scheider violently pulls back the shower curtain to reveal a
naked Janet Margolin in *Last Embrace*, the *Psycho* reference is
hilarious in its crudeness – all the more so for emerging from a
film that constitutes such an impeccably tidy homage to Hitchcock. (It's as though Demme is proving that he can play both
the reverent student and the class clown, trawling the murky
psychosexual undercurrents of Hitchcock's world, but also rais-
ing merry hell when the mood takes him.) And when the new
prisoners in *Caged Heat* are subjected to a strip search, the
tongues of the target audience may be hanging out, but
Demme's own is lodged firmly in his cheek, as indicated by the
supervising guard's unconvincing assurance that 'I don't enjoy
this any more than you do'.

Demme doesn't recognize the borders between good and
bad behaviour, or 'high' and 'low' culture. Anything that stim-
ulates the eye, the heart or the mind has automatically earned
its place on screen. In *Caged Heat*, the repressed warden (Barbara Steele) reprimands her charges by telling them, 'Given the

chance to express yourselves you went straight to the gutter,'
and there is something of their profane relish in Demme too.
He isn't out to shock: when he shows us something taboo or
unsavoury, the kick is in the gleeful breach of etiquette, as it is
in the films of John Waters or Russ Meyer (from whom Demme
'borrowed' two of the performers in *Caged Heat*: Erica Gavin,
who plays the film's heroine, and, as the leering doctor, Charles
Napier, who would later become a Demme regular). There are
shots in *Caged Heat* of an elderly matron's dentures slipping
from her mouth as she has a heart attack, and one of a severed
ear hitting the dust, and in those moments you detect a hint of
the giddiness that comes from absolute, anarchic freedom – the
same freedom that makes possible Waters' *Female Trouble* or
Meyer's *Faster, Pussycat, Kill! Kill!*, both of which share key
DNA with *Caged Heat*.

Where Demme differs from Waters and Meyer is in his ability to frame such disposable details within a broader social and
cinematic context. The lawless environments of those directors'
movies are an end in themselves; it is joy enough for Waters
and Meyer to execute affronts to polite society, whereas
Demme is more interested in how misfits negotiate a world that
hasn't been designed to their specifications, whether it's the
prisoners challenging the brainwashing regime of the sinister
Behavioural Correction Department in *Caged Heat*, or the dis-
enfranchised landowners in *Crazy Mama* and *Fighting Mad*.
(The respective heroes of *Melvin and Howard* and *Philadelphia*
would continue this struggle by more peaceful means.)

Crazy Mama, which Demme grudgingly took on in 1975 at
Corman's insistence after its original director Shirley Clarke
dropped out, is as near to a John Waters film as you will find in
his oeuvre, and it shares some of Waters' limitations – a sequence in Las Vegas seems to have little purpose other than to
showcase some garish production design, but the chandeliers
and gold leaf linger on screen long after we have finished cring-
ing at them. In other scenes, it becomes clear that the director

doesn't have it in him to be as casually callous as Waters might have been. When an elderly woman is shot by cops through the grocery bag that she is offering up in surrender, the film appears poised to turn several shades darker, a prediction that is undermined by a shot of Lena (Cloris Leachman) tottering along in unsuitable heels and a pair of zebra-stripe leggings paraded for our amusement. That the audience should find itself in a cleft stick is hardly surprising since the director is similarly divided: Demme doesn't want to scandalize us, and having done so he isn't certain what to do next. The humour that is intended to serve as a balm only succeeds in introducing another jarring flavour into the brew.

A different breed of conflict prevails through Demme's next film, *Fighting Mad*. The picture seems almost apologetic for the frivolity of *Crazy Mama*. Despite the merciless tone, it can be tough to suppress your appalled amusement at its slavish adherence to the genre template. We know that substantial motivation will be required before full retribution can be visited upon unscrupulous capitalists by the rural avenger Tom Hunter (Peter Fonda, cast as much for his iconic status as warrior of the common man as for his acting ability). But not only are Hunter's brother and sister-in-law attacked – as they are about to make love – and savagely beaten, they are then pumped full of booze and locked in a car, which is tipped off a cliff. And they're still not dead. It's not so much a question of how much punishment the characters can withstand, as how much will the audience endure?

Just as the plucky abandon of *Crazy Mama* jars with scenes of violence from which the director himself seems to retreat, the brutality in *Fighting Mad* sits uneasily with its supposed liberalism. The hero's son is named Dylan (spelt out in case we have missed the point), while the villains of the piece are dastardly developers who plan to bury the countryside beneath power plants and shopping malls. But the picture appeals too persuasively to its audience's basest instincts to claim liberal credentials of its own. It remains an instructive precursor to *Something Wild*, where a man who rejects conformity also has to confront the demons attached to his new lifestyle, but it has yet to develop the interplay between form and content achieved in the later movie, where fun and horror are two sides of the same blade. In *Fighting Mad*, violence provides character motivation and audience gratification, and nothing in between.

Still, there is a pleasing hint that the conflicts and ambiguities in the film's tone are reflected in its self-righteous hero. As Hunter drives to the family ranch with his young son, after a messy separation that has instigated his escape from city life, he pauses to intervene in a roadside dispute. When he wades in with busy fists, the boy turns away with an audible sigh of disapproval, as if to say: Dad's at it again. The suggestion that the supposedly peaceful Hunter may be disproportionately keen to resort to physical aggression corresponds with the movie itself, which is torn between fighting the good fight, and fetishizing every punch thrown and every drop of blood spilt in its course.

The same distrust of the establishment is evident in both *Fighting Mad* and *Crazy Mama*, but for all its ramshackle zaniness it is the earlier movie that represents the most enduring challenge to the patriarchal, reactionary bias of the action genre. In *Crazy Mama*'s story of three generations of white-trash women – Melba (Ann Sothern), her daughter Lena and her own pregnant offspring Cheryl (Linda Purl) – who embark upon an improvised crime spree en route to retrieving their land, you can find Demme's characteristically generous interpretation of family values. This lawless trio, any one of whom could have lent the film its title, accumulates new family members and hangers-on at every turn, from a bewildered grandmother discovered among the one-armed bandits in Vegas, to a rockabilly suitor for Cheryl to add to the beach-bum who is already panting in her wake. (This impromptu threesome shares a bed without complaint or, for that matter, carnality.) Family here is not the sealed unit promoted by society, but an open-ended organism that expands or contracts to suit the available space. Even its fundamental components are not rigidly defined. Reminding her boyfriend that the baby she is carrying may not be his, Cheryl discloses a certain vagueness in her own family tree – 'I've always had my choice of five fathers,' she says blithely.

Demme's exploitation background is intriguingly complicated by this baggy approach to orthodox morality. It marks him out from other Corman disciples who lacked his inclusive sensibility, and therefore his opportunities for advancement, such as Lewis Teague, who took several cautious sideways steps after editing *Crazy Mama* by going on to direct schlock thrillers like *Alligator* and *Cujo*. Demme's affinities lie instead with some of Europe's modern imps of irreverence – in particular Bertrand Blier and Pedro Almodóvar. There's something of Blier's insouciant, slaphappy cheerfulness in *Crazy Mama*, and in the ménage à trois at the heart of Demme's 1977 film *Citizens Band*, in which a bigamous truck driver named Harold (the granite-faced Napier again) and his two wives arrive without any fanfare at a harmonious living arrangement helpfully suggested by the prostitute with whom Harold has been dallying. In the same year, Blier's most dazzling and daring sex comedy, *Get Out Your Handkerchiefs*, was released, positing an equally unconventional solution to marital stalemate, with a man (Gerard Depardieu) making good on his wish to see his morose wife happy by imploring other courtiers to bestow upon her the bliss that he evidently cannot (she eventually finds its nearest equivalent in the arms of a thirteen-year-old boy genius).

Get Out Your Handkerchiefs won the 1978 Academy Award for Best Foreign Film, but *Citizens Band* was met with crushing indifference by cinemagoers everywhere, even when one US cinema waived its admission price. Paramount renamed the picture *Handle With Care*, but in their treatment of it failed to adhere to the advice of that new title. The studio released the film without its original ending, in which the CB enthusiasts

Pam (Candy Clark) and Blaine (Paul Le Mat), the closest thing
the film has to romantic leads, are married in a wacky highway
ceremony conducted by radio. Presumably this was considered
an idiosyncrasy too far. In Paramount's preferred version, the
film closes on a freeze-frame of Pam and Blaine kissing, a more
conventional sign-off that denies the characters' unforced ec-
centricities. After protests from influential critics, Demme's ending was reinstated, but to little commercial good. Context is
one explanation for the disparities between the receptions that
greeted *Get Out Your Handkerchiefs* and *Citizens Band*. What
feels alluringly exotic in a European location, in a foreign language, can to some audiences look plain incongruous when
transposed to a parochial setting about which they harbour less
generous or romantic preconceptions. Likewise, a viewer who
whoops through Almodóvar's 1983 convent comedy *Dark
Habits* – essentially a prison movie with wimples – might well
recoil from the shrill farce of *Caged Heat* or *Crazy Mama*,
which offers pleasures not readily tolerated or appreciated by
English-speaking audiences outside the realm of exploitation.

But the key to appreciating Demme's film-making lies in understanding how invidious these definitions can be, and the extent to which they can impede our relationship with movies.
After Demme experienced his first box-office hit with *The Silence of the Lambs*, he reflected on his former inability to find
mainstream acceptance. '[A]t a certain point,' he said, 'I started
wondering, "What is my problem? I can do films that are appreciated in some quarters, and so on, but either there's something that I find interesting which is getting in the way of my
sharing my work with a lot of people, or there's some ingredient that I'm simply missing."'[5] That mysterious something that
he found interesting was life, all its manifestations and peculi-
arities, rendered without bias or rhetoric. That elusive missing
ingredient was the capacity for manipulation that instructs an
audience in its responses. It has to be said that there are worse
qualities for a director to be lacking.

It's debatable whether Demme has since learned to play

babysitter as well as storyteller to his audience, or at least learned to fake it, but a viewer who comes to his work in need of explicit guidelines is bound to feel stranded. *Caged Heat*, *Crazy Mama* and *Fighting Mad* all have a rudimentary governing morality consistent with their genre specifications: individual spirit is good, authority (especially in the form of law enforcement) is bad. But *Citizens Band* is a quieter and more rewarding piece, less redolent of any cinematic archetypes, less forceful in parading its enticements. It's ironic that Paramount hoped the movie might exploit the CB radio boom, when in fact that fad is a mere springboard for the plot, and a metaphor for the characters' inabilities to express themselves. In *Citizens Band*, everyone is someone else when they pick up the radio, and not just because of the 'handles' by which they are known (and by which each character is, somewhat sweetly, listed in the end credits). CB becomes a vessel for their fantasies, a conduit for their desires. Pam can't talk to her by-the-book boyfriend Blaine, so she reinvents herself on the airwaves as Electra, and enjoys innocently dirty chit-chat with a voice identified to her as Warlock, but known to us as a teenage nerd in his daddy's car. Blaine's brother uses CB to express to his sibling the contempt that can't be articulated in person, while their taciturn father (Roberts Blossom) only comes alive on air – over the breakfast table, he can barely bring himself to speak, unless it's to issue morbidly convincing death threats to Blaine's mutt.

Then there are the assorted disembodied voices ringing out in the night, each of which is, most likely, only tenuously related to its radio persona. When this unseen supporting cast is finally revealed in the movie's climax, together with Harold's cows, who had wandered out into the night, and the jaunty prostitute Debbie, who turns up to hand out trays of her home-brewed coffee, the scene has the euphoria of an unexpected family reunion. You can't predict the gentle force that it delivers because you don't even notice Demme building toward it. Suddenly it's there, providing an emotional release that you didn't realize you needed.

There is the danger that a film as elegantly constructed as
Citizens Band can fall apart under examination, because no
synopsis can do justice to the lightness of Demme's touch.
Reading Harold's line to his wives as they attempt to wring
harmony from bigamy – 'What we've got here is a communication problem' – you would be forgiven for thinking that the
movie's subtext was being splashed across the screen in undignified graffiti. In fact, the opposite is true: nothing in the movie
feels contrived, except perhaps the last-minute effort to integrate the separate stories of Blaine and Harold. Even the farci-
cal jolt that we experience when Harold's wives run into one
another is lovingly handled. We can see that plot twist coming
from some distance away, but our expectations are teased by
Demme, who keeps the characters from sharing our knowledge
until the last possible moment – until we are helplessly squirming through our giggles. And just when the comedy seems to
have dissipated with the wives' realization of their mutual interest ('Does this mean we're related?'), it is transformed into a
kind of knockabout melancholy, as the women get drunk and
compare Harold's romantic techniques. Their raucous laughter
lights up the drab motel room.

The scenes unfold casually, as though they had just occurred
to Demme a moment before shouting 'Action', which accounts
too for that freewheeling attitude toward the characters' emotional complications; there seems neither the time nor the inclination to pass judgement. Everything here has the zing of
freshness, from the off-the-cuff dialogue (upon being informed
that her new mobile home sleeps three, Debbie coos excitedly,
'I've never even done a three before!') to the early morning sunlight that twinkles through the perforations in Harold's straw
Stetson. Almost without our noticing, that hat becomes a symbol of Harold's relaxed masculinity; the way it takes up the
whole surface of the table when he lays it down during the
summit meeting with his spouses seems to say so much about
him, and the warmth he has brought to both his marriages.

Demme is a whiz at these apparently throwaway touches.

Some of the scenes are no more than doodles. The montage in which Blaine visits those users whom he deems to have violated the CB code, from schoolboys and decrepit old women to neo-Nazis, is like a page torn out of the funnies – each skit has its own miniature pay-off. You can see Demme's sensibility developing before your eyes. In *Caged Heat*, there is a sequence where a gang of escaped convicts turn up at a bank with the intention of robbing it, only to find that rival crooks have beaten them to the scene of the heist, and Demme choreographs this burst of loopiness so coolly, so casually, that the manner of its execution becomes as dotty as the gag itself. No other American film-maker since Preston Sturges has been so consistently gripped with glee, so high on human foibles. Demme looks at life and smacks his lips; his motto might be 'Anything goes'. When *Last Embrace* punishes its psychopathic but very human killer – a woman who tracks down the descendants of her grandmother's oppressors and murders them mid-coitus – that simple genre requirement seems unduly harsh. Could there not be room in Demme's universe for this particular alternative lifestyle, you find yourself wondering, in the manner of a lawyer pleading for clemency.

Citizens Band rarely resorts to the common vocabulary of cinema, where a camera movement or an orchestral augmentation provides the emphasis necessary for a scene to be processed by the viewer. We are, by and large, left to our own devices. *Citizens Band* was the first of Demme's features that he hadn't written himself (he collaborated with Paul Brickman on a rewrite of Brickman's original script), but in keeping with the director's natural inclinations the film obeys the rhythms of its characters' lives, best described as harmonious in the face of hysteria. Brickman reputedly deplored Demme's handling of his script ('First of all,' said Demme, 'he was horrified that a Roger Corman director was being attached to his screenplay'[6]). And though the precise nature of his objections are unknown, the evidence of the movies that Brickman subsequently directed,

Risky Business and *Men Don't Leave*, would indicate that he didn't share Demme's faith in the audience's ability to watch a film unaided by editorial inference.

But that's the essence of this film-maker's genius. It isn't that he's hands-off. The convicts' triumph over their oppressors in *Caged Heat*, for instance, was pivotal to Demme's vision of the movie. 'I insisted [to New World] that all the women be allowed to escape,' he said[7] – hence the final shoot-out in which a truck is riddled with bullets which only strike those passengers who have been revealed as corrupt or sadistic, leaving the prisoners to flee unharmed. But he's a director whose technique can sometimes be so invisible, so effortless, that you have the uncanny experience of being lulled and stimulated at the same time. The actors – especially the former boxer Paul Le Mat, a pleasantly reined-in, mild-mannered goofball who starred in *American Graffiti*, and whom Demme later cast in *Melvin and Howard* – are instantly convivial and familiar. Even the extras who call out a line each to Blaine when he's in the diner buzz with energy; you can believe that they have lives outside that diner, and that scene. You warm to the characters in *Citizens Band* before you know them, and you know them before you realize it.

The generosity of *Citizens Band* was present, in a disguised form, in the 1979 thriller *Last Embrace*, though Demme – at that point practically unemployable – had been forced to plug the gap between the two pictures by directing an episode of *Columbo*. He maintains that the script, which he once again reshaped with the original writer (David Shaber), went into production before its narrative discrepancies could be repaired. But it still bubbles with wit and affection, two qualities that had by the end of the 1970s largely vanished from the thriller genre, not to return in any coherent form until the likes of John Dahl and Quentin Tarantino applied the lessons of the past to cinema of the present in the early 1990s.

There is in much of *Last Embrace* that streak of gloriously perverse humour characteristic not only of Hitchcock but of Roman Polanski too, in which human vanity or vulnerability is transformed into an ongoing punchline. Think of the paranoia of Harry (Roy Scheider) in the early scenes of *Last Embrace*, and how oddly self-aggrandizing it seems, as though the fact that someone might be out to kill him gives him unique purpose and import (of course, someone *is* out to kill him, but what punctures that self-aggrandizement is that it's the one person that he fails to suspect – the one person whom he believes to be wholly benevolent). Polanski had appeared for a time to be the saviour of the modern thriller, after films like *Rosemary's Baby* and *Chinatown*. But following the near-operatic horror of his underrated film *The Tenant*, those hopes receded. It would not be stretching a point to find in *Something Wild* and *The Silence of the Lambs* that raw intimacy between beauty and deformity, civility and psychosis, which had made *Repulsion*, *Cul-de-Sac* and *The Tenant* so searing to the touch.

Hitchcock and Polanski's pedantic attention to detail, and the obsessive inquisitiveness of their cameras, can also be discerned in *Last Embrace*, mingled with the sensitivity that had become Demme's signature quality. It's an unexpected ingredient to bring to a Hitchcock homage. Brian De Palma was replaying many of Hitchcock's trademark tricks in altered forms to undermine the security of newly sophisticated audiences ('You think you've seen this before?' he seemed to be taunting them in *Sisters* and *Carrie*. 'Well, think again.') but it would be a generous viewer who received his work as humanistic, at least prior to the traumatized horror of *Blow Out* in 1981. Demme, on the other hand, seems to approach his material with the lingering question, What if Hitchcock had been really fond of his characters? The role of the impotent hero played by James Stewart in *Rear Window* and *Vertigo*, and by Cary Grant in *North by Northwest*, is here taken by Scheider as Harry (a name with Hitchcockian baggage), but there's no feeling that Demme will exploit his own position as puppet-master in Harry's fate. That cruelty isn't in his repertoire.

Instead, Demme works with Scheider to accentuate Harry's forlorn frailty. The brilliant white suit in which Scheider spends much of the picture ensconced – or rather mummified, given the protective bandaging of grief that Harry wears – cries out to be crumpled and torn, splattered with mud or blood, just as the worsening state of Grant's suit in *North by Northwest* represents the extent of the indignities to which his debonair persona is subjected. But Harry's clothes instead convey how lost he is in the new world into which he has emerged following a nervous breakdown over his wife's death. One of Harry's earliest lines in the movie – 'It's like a string of bad jokes, only I don't get the punchline' – establishes the bewilderment and paranoia that defines him, and it also carries strong film noir echoes. Demme had expressed the view that Scheider 'could be the Humphrey Bogart of the 1970s',[8] and you can just hear Bogart reciting those lines, sounding as ever like a man with lockjaw talking in his sleep.

It makes sense to read the film as the story of Bogart frozen shortly after completing *In a Lonely Place* in 1950, and then decanted into the muddled, frazzled America of 1979. Scheider looks fabulously lost and, unfortunately, so untrustworthy that surely no one would want to help him find his way again. With that flat face (he has no profile) and oily skin, it's clear now that he was an endangered species. In the same year, Richard Gere would manage to look swell while also falling apart in Paul Schrader's *American Gigolo*, and the preppy locker-room blandness of Tom Cruise and his brat-pack siblings was only a few years away. How could Scheider have hoped to survive? The fact that he didn't, and was more stubborn and gnarled than heroic by the time he played the lead in *Blue Thunder* in 1983, lends *Last Embrace* an uninvited poignancy. When Harry visits the graveyard, the New York skyline is set high in the distance behind him, and beyond it stands a rusty sunset: he seems to be saying goodbye to more than just his wife. (Scheider might be bidding farewell to his own popularity, and also to the era of *Jaws*, his greatest success.) When he steps out on to the viewing deck next to Niagara Falls in the film's climax, he lets out an involuntary groan that corresponds to the visual shock of his white suit infiltrating a throng of banana-yellow sou'westers, and you imagine that Scheider's reaction to the encroaching generation of pretty-boys, flawless and homogenous, was similarly fraught.

The film is studded with these disorientating images, from the tunnel along which the camera retreats to reveal unexpectedly its place beneath an ornamental waterfall, to the woozy handheld photography in the opening flashback, and on the station platform where Harry becomes convinced that he is about to be murdered (even the public address system seems complicit). And while there are reminders of the kinkiness of Demme's earlier movies (the fur-trimmed kitten heels languishing by the bathtub in which a woman is drowning her lover could have come straight from the *Crazy Mama* props box), the tone is, right from that elegiac title simultaneously suggesting passion and death, one of strangled nostalgia.

The distant past does, after all, play a defining role in the plot, since it provides the killer with motivation. The movie implicitly suggests that no matter how effectively we feel we have outrun the achievements and errors of the past, they remain on our doorstep, at our side – or literally close to the surface, in the case of the architectural evidence of New York's early twentieth-century white slave trade uncovered by Harry. The past is tangled up with the present, thereby rendering redundant the very definition of it as the past. If this admission serves a portentous function in the plot of *Last Embrace*, it is nutritious in the broader context of cinema itself, where past, present and future can be seen as reels of the same movie, scenes in the same reel, frames in the same scene.

It is often said that a film-maker whose work is influenced by other, earlier practitioners owes a debt to those who have gone before. But we should perhaps cease to consider cinema in such punitive financial terms, where influences are like mortgages to be painstakingly settled, and artistic worth is measured in hard-earned collateral. Better to see this most fluid and democratic of art forms not as something proprietary, but as an unpolluted atmosphere continually replenished by those who move through it, so that Demme's insights and triumphs, inherited from the contributions of Jean Renoir or Roger Corman or Bertrand Blier, are in turn adopted and cultivated by Paul Thomas Anderson (*Magnolia, Punch-Drunk Love*), Richard Linklater (*Waking Life, Before Sunrise*) and Mira Nair (*Salaam, Bombay!, Monsoon Wedding*) – as well as anyone else too elusive and amorphous to be pinned down in a simple game of spot-the-influences.

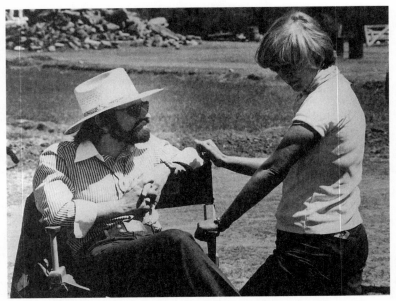

Making *Alice Doesn't Live Here Anymore* (1974): Martin Scorsese directs Ellen Burstyn (as Alice Hyatt). (© Warner Bros)

New York, New York (1977): Francine Evans (Liza Minnelli) and Jimmy Doyle (Robert De Niro). (© United Artists)

10. Martin Scorsese

This chapter is dedicated to the task of reclaiming Martin Scorsese from his reputation, and from himself. Of all the film-makers who came to prominence in the 1970s, it is only Scorsese who has been severely misrepresented by subsequent assessments of his work. Not that his most paranoid supporter could uphold a case for his movies being underrated. If anything, the less convincing pictures of his later years – in particular *The King of Comedy*, *After Hours*, *Bringing Out the Dead* – have generated undeserved acclaim because of the lustre associated with their director's name. But he is known now as the gangster's ambassador, the pre-eminent chronicler of life on New York's nastier sidewalks, an appointment nicely ridiculed in the first season of the HBO series *The Sopranos*, when a minor Mafioso spotted him entering a nightclub and called out 'Hey Marty! Loved *Kundun*!', a reference to the director's becalming 1998 Dalai Lama film.

That *Kundun* – and the 1993 Edith Wharton adaptation *The Age of Innocence* – were considered upon their release to be radical departures from home turf only reinforces the problem with the received wisdom about Scorsese. Even using his 1970s output as a representative example of his diversity reveals that violence is not high on his list of priorities: out of

eight films, only three in any way support his image as a suc-
cessor to Sam Peckinpah, or a forerunner to Quentin Tarantino
(and one of those – *Taxi Driver* – is less concerned with the actual explosion of rage than its day-to-day maintenance). In this
director's entire oeuvre, that number rises to a mere eight out of
more than twenty titles. Of course, violence has different manifestations, and it is certainly the case that one of Scorsese's
most fascinating and misunderstood films, *New York, New
York*, is also one of his most brutal, despite being free of gunfire. It is the case too that this is not a film that has made much
contribution to the Scorsese image; film history is not as forgiving as we might hope of financial failures, or of works which
jeopardize a commonly held misconception.

It may be that the majority of audiences genuinely believe
that explicitly violent films such as *Raging Bull* and *GoodFellas*
represent Scorsese's finest work. Or perhaps it is that the adren-
aline fix administered by these pictures remains in the bloodstream longer than, say, the restraint and compassion of *Alice
Doesn't Live Here Anymore* lingers in the mind. It is also likely
that Scorsese's lopsided reputation has been fostered by numerous articles in the men's magazine market celebrating the likes
of *Taxi Driver* and *Raging Bull* as hymns to the savage, inartic-
ulate male – a construct designed to flatter untapped fantasies
of alienation or fury in those publications' target audience, to
the detriment of the movies themselves. You can witness the
same response to Tarantino, whose third feature *Jackie Brown*
was never going to generate the same obsessive levels of worship as his earlier, less mature movies – *Reservoir Dogs* and
Pulp Fiction – because it traded in middle-aged characters
dawdling in the door of the last-chance saloon, as opposed to
young gunslingers in love with their own capacity for quick
talk. Indeed, *Jackie Brown* might have been written with the
assistance of a computer programme designed to delete automatically any monologues likely to be quoted by Jack the Lad
in his Reebok Classics.

Those parts of Scorsese's career that fail to correspond to the prevalent view of him as a guy's director have been discarded in the routine rewriting of his career in the media, and Tarantino will undoubtedly fall foul of this same process, which cannot help but diminish a complex film-maker (though it can turn a Guy Ritchie into an *auteur*). Scorsese has had a bum rap, but for an unusual reason: he has proved himself such a virtuoso stylist of film violence, and so comprehensive in his understanding of male neuroses, that his other capabilities have been entirely eclipsed. *GoodFellas* is curious in introducing into the male-dominated crime genre a potent and plausible female voice (Lorraine Bracco, as the hero's wife, briefly wrests control of voice-over duties from Ray Liotta). But on the evidence of Scorsese's machocentric reputation, you would never guess that he is an assured director of women, naturally drawn to the mechanics of camaraderie, irrespective of genre.

He shot a series of short films while at NYU before making his feature debut in 1969 with *Who's That Knocking at My Door?*, a story of male sexual and religious angst which would later be partially transformed into his third film, *Mean Streets*. Both movies are set in his native New York neighbourhood of Little Italy, and like George Lucas immortalizing his own formative years in *American Graffiti*, there is a sense of Scorsese preserving an era that was slipping away. That mission didn't end with *Mean Streets*. In 1974, between *Alice Doesn't Live Here Anymore* and *Taxi Driver*, Scorsese made the documentary short *Italianamerican*, a touching and unashamedly nostalgic interview with his parents, Charles and Catherine Scorsese, which incorporates his mother's recipe for spaghetti and meatballs. This was Scorsese Jr. unambiguously committing his history to film, and advertising his ethnicity, just as he had used *Who's That Knocking at My Door?* and *Mean Streets* to stake out his own geographical territory, shedding light on a strip of the East Coast largely neglected by cinema.

The immediacy of autobiographical experience is striking in

those New York movies. Later, for *Taxi Driver*, he would hire
Bernard Herrmann, who had scored two films by Scorsese's
friend Brian De Palma, but was best known for his work with
Hitchcock. Herrmann's score for *Taxi Driver* was ripe and in-
toxicating; like the paranoia of that film's hero, Travis Bickle,
there's no escaping it. But a subtler reflection of Travis's damaged interior life can be found in that film's sound design, its relentless bustle of ghoulish cries and anonymous protestations,
which transforms an area known as 'noises off' into an entire
score in itself. In those details, those sounds, is the authenticity
of city life and madness.

Besides fashioning a sense of identity with his early movies,
Scorsese was also challenging an established hierarchy that had
left New York film students feeling at a disadvantage to their
Californian counterparts. It was New York as much as Scorsese
that was being promoted in *Italianamerican* and *Mean Streets*
(most of which, ironically, was shot in Los Angeles for budget-
ary reasons), and there was the feeling of a balance being re-
dressed in that work, and in De Palma's early features. USC
would later claim 'as of December 1983, 41 of the 42 all-time
highest grossing films have USC alumni affiliated with them',[1]
and students from other corners of America would already
have been aware of this imbalance. 'The student films from
California are much slicker, more professional-looking,' Scorsese had observed. 'In New York it's handheld quickie shooting; the difference in equipment is amazing.'[2] If there was
admiration, there was bitterness too. '[Independent features]
are looked down upon, especially independent features made in
New York. They look down on most non-Hollywood-produced
stuff except foreign films. They have that aura of "art".'[3]

But after graduating from NYU, Scorsese found employ-
ment, like De Palma and Lucas, with Warner Bros in Los Angeles, where he edited music films such as *Woodstock* and
Medicine Ball Caravan. 'One short cut might be to come to
California sooner,' he reflected later, 'because, in a sense, you

take the cue from the people at USC like John Milius and Coppola. These people went from the schools right to [Roger] Corman. You're fed right into the industry, and the industry is right here. If you make cars, you've got to be in Detroit.'⁴ Corman, the patron saint of struggling young film-makers, and an early admirer of *Who's That Knocking at My Door?*, took Scorsese under his wing and gave him the chance to make his second feature in 1971.

Boxcar Bertha, set in Depression-era Arkansas, was to be the latest of American International Pictures' exploitation quickies. Corman was chasing the success of Arthur Penn's *Bonnie and Clyde*; once the gunfire of that movie's final scene had been greeted by the jangle of box-office cash registers, Corman began devoting his time to rushing out variations on the theme of itinerant criminals – like *Bloody Mama* which starred Robert De Niro, the young livewire who had brought his considerable voltage to Brian De Palma's early films. *Bonnie and Clyde* at least bore a passing resemblance to the true story upon which it was based, but the advertised historical connection in Corman's rush-jobs was as spurious as the incongruous inserts of sex and violence which occurred at regular intervals. That loose phrase 'regular intervals' doesn't really do justice to the rigour of the formula to which Scorsese was required to adhere. From the moment that Barbara Hershey, as Bertha, hitches up her dress to expose a stretch of thigh, it is possible to set your watch by each flash of flesh, each right hook or shotgun blast.

But the discipline was instructive. (Those not inclined toward the films of John Cassavetes might reasonably speculate on how he would have progressed had such constraints been imposed in the early stages of his career.) And only a viewer of wilful ignorance could pretend that other, more prestigious movies don't observe the same formula. As Jonathan Demme noted of *The Godfather*: 'It's a classical Roger Corman movie. All the Corman moves are there – a little sex, a little violence, a little social comment.'⁵

Scorsese still finds ample room for manoeuvre in *Boxcar Bertha*. The movie gets up to speed when Bertha, whose father's death in a plane crash was caused by unscrupulous businessmen, joins Big Bill Shelley (David Carradine), an aggrieved union leader, in a spree of robberies and murders; in the gaps between these brash set-pieces, Scorsese preserves a touching mood of intimacy. The bond between Bertha and Bill doesn't bear – nor for that matter, does it get – much scrutiny, but Scorsese directs Hershey and Carradine with a leisurely generosity that belies AIP's penny-pinching budget and schedule. The movie is nothing if not brisk, but there is time to luxuriate in the characters. The most enduring scenes are those that don't seem harnessed to the action. A dissolve between two separate shots of Bertha sleeping after she and Bill have made love has a hesitant tenderness – as though Scorsese was striving for a gentler version of jump-cuts that he was to use in the bedroom scene in *Mean Streets*.

The humour is mostly of the hayseed variety, with the exception of one sliver of pointed irony, when the film cuts from Bertha playfully ordering two captive policemen to repeatedly stand up and sit down under the gaze of her gun, to the freed men receiving precisely the same instruction upon returning to their gruff superior. Not a subtle criticism of the intimidation commonly found on both sides of the law, but a funny one.

Elsewhere, there are fleeting indications of where Scorsese's real expertise resides. The opening sequence, for example, as Bertha watches her father soaring overhead in his cropdusting plane, shows an early mastery of ambiguous tension, with its dreamy atmosphere of distant foreboding, and the confident crosscutting between opposing perspectives. Bertha watches the plane; Bill, working on the railroad, watches Bertha. There are cuts to the point of view of Bertha's father; and the businessmen survey the entire scene. An urgent, pulsing harmonica soundtrack is layered over the montage. The focus of the scene is kept deliberately indistinct. When tragedy arrives, it is sudden, greeted with Bertha's bestial screams and immediate retribution. And then the film dusts itself off and marches on, like its heroine.

Making *Boxcar Bertha* got Scorsese noticed, and it suited his natural on-the-hoof vitality that was always verging on impatience – 'Four words in the space God made for one' was how the screenwriter Paul Attanasio described his verbal rhythms.[6] Scorsese utilized what he learned on *Boxcar Bertha* when he finally came to make the more personal and much-brooded over *Mean Streets*. 'We used the same ideas, the same fast-paced work, except for a different kind of film. [The crew] didn't understand the film this time, but it paid off anyway because they knew how to shoot pretty fast.'[7]

Watching the two movies back to back is instructive. Where the earlier film is an enthusiastic display of painting by numbers that's not afraid occasionally to go over the lines, *Mean Streets* is splashed with newly invented colours on a homemade canvas. Its energy and abrasiveness owed something to Scorsese's new-found friend and supporter John Cassavetes – a poster for his picture *Husbands* can be glimpsed in Scorsese's film, alongside one for John Boorman's *Point Blank*, a less obvious influence than the braggadocio-heavy *Husbands*, but one which scrutinized, in different ways from *Mean Streets*, the relationship between men, guns and guilt. Cassavetes' films, such as *Shadows* and *Faces*, had brought a new edginess to American cinema, or had dragged to the surface an edginess that already thrived in the work of other directors (Nicholas Ray, Samuel Fuller) who had made an impression upon Scorsese. Meanwhile, Boorman's *Point Blank* had introduced into American cinema a European sensibility – stark, contemplative, analytical – which would flourish in such films as Coppola's *The Conversation*, with its echoes of Antonioni, or *Taxi Driver*, with its shades of Robert Bresson.

But *Mean Streets* is more than the sum of its creator's influences. Scorsese also adds important elements of his own,

thereby continuing the honourable artistic tradition that I have
mentioned, of replenishing the atmosphere from which you
draw sustenance (compared to film-makers like Guy Ritchie or
Neil LaBute or M. Night Shyamalan who are all take, take,
take). Viewers in 1973 would not have been as familiar with
the scuzzy, twilight world of *Mean Streets* as we are today,
while the giddy camerawork created genuine disorientation.
Audiences had not become acclimatized, as we are, to the anarchy of the handheld camera by TV shows like *ER* and *NYPD
Blue*. So many of the techniques used in *Mean Streets* have
since been absorbed into the common idiom of mainstream cinema and television – the use of titles to introduce characters,
the home movie excerpts which create an automatic familiarity
(and which Scorsese would use again in *American Boy* and
Raging Bull). And, most of all, the unity of music and movement. Scorsese was not the first film-maker to seize on slow-
motion as an ideal form for visualizing the macho tendency
toward self-mythology – Boorman in *Point Blank* and Sam
Peckinpah in *The Wild Bunch* had already picked up on that
while Kenneth Anger had long ago whipped up his own cock-
tail of machismo, music and motorcycles. But Scorsese did in-
vent the idea of men walking slowly to the sound of jangling
guitars. It takes Johnny Boy (Robert De Niro) forever to swag-
ger from one end of the short bar to the other, but from our
cinema seats we are willing it to take even longer, the better to
relish his roughed-up alley-cat elegance for another moment –
heaven knows we will never again see him so close to repose –
and to soak up a few more bars of the Stones' 'Jumpin' Jack
Flash'.

If the camera makes heroes out of the lowliest of us, then
slow-motion provides even greater commendation. Johnny Boy
looks immortal; he could be walking on water. That's how he
sees himself: like a movie star suspended in an endless close-up,
he doesn't think ahead to the next shot, the next scene; he has
no understanding of consequences, which is how he accumu-

lates the debts that will eventually bring down him and his friends. Whereas Charlie (Harvey Keitel), who is troubled by the conflict between his own devout Catholicism and his life as a petty crook and loan shark, is all consequences. Scorsese whacks us with this contrast quickly and brutally. The film's opening words, spoken by Scorsese over a black screen, fix the mood of agonized guilt that will dog Charlie, whom we first see sitting bolt upright in bed, as if from a nightmare. When his head returns to the pillow, it is greeted by the hard, summoning drums that kick off the Ronettes' yearning pop song 'Be My Baby'.

Scorsese might not have directed his first bona-fide musical until *New York, New York*, or his first concert film until *The Last Waltz*, but both movies represented an organic progression from his earlier work, where a pop song can be one of the profoundest expressions of identity. Music is so integral to *Mean Streets*, so eloquent in articulating the characters' desires and establishing the textures and contours of their environment, that the movie sometimes seems a heartbeat away from being a musical. In the first few minutes of *Alice Doesn't Live Here Anymore*, pop music similarly becomes both a commentary on character and a statement of intent. The glam-rock punch of Mott the Hoople's 'All the Way to Memphis' is a compelling and unexpected introduction to that film's suburban grind, informing us in no uncertain terms that this character's identity is not necessarily consistent with her surroundings. It's also the first indication that Scorsese will be averse to the opportunities for soap-opera that are implicit in the material. And if you're looking for a single telling sign that Scorsese instinctively resists banality in the application of music, consider the soundtrack space that is afforded to Mott the Hoople and T-Rex, while a little ditty called 'I Will Always Love You' by Dolly Parton (which would later provide a hilariously overblown sign-off to *The Best Little Whorehouse in Texas* before being re-recorded in a pumped-full-of-steroids version by

Whitney Houston for use in *The Bodyguard*) plays almost unnoticed in the background of one scene.

The juxtaposition in *Mean Streets* of religion and pop music, high culture and low culture, establishes the film's roster of
mismatched marriages: between the sacred and profane, when
Charlie's expressions of religious torment are layered over shots
of the lurid, red-soaked bar; or between tenderness and violence, such as when the spick-and-span hitman (played by
Scorsese) tends to his gun with a wordless kiss. The crime genre
had always accommodated moral lessons in the final reel, to
cleanse the audience after the preceding ninety minutes of illicit
excitement, but *Mean Streets* mixes up the formula until it isn't
a formula at all – until it isn't a gangster film anymore. Every
explosion of energy, like the thrilling pool-hall brawl in which
the handheld camera reels around the tables while the jukebox
pumps out 'Please Mr Postman' by The Marvelettes, is undercut by a corresponding passage of contemplation. You don't get
your kicks straight in this film, but then you don't get them
with a simple redemptive chaser either. Charlie is no cut-and-
dried good-guy in gangster's clothing, but something of a subtle
schemer who manipulates his friends and modulates his own
ambitions for temporary advantage, then tries to pay for his
misdeeds by holding his hand over a naked flame.

Scorsese had written the part for Harvey Keitel, essentially
as a continuation of Keitel's role in *Who's That Knocking at
My Door?* For Johnny Boy he chose this wiry kid De Niro on
the strength of recommendations from De Palma. You can read
the relationship between Keitel and De Niro before they exchange a word. Keitel looks so overburdened; he was born with
something on his mind. He's like a philanderer trying to appear
debonair to his latest catch, all the while transparently unable
to forget about what's waiting for him at home – a wife, a
child, a puppy dog, a hot meal growing cold on the table.
Everything he does is filtered through that inner conflict. He
was eventually cast in roughly that role in Scorsese's next film,

Alice Doesn't Live Here Anymore, and long before you discover that Sam the cool-cat cowboy has trouble back at the ranch, you know there is something off-key about his forced breeziness. Even in *Taxi Driver*, where he plays the languid pimp Sport to De Niro's coiled Travis Bickle, you are always aware of the aggression behind the apparent apathy; the limbs might be loose, the mane falling about his shoulders, but his true nature can be betrayed by a single giveaway detail – that long, sharpened fingernail, or the false funkiness ('Be cool, bitch') affected to calm the young prostitute Iris, played by Jodie Foster.

In *Mean Streets*, he plays a man who would dearly love to run with the pack, if only he hadn't expended all his energies assessing the implications of running with the pack. Charlie's contemplative nature removes him from the criminal life, but not far enough to escape its ramifications. He has sufficient wherewithal to know that his lifestyle is morally dubious, but not to denounce it. Charlie is constantly postponing his commitments – to the future, to his happiness, to his friends, to the woman he loves (Johnny Boy's cousin Teresa) but whom he must conceal in order to maintain his respectability in front of his uncle, who disapproves of Johnny Boy. Charlie can't display allegiance to any corner of his life; there's no nobility to him. When Teresa has an epileptic fit, he runs out on her because his priority at that moment is placating Johnny Boy. Charlie doesn't know which way is up.

In his later roles, such as the tender cop in *Thelma and Louise* or the foolishly trusting Mr White in *Reservoir Dogs*, Keitel has tended toward the avuncular, while his celebrated performance in Abel Ferrara's *Bad Lieutenant* was an exorcism of the same guilt and self-disgust that had seemed so much more monstrous in *Mean Streets* for having been kept under wraps, concealed by an unconvincing bonhomie or buried beneath his concern for Johnny Boy. The threat of rage in an actor is most intimidating as just that – a threat, an insinuation, something half-registered. Jack Nicholson choking back his anger in *Five Easy Pieces* promises untold horrors, but the same performer spitting bile in *Carnal Knowledge* offers the audience an emotional release – the storm after the calm. Similarly, the Keitel we see in *Mean Streets* is a mine of unresolved agitation: Charlie doesn't even seem to realize how distressed he is, galumphing through much of the movie as though in mourning. Who knows now what a Willard this actor would have made had Martin Sheen not replaced him on *Apocalypse Now*? It is possible that Keitel, in that role, and Brando, as Kurtz, would have caused thunderstorms if they'd appeared in the same shot. Certainly the audience could not have swallowed Kurtz's assessment of Willard as 'an errand boy sent by grocery clerks' if it had been directed at Keitel, a man who, in contrast to Sheen, could never be mistaken for anyone's dogsbody.

Those collaborations in the 1970s between Keitel and Scorsese have an impressive continuity: Charlie, Sam and Sport collectively represent an insightful study in the way a certain type of man handles those shortcomings that are most mercilessly illuminated in the presence of women. It's no accident that the character of Teresa is epileptic: it makes her unpredictable, unmanageable, even volatile – a physical manifestation of the hazard that she poses to Charlie's reputation. There is real shame there. When Johnny Boy taunts Charlie with sexual insults relating to Teresa's epilepsy ('What's she like when she comes?'), Charlie's violent response suggests that his own sense of disgrace has been revealed. He wants to keep Teresa quiet, to make it easy for him to see her secretly or else to dump her. But she won't be dumped, and when Charlie tries to offload her, Teresa's instinctive reaction is pre-verbal – an unformed, helpless whimper that for a moment makes us share Charlie's embarrassment, his need to stifle her. He panics in the glare of her vitality, just as Sam in *Alice Doesn't Live Here Anymore* throws off his charming disguise when it becomes necessary to humiliate a woman who has contravened his orders; just as

Sport in *Taxi Driver* can only be truly relaxed when he is slow-dancing with his ward, Iris, in an embrace that is also a stranglehold. (The fact that this monster is also capable of tenderness only makes him more monstrous.) It's ironic that *Mean Streets* and *Taxi Driver* have become objects of male worship and obsession in early twenty-first-century culture: these films to a large extent analyse the poverty of the worlds that men construct in order that they might live independently of the love and judgement of women.

Scorsese would pursue that theme with De Niro in *New York, New York*, and later in *Raging Bull*. But there is something less obviously cinematic, less aggressive, in Keitel's acting style, which makes his work more challenging. He doesn't rise to greet the audience forcefully like De Niro: he'll hang back if it helps the film. Take *Mean Streets*: Charlie is no one to aspire to, he has all the straight lines; Johnny Boy is the one cracking them up. But it's Charlie's frustration at Johnny Boy that makes the movie crackle. It's never broached in the script, but when Charlie goes to sleep at night, he must dream of being as footloose as his snarling young buddy. And in Keitel's performance, you can feel that disparity, that regret, and its cost to restful slumber.

While Keitel is almost doubled-up with the weight of his own thoughts, De Niro is playing a character who can only get through life by not thinking. When he waves crisp new bills under the nose of an impatient creditor, and then wonders aloud why this rankles, you can believe that there is genuine ignorance mixed in with the arrogance. Johnny Boy holds everything in equal disregard, from his ratty hairdo, which surely sits on his head just as it does on the pillow each morning, to the women that he picks up in Greenwich Village, to the lies he tells Charlie about the debts that he will never settle. And yet because he is the opposite of his worryguts chum, and to some extent the film's only release from Charlie's woes, we respond viscerally to him. He is as much a conduit for our antisocial fantasies as a Jerry Lewis or a John Belushi. Even in death, Johnny Boy refuses to go down quietly or nobly; his exit is marked by lycanthropic howls and an unfeasible amount of bloodletting.

It was the last time De Niro would play someone so full of uncomplicated abandon. In *New York, New York* his lunges at lightness are as intentionally savage and mortifying as his imitation of etiquette in *The King of Comedy*; popular successes like *Midnight Run* or *Meet the Parents* both find comic mileage in exploiting our fear of De Niro's scorn without ever actually dispelling it.

While *Mean Streets* highlights facets of Keitel and De Niro that have receded or been eclipsed by subsequent roles, it provides something of a foundation for what Scorsese did next. He shifted to a completely different environment for *Alice Doesn't Live Here Anymore*, a road movie-cum-melodrama about an ex-singer, Alice (Ellen Burstyn), who ups stumps with her wise-owl son Tommy (Alfred Lutter) after the death of her husband. But it would not take a rigorous investigation to unearth similarities between the two films. Scorsese is interested in the dynamics of relationships, the excuses that people make to themselves and one another when things don't go according to plan. The project had been kicking around at Warner Bros for a time, initially with Diana Ross attached to star (which explains the moment when Alice knocks at the door and Tommy asks who's there, to which she sarcastically replies: 'It's Diana Ross'). Scorsese landed the job after endorsements from famous friends. Cassavetes, who had admired *Who's That Knocking at My Door?* and *Mean Streets*, and had employed the young director as assistant sound editor on *Minnie and Moskowitz*, advised friends at Warner Bros to hire him. Meanwhile, Francis Ford Coppola, who had just cast De Niro in *The Godfather Part II* on the back of *Mean Streets*, recommended Scorsese to the new Alice, Ellen Burstyn.

He was an inspired choice, if not an obvious one, and it's

easy now to imagine the kind of film it might have become
without a director of Scorsese's assurance – if only because that
kind of film has been made and remade in various forms over
the years (you can glimpse the *Alice*-that-thankfully-never-was,
or parts of it, in movies like *Mermaids*, *Anywhere But Here*
and *Tumbleweeds*). From the opening frame of the lush title sequence, which with its ornate lettering descending the screen
against a silk backdrop evokes a 1940s melodrama, Scorsese
makes his presence felt.

He was part of the first generation to establish an ongoing
dialogue with movie history, and to have worn its eclectic influences proudly and publicly. Scorsese observed, 'We seemed to
be more cine-literate than our predecessors, who came from
many different backgrounds, like literature, the theatre or live
television.'[8] When Scorsese sprinkles throughout his own work
tributes to the films of Michael Powell and Emeric Pressburger,
he is in effect taking his place in line, defining himself by his
loyalties. This can take the form of the prominent use of the
colour red as a character in its own right in *Mean Streets*, a
spiritual cousin of *The Red Shoes*, and in *New York, New
York*, where Liza Minnelli's lips might not have been quite so
rich and red without the overheated influence of *Black Narcis-
sus*. Then there are the throwaway details: Robert De Niro in
New York, New York signing himself 'M Powell', or Scorsese
naming a pair of characters after Powell and Pressburger in
Boxcar Bertha. Each of these choices helps define Scorsese, just
as De Palma's devotion to Hitchcock becomes an autonomous
quality that transcends homage. This generation was working
with tools not previously available, drawing on memory banks
crammed with fresh reserves of cinematic pleasures.

Scorsese's closest compatriot in the early 1970s appeared to
be the critic-turned-director Peter Bogdanovich, who for a time
promised to be Scorsese's equal in his ability to channel an
obsession with dynamic old movies into the art of making
dynamic new ones. They had sprung from the same soil: Bog-

danovich had toiled for Roger Corman on *The Wild Angels*, scouting locations, rewriting dialogue and directing second unit; Corman then helped finance Bogdanovich's debut film, *Targets*, on the condition that the first-time director incorporated footage from Corman's 1962 film *The Terror*. But while both attracted acclaim for auspicious early works – Bogdanovich for his poignant and visually arresting second feature *The Last Picture Show*, Scorsese for *Mean Streets* – the nature of their gradual divergence clarifies Scorsese's vitality, as well as Bogdanovich's limitations.

Bogdanovich was drawn to the cul-de-sac of uncomplicated homage – he rejoiced in screwball comedy in *What's Up, Doc?*, and celebrated the musical in *At Long Last Love*, without augmenting the scope or appreciation of either genre. *What's Up, Doc?* is a glittering, lovingly crafted work, fit to share the bottom half of a double-bill with the finest examples of the genre to which it pays tribute – *The Palm Beach Story* or *His Girl Friday* or its main influence, *Bringing Up Baby*. As an entertainment it is beyond reproach. But Bogdanovich's skill at reviving rhythms and patterns that had long been foolishly disregarded by modern cinema hinted at where he would come unstuck: he was an accomplished handyman, adept at getting fresh water flowing through rusty pipes, but reluctant to try out any innovative new system of his own. Soon after *The Last Picture Show* it became apparent that he simply wasn't that way inclined. Like Herbert Ross, whose propensity for the immaculate homage might yield occasional bursts of brilliance – a *Funny Lady* here or a *Pennies from Heaven* there – but who was otherwise stultified by an inability to animate his nostalgia, Bogdanovich's talent for recreating the past looked set to embalm him.

In Scorsese's hands the homage becomes an act of simultaneous affection and inquiry, paying tribute to genre conventions whilst pulling away from them, or questioning their validity. His stylized prologue for *Alice Doesn't Live Here Anymore*, shot in saturated colours on an artificial *Wizard of Oz-*

style farmyard set, honours Alice's dreams for her own life
while preparing us for the chasm between those dreams and
how that life eventually transpired. The clash between cinema
and life returns in *New York, New York* and is what ultimately
makes that movie so fraught: the spectacle of the traditional
Hollywood musical is painstakingly recreated one moment,
only to be cruelly dismantled, lightbulb by lightbulb, the next.
Literally so in one scene, where a shimmering tunnel studded
from floor to ceiling with glowing lights – the kind of corridor
that might usher patrons into the Korova Milk Bar in *A Clockwork Orange* – provides the setting for a scuffle in which
bouncers eject an unruly customer who kicks at the walls,
smashing bulbs with each stamp of his heels. Scorsese is so
mindful of the suffering behind every love story that it becomes
impossible for him to serve up the generic pleasures of the musical without undermining them with pain. In *Taxi Driver* too
the distance between Travis Bickle's heroic vision of himself as
an avenging angel and the squalid reality is beyond negotiation,
though the film is exhilarating enough to provide vicarious
thrills for anyone who wants them.

Alice Doesn't Live Here Anymore is a less distressed movie,
adhering to the carefree rhythms of its heroine. Scorsese's confidence with his actors here is as purely enjoyable as anything in
his films. His grasp of the emotional telepathy between Alice
and Tommy is splendidly intuitive, particularly in the scene
where the boy nudges his mother to the tearful brink of insanity simply by repeatedly explaining the meaning of a joke. But
for all the buoyant realism of the performances, the film's
world of Arizona motel rooms and diners is in its own way as
exaggerated as the balmy New York of *Taxi Driver*. The cinematography (by Kent Wakeford, who shot *Mean Streets*) manipulates the limited space in Alice's new lifestyle to reflect her
shifts in mood, her varying chances for happiness, just as New
York seems to grow more repellent with Travis's increasing im-
mersion in his own diseased mind.

When Alice first hits the road after being widowed – the

(off-screen) death of her husband being as sudden, and as briskly recovered from, as the demise of Bertha's father in *Boxcar Bertha* – the wide-angle lens makes everything look grand and daunting, and not only on the highway that rolls off toward the horizon like the Yellow Brick Road. The interiors of the crummy motels are like treasure troves; you know they must be cramped, yet the camera bestows upon them impossibly generous dimensions – those rooms promise the world. Toby Rafelson has a short list of credits, mostly on the films of her husband Bob Rafelson – including *Five Easy Pieces* and *The King of Marvin Gardens* (she also has an acting cameo as Pinter, the warden's adoring assistant in Jonathan Demme's *Caged Heat*). But her production design work here and on Demme's *Melvin and Howard* is truly joyous, maintaining a lively rapport between the characters and their surroundings. The happy clutter of cheap bric-à-brac, the bright orange walls, the majestic skyline of table lamps and ornaments reflected in dressing-table mirrors, all seem to point toward what Alice can have if she climbs into her natty green dress and spills out on to the street. In the seamy bars and clubs and hotels that she visits in her search for a singing job, that dress is as pivotal to who she is as the ruby slippers are to Dorothy: when Alice puts it on, she's a verdant, vibrant tonic, something zesty and nutritious in a sea of soda pops and oozing hamburgers.

When her prospects narrow, the world narrows with her. At her lowest ebb, she's working as a waitress, crying on the shoulder of a colleague in an arctic blue cubicle. A new motel in Tucson has the comfort of a broom cupboard until Alice settles into her job, then suddenly there seems to be space for her and Tommy to chase one another along its passageways, and in and out of rooms that we didn't know existed. Scorsese's manipulation of space is masterful. He puts a dramatic spin on perspective in *Raging Bull*, where a boxing ring can seem as vast as a football field in one match, and as tiny as the head of a pin in the next, but his work in *Alice Doesn't Live Here Any-*

more is just as attentive to the relationship between a character's inner and outer worlds. By the end of the film Scorsese has silently tutored us to read the *mise-en-scène* and the position of the camera as keenly as we read the expression on an actor's face or an ambiguous line of dialogue. Space has become such a primary means of communication that, when we notice the streamers dangling from the ceiling in the house of Alice's new lover David (Kris Kristofferson), we may brace ourselves for an abrupt end to the couple's hitherto tranquil romance. In the film's vocabulary, happiness usually descends when the characters have room to roam, even if that only means forging personal freedom in unpromising spaces – playing tag in a tiny motel room, or sprawling on the floor between two booming hi-fi speakers, as Tommy is doing when the camera first happens upon him.

Those streamers are like a net in which anyone might become suddenly entangled, and sure enough the image precedes a domestic spat rooted in a misreading of signals. David takes Tommy's single-mindedness, the quality that most connects the boy to his mother, as simple impudence and punishes him accordingly. But that is the old way, the patriarchal way which Alice rejects, and which she might have hoped had died along with her husband. The film is about learning new patterns of behaviour, which makes it sound terribly therapeutic, when in fact it readily concedes that this re-education is rife with turmoil. In fleeing the confines of domesticity, Alice has not simply traded her oven gloves for a one-way ticket to freedom: when the ingrained misogyny of Sam is revealed to her, it becomes apparent that on her journey to emancipation she will have to deal with fellow travellers whose reasons for eschewing a domestic structure may run counter to her own.

Although Scorsese sought to discourage exclusively feminist interpretations of *Alice Doesn't Live Here Anymore*, the film captures a feeling of shifting dynamics and gender roles in flux, even in its throwaway details, like the scenes of Tommy being quietly and playfully intimidated by a tomboyish schoolfriend (Jodie Foster) and enjoying it into the bargain. The movie does spring upon us a rather contrived reconciliation scene between David and Alice, played out in the restaurant where Alice works, and which has become an unofficial meeting place for the characters, like the bar in *Mean Streets* and the all-night diner in *Taxi Driver*. But despite this surrender to resolution, the actual parting shot restores those notes of uncertainty and opportunity that have been sounding throughout the picture – the image of Alice and Tommy walking away from the camera toward a messy collage of street signs, lamp-posts and billboards suggests that their future has not been dictated by Alice's reunion with David, but is instead as alive as ever with a jumble of possibilities.

Of course, it also inadvertently foreshadows what would become the signature shot of Scorsese's next feature, *Taxi Driver*. When Travis Bickle ambles along the sidewalk, away from those same possibilities, his journey is toward the camera's eye, fittingly enough for an individual whose conception of himself is so rooted in notions of singularity and narcissism – man as a heroic self-sufficient loner, defined by his physical and emotional austerity and devoted to a sole cause, no matter how misguided.

Until the release of *GoodFellas*, *Taxi Driver* was arguably the work by which Scorsese was most readily defined, and it is a film which, like its director, has been dwarfed by its own effectiveness, its own influential power. The movie is superficially about the efforts of a lonely cabbie, Travis Bickle, to rescue a teenage prostitute from her pimp. Beyond that, it is a painstaking analysis of that cabbie's mental disintegration. The film is firmly rooted in Travis's perspective; it functions as an act of extended defiance to the viewer, daring us to pull away, daring us not to empathize. The camera is such a persuasive tool and the absurd idea in fiction of a 'central character' so flattering to our sense of individuality that we respond intuitively to anyone who is deemed worthy of close-ups, or who is honoured with the responsibility of providing a voice-over. To reject that character's perspective, or their morality, therefore becomes an assertive act contrary to the passive nature of watching a film.

When those gifts are corrupted – when the narrator turns out to be dead, as in *Sunset Boulevard*, or unreliable, as in the various accounts that comprise *Citizen Kane*, or unversed in narrative conventions, as in *Badlands* and *Days of Heaven* – we are likely to feel vulnerable or undermined. *Taxi Driver* is a more extreme version of this disorientation technique because it only gradually reveals Travis's perspective to be damaged and does not do so until we have been seduced by his awkwardness and lulled by his importance as the subject of the movie. To the first-time viewer, this claustrophobic picture offers little breathing space between Travis's perspective and any objective reality: you have to take what you see on trust, until you can't take it any more.

For example, the camera only notices the high proportion of sinister or threatening African-American men on the New York streets because that is the way that Travis sees the world, just as the division of women into virgins and whores conforms to Travis's limited moral scale. The brusque cashier (Diahnne Abbott, a Scorsese regular for a while) who sneers at Travis's pick-up line seems unduly harsh, both to Travis's eyes and our own, so closely are we forced to empathize with him. We have to remind ourselves that Travis cannot interact with other people. The sweet-talk chosen to charm Abbott away from her daydreams is that old favourite 'What's your name?' – he's like the Terminator drawing on an inadequate supply of ice-breakers. And we must remember too, if Travis feels unjustly spurned, that he is hitting on a porno-theatre cashier, of all people.

Even if you can resist Travis's rancid worldview, it is not always possible to ascertain whether something is really happening, or just feeding through the whirring projector in his mind. He surely conjures for himself the simpering return of his despised dream-girl Betsy (Cybill Shepherd) – only Travis could conceive that the murders he committed would make a sophisticated woman succumb to him. And if he can summon the mirage of Betsy, who is to say that Travis hasn't also created the toxic goblin who rides in the back of the cab? Scorsese himself plays him, with the jabbering jaw of a ventriloquist's dummy partially concealed by a neat beard that suggests this fellow spends hours before the mirror in preparation for an evening of malevolence – not unlike Travis, in fact.

Scorsese apparently took the part because the original actor dropped out. But the appointment of the director to portray a character who is most likely a figment of Travis's imagination seems somehow symbolic, as though such a vivid projection of subconscious fears and desires could not be rendered by a mere actor. That passenger's invective against the sexual potency that he sees in women and in black men is a distillation of all the hostility and horror that runs through the picture. And like Bernard Herrmann's score, this septic monologue can be difficult to withstand. It serves up in undiluted form the venom that the rest of the film administers cumulatively, drop-by-drop.

But that scene also draws us closer to Travis at the very point that we are likely to be recoiling from him. Just as Hitchcock deprives us of our point of identification by killing off Marion Crane in *Psycho*, leaving us no one to cling to but Norman Bates, so Scorsese and Schrader introduce this hateful demon, and later the creepy gun salesman played by Steven Prince (the subject of Scorsese's documentary *American Boy*), to kid us into thinking that maybe Travis isn't so bad after all, that there are worse monsters in the shadows. The film persists in playing these complicated games with our sympathies. How we want things to work out between Travis and Betsy, even after he has convinced her to join him at a porno movie; how we hope that she will somehow not reject him! If she rejects him, she rejects something in us, the viewers who have been tricked into empathizing with him.

When that inevitable rejection comes, it disrupts the film, which now has to start all over again, just as *Psycho* must after the disappearance of its own blonde-haired dream-girl. Marion is dead, and Travis has banished Betsy to hell. Now he must find another mission by which to define himself. And the film, which obediently runs to Travis's rhythms, incorporates this temporary respite just as it faithfully reproduces his hallucinations and neuroses. Travis is the author of the movie; our only way into the film's world is through those sleepless eyes that flood the screen in extreme close-up. He invites us into his diary and into his head. He lets us see him rehearsing his fragile macho fantasies before the mirror, a performance more intimate than sex since it was never meant to involve more than one person – albeit one person cleaved in two (his 'You talkin' to me . . .?' soliloquy being a succinct expression of both his confused identity and our own feelings of isolation sitting in the dark).

When he chances upon Iris, he is like a blocked writer whose muse has finally materialized. He sees his quest to save her as something moral, but it is more the case that he needs a hobby, and to be cleansed, and so the act of rescuing Iris takes care of both requirements. The smartest idea in the movie was to play the whole thing straight, as though Travis really is who he thinks he is, as though his vigilante mission has the poker-faced integrity of Charles Bronson in *The Stone Killer* and *Death Wish*.

It's a dangerous game. To many viewers the film will indeed play like a continuation of *Death Wish*. Its sleazy climax, in which Travis shoots at a succession of pimps and johns who, maddeningly, refuse to lie down and die, will be transformed in those viewers' eyes into a triumph of good over evil, rather than a further confusion of such arbitrary definitions. Any picture that adheres to the perspective of its protagonist, without somehow introducing the counterpoint of external commentary, runs the risk of being interpreted as an endorsement of that character. Mike Leigh's *Naked* was reviled in some quarters because its representation of women confirmed the misogynistic viewpoint of its hero, Johnny (David Thewlis). If anything, that film's fatal flaw is that it isn't ruthless enough: the departures from Johnny's perspective weaken the case to be made for the movie as an extension of his identity. *Taxi Driver* seems to fall foul of this only once, when Travis miraculously acquires the wherewithal to be perfectly charming to a secret service agent with whom he falls into conversation. We have never seen that side of Travis, and there is no proof that he has the reserves of confidence required to summon it up. That lapse aside, the film's single-mindedness can be horrifying, and horrifyingly seductive.

Few film-makers would so recklessly immerse a movie, and an audience, in the perspective of a single character, let alone a psychotic one, and none of those pictures directly inspired by *Taxi Driver* have dared to attempt the feat. *Falling Down* converts Travis Bickle's explosions of violence into crowd-pleasing set-pieces but ultimately locates its antisocial hero on the side of righteousness; *I Love a Man in Uniform* makes its own protagonist even more unstable than Travis, while introducing irony to preclude the audience's identification with him, in effect preventing us from getting too close. *Seul contre tous* is the picture that has been most fearless in the face of Scorsese's imposing influence and it cleverly teases those audience members who had been swept along by the awful polemic of its main character. That is a different species of film, ready at a moment's notice to concede its own status as a fiction. For Scorsese's movie, there is no such loophole. Look how the camera probes intimate spaces – the cinema projection booth, the Alka Seltzer noisily dissolving in a glass of water. The excerpts from pornographic movies feel strangely like a relief from the picture's violations; those writhing bodies are just flesh, just sex, whereas Scorsese's camera leads us into the dank catacombs of Travis's mind. How can pornography shock us once we've seen that?

The question 'how did that ever get financed?' is often voiced whenever a major studio pumps money into a project that deviates from a proven formula, but the enquiry is less pertinent to the early part of the 1970s, when studios had cottoned on to the idea of using young talent to make lower-budget movies that would have a greater chance of showing a profit. *Taxi Driver* might have seemed less risky than some. In De Niro, the film had an actor who, if not quite a star, had just won an Academy Award (for *The Godfather Part II*), as well as a director who had presided over a popular success (in the same year, Ellen Burstyn had won the Best Actress Oscar for *Alice Doesn't Live Here Anymore*). Paul Schrader was a sparky young screenwriter, having sold his script for *The Yakuza*, eventually filmed by Sydney Pollack, for a record-breaking sum. And the producers Julia and Michael Phillips had a keen commercial sense: they had backed *The Sting*, a slab of Oscarwinning baloney, and were busy producing Spielberg's *Close Encounters of the Third Kind* – for which Schrader had written a first-draft screenplay – when *Taxi Driver* won the Palme d'Or at the 1976 Cannes Film Festival.

Despite the concurrent glories of these collaborators, it is still something of a marvel, and a testament to how different the Hollywood climate was in the 1970s, that *Taxi Driver* could get made and released. In 1976, it caught a mood, and helped define one. Studio executives were approving projects that would have been box-office poison a decade earlier: disillusionment was now something to be marketed, like a goodlooking pin-up. If that sounds cynical, it is intended only to suggest how fully the unforgiving stance of these young filmmakers was embraced and nurtured and how happily it coincided with the public mood. It made possible the narcissistic hero of Elaine May's *The Heartbreak Kid*, a real precursor to Travis in more than just his infatuation with Cybill Shepherd. This romantic comedy, which employs extreme social embarrassment to torture its audience, brutally undermines the conventional happy ending: the hero ends up with what he wants, only to realize, long after we have, that he doesn't want it any more. Self-doubt wracks Jack Nicholson's character in *Five Easy Pieces*, a former pianist who has rejected his bourgeois upbringing, and the athletes in Nicholson's *Drive, He Said*, who harbour similarly conflicted ideas about identity. Conspiracy theory thrillers like *Klute* and *The Parallax View* flout the stipulation that the hero must walk off with the girl into the sunset, or even walk off at all.

Disenchantment in American cinema was not patented in the 1970s. Sidney Lumet had already devoted a large portion of his career to exposing the fallen or ambiguous hero in character studies like *Twelve Angry Men* and *The Pawnbroker*, before swooping in on the flaws of law enforcement in *The Offence* and *Serpico*, the former a still-stinging rebuke to the reactionary excesses of Don Siegel's *Dirty Harry*. But there was a synchronicity between the rebellious instincts of the young American directors and the current flavour for subversion, which made their movies uniquely pertinent. Part of what differentiated this new generation was their active response to the movies that had preceded them. These are not iconoclastic directors. Scorsese and De Palma and Spielberg, like Quentin Tarantino, Tim Burton or Wes Anderson in recent times, refer constantly to the films of the past. Their cinema is not about rejecting film history but keeping it alive, drawing on it for sustenance and inspiration, and advancing it frame by frame.

This process of communication visibly energizes Scorsese. Nothing in his work is more prevalent than the conflict between a desire to recreate the past, and the bitter realization that such a craving will inevitably be thwarted. *New York, New York* might have been created solely to illustrate this paradox. It begins with a stock shot of the city skyline, before withdrawing into a series of pointedly artificial and often claustrophobic studio sets – a contrast so symbolic of the film's identity and so beloved by Scorsese that a full three years before the picture was released he had already described that opening in detail to any interviewer who would listen.

New York, New York is about conflicts and contrasts, two species of New York, two species of reality. This motif manifests itself in everything from the repetition of the title to the subtle clash in acting styles between Liza Minnelli and Robert De Niro. Minnelli's casting in *New York, New York* was in some ways symbolic. As the daughter of Vincente Minnelli and Judy Garland, and a woman who had observed first-hand the precise manner in which reality can be ravaged by celebrity (perhaps even without being certain of what she had witnessed – her huge, hopeful eyes seem incapable of registering anything bleaker than bunny rabbits and rainbows), Liza Minnelli personified both old-school showbiz in all its sequinned, fur-trimmed corniness, and the kind of wilted existence that this blistering entity leaves in its wake. She doesn't have the physical frailty that characterized her mother, but you sense the danger that Minnelli might easily be scandalized or violated by an unkind word or an uncouth gesture. A glass inadvertently upset might put her in a blue funk.

In this light, the pairing of Minnelli and De Niro looks like a scientific experiment destined to end in the destruction of the laboratory. Minnelli's acting technique, like her mother's before her, embodies the Hollywood tradition, where emotions are worn and paraded like diamonds and minks. Acting becomes external, in contrast to the Method technique which had been seeping into cinema since Brando and Dean made their movie debuts in the 1950s. An actor like De Niro visibly feels everything; the camera just happens to capture it. But Minnelli plays toward the camera – it defines her behaviour. Which is not to say that she is any less sincere than De Niro. Some detractors have even argued that the Method makes the acting process too transparent: 'When you see De Niro or Daniel Day-Lewis acting, there might as well be a "Men at Work" sign on the screen,' complained Paul Morrissey, the director whose own films with Andy Warhol (including *Heat* and *Trash*) counter the sobriety of the Method.[9]

Both performers in their own way exude discomfort in the

film. De Niro is antagonized by his glitzy surroundings; there's
something in the decadence that he seems to despise. And Minnelli looks so vulnerable in his presence, when she should feel
right at home. Audiences were already in little doubt that a
sideways glance from De Niro could inflict greater injury than
an upper-cut from any of the decade's bantamweight tough
guys like Clint Eastwood or even Steve McQueen, whose surli-
ness had turned to paralysis. Those performers released their
aggression in bar-room brawls or storefront shoot-outs. Even at
this stage in his career, De Niro had already started exploiting
the possibilities for intimidation in scenarios that might not
naturally lend themselves to violence, such as the standard boy-
meets-girl set-up. By the time he had bitten a hole in a woman's cheek in Scorsese's 1991 remake of *Cape Fear*, it was a
case of boy-eats-girl. But the most disturbing scene in that
movie, where he prowled around a giggly, finger-sucking Juli-
ette Lewis, caressing her curiosity with his insinuations, represented a ghastly advancement on his courtship with Cybill
Shepherd in *Taxi Driver* and with Liza Minnelli in *New York,
New York*. Now the man who had crushed women through
sheer ineptitude had learned to perform the same trick with patience and skill.

Any actor who builds a substantial body of work naturally
has increased resonance to play with, but De Niro more than
any other performer remains in constant communication with
his past. Sometimes the effect is dazzling: only De Niro, with
his baggage, could have pulled off the unheralded murder in
Jackie Brown with such conviction. Sometimes not: the world
could well have lived without his reprise of the 'You talkin' to
me?' speech in *The Adventures of Rocky and Bullwinkle*. But
even by 1977 De Niro could draw on the itchy unpredictability
of Johnny Boy and the concentrated menace of Travis Bickle to
bring to Jimmy Doyle, his character in *New York, New York*,
an undertow of horror. Throughout the first third of the movie
you feel a sense of cautious amazement – perhaps it's Scorsese's
own at having captured in the same frame these torchbearers

for different provinces of showbusiness – which in the later scenes has endured such a beating that the remainder of the picture is watched in appalled sorrow.

More integral to the film even than that collision between Minnelli and De Niro is the thematic struggle between a yearning to uphold the glory of classic Hollywood musicals and an acknowledgement of the pain that rushes through the genre's arteries like a fatal blood clot. The movie is torn between splendour and seediness, just as its doomed lovers zig-zag between romantic idealism and curdled self-hatred. While preparing the film, Scorsese remarked, 'I was curious about the murky quality of those old Warners musicals,' before promising, 'but my film will be lighter, more fun.'[10]

No film-maker's assessment of his own work can ever have been so wide of the mark. *New York, New York* doesn't fit the loosest definition of light and it's not like any kind of fun that you would ever want to have.

Jimmy (De Niro) is a saxophonist hunting for a woman on V-J Day, 1945, in New York City. I mean, literally hunting. His technique is coarse: he jabs at women with words and when he meets resistance he jabs harder. One of his attempted conquests, the singer Francine Evans (Minnelli), rebuffs him from the word 'go'. Or rather, the word 'no'. She uses that word like a baseball bat, to casually deter each hopeful missile that he pitches her way. No, no, no, *no* – every time she utters the word it has a fresh nuance, a subtly altered inflection, to suggest gradations of disdain, boredom or exasperation. And when those rebuttals fail and she realizes that Jimmy is pestering her for sport, she contemptuously bats her eyelashes at him, as though he were an insect that could be shooed away or swatted. 'I wanna stay here and annoy you,' he tells her. Once it seems she has slipped through his grabbing fingers, he makes a promise to himself. 'I'll get her,' he hisses. No stalker, no serial killer ever dreamed up by the movies, has been more single-minded on his mission of extermination.

In many ways, Jimmy is a more hazardous, insidious incar-

nation of Travis Bickle – a Travis who has not isolated himself
from the rest of society by wearing a Mohawk cut, or driving a
cab, or hanging out in porno-houses, but who has learned to
temper his antisocial tendencies just enough to blend into normal life. There he is in the film's opening tour of the V-J Day
celebrations, integrating himself so successfully into the throng
that the camera loses sight of him, until Scorsese signs off from
this wide shot with a stunning *coup de théâtre* – a neon arrow
attached to the storefront architecture has jutted into view
without us even noticing, and it is pointing directly at Jimmy,
picking him out of the hubbub, like the You Are Here caption
on a street map. More likely, the effect will remind modern audiences of those CCTV pictures in which an optical emphasis
selects from the anonymous crowd one man who is about to
commit a terrible crime. That just about sums up Jimmy. If
Travis is a controlled explosion in a bad part of town, Jimmy is
something altogether more destructive. He's wired to go off in a
public place.

It's a long picture – 136 minutes in its original theatrical version, pushed up to 163 in the commonly available restored cut
that includes the muted spectacle of the eleven-minute 'Happy
Endings' sequence in which we are taken inside one of
Francine's own movies. But it is possible to watch the entire
thing through splayed fingers, grinding your teeth, clenching
your toes. This is one of the most uncomfortable experiences in
cinema – *Who's Afraid of Virginia Woolf?* with songs – and yet
the manner of its cruelty is part of the point. The film depicts in
excruciating close-up the pressures exerted on us by the romantic aspirations expressed in movies and music; squirming is expected and required.

After Francine performs with Jimmy to help him through an
audition, he is hired on the condition that she joins him on
tour, which intensifies the unspoken competitiveness between
them. It's true that when they perform together for the first
time, our urgent enquiries about their mutual attraction – Why

would so classy a woman waste her time with such a vulgar thug? Why would a make-out artist pursue someone who clearly demands so much more than he wants to give? – are postponed. Clarity descends within a few bars of music. Then we understand why she flashed him an admiring smile when he was making such a shrill song and dance about wriggling out of his hotel bill. And why she didn't sock him in the jaw when he pressed his half-chewed gum into her dainty white-gloved hand. When she responds intuitively to his playing and he begins to tailor and modify its primitive vigour to suit her style, then we see why they are together. But that's also when we understand why they will never be happy.

Both of them are enslaved to the pre-packaged romantic ideals represented by their respective musical styles. Francine is sweet for the sanitized version of love symbolized by her penchant for ballads and show-tunes, while Jimmy is hooked on the heady rush of black Harlem jazz, and to this end becomes hooked on heroin too, as though traces of blackness might find their way into his bloodstream on a shared needle – as though a willingness to suffer might make him Charlie Parker.

In choosing one another, they have guaranteed their own unhappiness. Francine wants romance. But everything Jimmy touches, no matter how pure, becomes contaminated by his self-loathing, just as Travis feels compelled to punish Betsy for the crime of enjoying his company. In Jimmy's hands, the act of ordering a drink or parking a car is an opportunity to intimidate someone. His clinches with Francine border on assault; a kiss has the force of a punch. The film plugs on bravely under the weight of his psychosis, rejuvenating the old Hollywood conventions, like the spinning newspaper headlines, or the multi-layered montages of neon signs that act as shorthand for a night on the town.

But there's disquiet mere inches below the surface, waiting to erupt. A simple proposal of marriage becomes an act of unfettered hostility in which a window is broken, voices are raised

and the subject of suicide is entertained, but not before Jimmy
has dragged Francine out in the middle of the night without
telling her where she's going, like a kidnapper trying to disori-
entate his hostage. When their destination transpires to be the
home of the local Justice of the Peace, that punchline feels almost too pitiless. Yes, Francine can get what she wants – that
marriage proposal – but only after a bewildering journey in
which it seems plausible that Jimmy is taking her into the
woods for an execution by moonlight. On this and every level,
the relationship between Francine and Jimmy mirrors our relationship with the movie. Yes, we too can get what we want; we
can have the nostalgic, glamorous, big-budget musical that
New York, New York proclaims itself to be from its opening
frame; but it will come at a price.

In a less conflicted picture, the 'Happy Endings' sequence
would be a blessed high, but here it is soothing, not surging.
Scorsese has already comprehensively dissected the misery leading up to this ironically-titled number, severely diminishing any
triumphant connotations it may otherwise have possessed. Immediately prior to it we have seen everything of worth between
Francine and Jimmy being burnt to cinders before our eyes. In
one of the most agonizing scenes, Jimmy is playing on stage at
the Harlem Club while the pregnant Francine watches from the
audience. After several aborted attempts to raise a glass to her
lips, she finally manages it, guzzling down red wine as though it
were a poison that she has at last summoned the courage to
imbibe. When she makes a move to join Jimmy mid-number, he
suddenly manipulates the music against her, violently switching
tempo to force her off the stage. She recoils timidly; his eyes are
flooded with contempt. Not a word of dialogue is spoken. Was
music ever used so organically? A few scenes later, they are in
hospital following the birth of their child. 'Did you see him?'
asks Francine quietly. 'Who?' 'The baby.' 'Oh, the baby.' Cigars
are not passed around, bouquets are conspicuous by their absence. It could be the least joyous dawn of any life.

And then comes 'Happy Endings' with its vivid sets: decadent red splashed everywhere, as though Francine, whose lipstick has remained fiercely glossed and unsmudged throughout the picture, has kissed every wall from skirting board to ceiling; an oversized pack of cards that doubles as a dance floor; a never-ending banquet table carpeted in green baize along which the camera retreats, flanked on either side by anonymous corporate figures whose synchronized hand gestures are as gratifying to the eye as any impeccably choreographed chorus line. In a less scalding, scathing picture, this might have become a euphoric climax. Here, it is something of a reprieve, made bitter by the revelation that Jimmy is also watching it from his cinema seat (he looks like Travis devouring pornography with those unblinking eyes).

How can we succumb to the visual grandeur of this miniature version of Francine's success when we know what it has taken to get to this point? That's the essence of the movie: those dreams that Hollywood sold us, they weren't lies exactly, but they weren't the whole story either. The actors pretend that they're strolling along real New York sidewalks, not on a set in Los Angeles. They don't acknowledge that the snow is synthetic, the moving scenery in the car's rear windscreen is just back projection, or that the train pulling away from the station is made of cardboard, with painted silhouettes frozen in each window. Scorsese exaggerates the artificiality of these movie conventions, the better to hint at a deeper fraudulence.

He isn't alone in identifying the suffering that lurks behind, and even underpins, the songs. One of the bitterest of all musicals, the 1954 version of *A Star Is Born* directed by George Cukor, also confronts the savagery in showbusiness, and was clearly a strong influence on Scorsese, in its portrait of a doomed relationship between a flourishing star and her kamikaze lover. But Scorsese was the first film-maker to successfully utilize our troubled relationship with movie musicals as a fitting subject for a movie musical. You need only compare

New York, New York with two other music-oriented pictures released in the same period – the 1977 remake of *A Star Is Born* with Barbra Streisand, and *The Rose* from 1979, starring Bette Midler in a role modelled on Janis Joplin – to appreciate how seriously the film was out of sync with popular conceptions of the modern musical. All three movies are rise-and-fall stories set in the music industry, but while Scorsese's is the only period piece, it is also the only one which addresses the functions and failings of the genre to which it belongs. It has a life and a resonance beyond its immediate subject that has prevented it from ageing, unlike *A Star Is Born* and *The Rose*, which now have little to recommend them, other than the insights they provide into late-1970s fashion disasters.

Despite its period setting, *New York, New York* is not an era-specific work. Its anxieties speak to anyone who has believed in the images on a cinema screen as a version of reality that might be attained through hard work or persistent daydreaming, not unlike the heroine of *Alice Doesn't Live Here Anymore*. One of the last shots in the film is of the 'Exit' sign that could transport Francine back on to the streets and into Jimmy's callous arms, if she chooses to take it (no escape route ever offered fewer prospects for freedom). In that shot, we may also feel the reluctance of the film buff to venture into the harsh world while it's so safe inside the darkened theatre. *New York, New York* is a love letter to the movies, but one whose author partly appreciates the futility and foolishness of the tribute that he has penned.

The picture was not a hit. Had George Lucas been right in his prediction after all? Could Scorsese have boosted the commercial potential of *New York, New York* simply by pasting on the kind of happy ending that had already been proved defunct by the rest of the film? Maybe. But I for one would have lobbed my popcorn at the screen.

'Success is mainly a matter of chance,' Scorsese had said. 'To play it safe, you can take less risks. If I played it safe it wouldn't be hard at all to stay on top. All I'd have to do would be to direct the best properties of the year – you know, film that book. But that's wrong.'[11] He held firm to these convictions by following New York, New York with two pictures that risk being viewed as doodles. One, the documentary American Boy, deserves that tag, since its schoolboy fascination with a fast-talking, self-mythologizing sensationalist (Steven Prince) foreshadows the hero-worship that prevents Raging Bull and GoodFellas from reaching full maturity. But that same idolatry is suffused with cheery reverence in The Last Waltz, Scorsese's film of The Band's farewell concert at the San Francisco Winterland.

A problem for modern audiences might be, how do you watch this movie in the shadow of the 1984 mockumentary This is Spinal Tap? Marti DiBergi, the bearded, ingratiating documentary maker played in that comedy by its director Rob Reiner, is clearly a devilish riff on Scorsese's on-screen persona in The Last Waltz, which combines chumminess, dogged sobriety and manufactured ease. At one point in The Last Waltz, the façade of an unassuming film-maker shooting the breeze with a bunch of chilled-out musos even appears to be deliberately discredited. A supposedly impromptu tour of The Band's headquarters by vocalist-guitarist Robbie Robertson is preceded by a shot of Scorsese and Robertson nervously frozen before the camera, waiting to launch into their spontaneity. Those few seconds could easily have been trimmed, but there is clearly something about the tensions between reality and film that appeals to Scorsese, even at this considerable distance from the terrain of New York, New York.

The recognition of the camera and its disfiguring properties registers subtly, echoing the deforming use of spotlights in New York, New York, where the illuminated subject appears to float in the darkness like an apparition, but also pre-empting the indictment of fame in The King of Comedy. As a documentary piece, The Last Waltz is a more freewheeling work than either

of those films, but here and there you can detect some intriguing editorial touches. The picture begins with the encore, perhaps out of tongue-in-cheek deference to Robertson's claim that
this end-of-career show represents 'the beginning of the beginning of the end of the beginning'. We have scarcely settled in
our cinema seats before the frontman Rick Danko announces,
'We're gonna do one more song and that's it.' Opening the film
at the close of the show is consistent with the ceremonial significance of the swansong, but once again it reminds us that we
are watching a movie, not an imitation of life. The camera reinforces this by observing Danko from behind the keyboards at
the back of the stage, creating a sense of intimacy while forcefully undermining the standard concert-film practice of positioning the viewer among the audience.

Scorsese further disrupts the concert's momentum by inter-
spersing the songs, many of them featuring guest performers
(Bob Dylan, Neil Young, Eric Clapton and, sweating passion,
Van Morrison), with clips of the band reminiscing, most no-
tably about the simplicity of their name as a reaction against
the florid, indulgent style of the day. 'Everyone else was called
things like Chocolate Subway and Marshmallow Overcoats.'
Scorsese's own meat-and-potatoes style suggests a rejection of
the same excesses, which is especially striking given that MTV
and the age of the pop promo are just around the corner. His
preference is for relaxed takes, which give The Band space to be
themselves, on stage or off. Which is not to suggest that there
isn't alertness at work. The most audacious moment in the
movie is a single, simple cut. When a group member responds
to a question about women on tour with the answer 'I love
them: I guess that's why we've been on the road so long,' Scorsese cuts without missing a beat to Joni Mitchell gliding on to
the stage, leaving the viewer to decide whether this is intended
as rejoinder or corroboration.

The influence of *The Last Waltz* on cinema can most obviously be felt in concert films like Demme's Talking Heads movie

Stop Making Sense, which rendered the live music experience in even more skeletal terms, and Jim Jarmusch's *Year of the Horse*, about Neil Young and Crazy Horse. But more important than this formal influence is that the film testifies to the flexibility of Scorsese's powers. Self-consciously 'major' works like *Raging Bull* and *GoodFellas* and *Casino* have made it difficult for him to be seen as anything more complex than a portrait artist for tarnished machismo, but it is his restless, roaming quality which is most threatened by this unaccommodating reputation.

Eclecticism has always been something of an embarrassment both to mainstream cinema, which generally embraces familiarity and consistency, and the auteurist bias of film theory, where every work must constitute a piece of the same puzzle, or risk going without favour. The climate might be changing: some of the most thrilling directors working in current cinema can be categorized precisely by their immunity to categorization. Steven Soderbergh, Ang Lee and Todd Haynes in America, François Ozon in France, Mike Figgis, Michael Winterbottom and Lynne Ramsay in Britain, Lars von Trier in Denmark, Julio Medem in Spain, Edward Yang in China, Takeshi Kitano and Miike Takashi in Japan: all have moved gracefully between disparate methods and genres without being forced to swear allegiance to any single style of film-making, while the enduring miracle of Robert Altman is that he remains a law unto himself. We may have become more liberal in accepting a director's diversity, but still there seems a reluctance to apply this retrospectively to Scorsese's body of work. Perhaps we feel we know him already, or know him enough – that we have got the measure of him. But it is at precisely that point that complacency creeps in and the dust starts collecting.

In a culture crowded with competing images, people feel compelled more than ever to search out individual mementoes – iconic freeze-frames, resonant lines of dialogue – which encapsulate the more time-consuming experience of watching a film.

So in place of a familiarity with Scorsese's work, we are drawn to telling moments, defining gestures, in the mistaken belief that cinema can be succinctly summed-up and sold, like fabric softener or bleach. How much easier to reel off Travis Bickle's 'You talkin' to me?' soliloquy from *Taxi Driver*, or parrot Big Bill's boastful claim for his gun – 'This here's my Bible' – in *Boxcar Bertha*, than to assess the whole canvas, the entire screen, and confront the possibility that the spirit of Scorsese cannot be distilled into a quotable line, a t-shirt or a bumper sticker. These movies are kept alive not only by their own vitality, but by our curiosity, and our refusal to accept the received wisdom about them as anything except idle gossip.

Conclusion

This morning I came across a damning judgement on 1970s cinema in the pages of a 1980 issue of *Film Comment*: 'The decade has been the worst in history for American films.'[1] If you've just finished reading the preceding eleven chapters of this book, and have found yourself even moderately persuaded by my enthusiasm for 1970s American film-making, then this remark might strike you as alarming. Can one man's Golden Age really be another man's Depression?

Perhaps it looked that way in 1980. One of Hollywood's star pupils, Francis Ford Coppola, had just spent an obscene amount of money in an ostentatious fashion making *Apocalypse Now*, a film not nearly as warmly regarded upon its release as it is now. Another, Steven Spielberg, had demonstrated the damage that a bottomless bank account can wreak on a movie's coherence with his reviled comedy *1941*, while Martin Scorsese's *New York, New York* was considered an indulgence from a film-maker formerly prized for his leanness. No one in the industry likes a director who doesn't have respect for the dollar, as Michael Cimino would discover that year when he followed the Oscar glory of *The Deer Hunter* with *Heaven's Gate*.

Meanwhile, George Lucas was seen to have paid too much

heed to commerce and not enough to art. The reductive spectacle of *Star Wars* mortified fans of the director's early work, but
its success also made it harder for young George Lucases to get
their own *THX 1138s* or *American Graffitis* off the ground.
The blockbuster was king now and any movie that didn't have
crowds camping out on the forecourt of Mann's Chinese The-
ater three days before opening was deemed to be a failure. A
survey conducted in summer 1979 by the Motion Picture Association of America found that forty-nine per cent of filmgoers
were between the ages of twelve and twenty, while another
twenty-seven per cent were between twenty-one and twenty-
nine.[2] This statistic, combined with the runaway popularity of
the special-effects-laden 'event movie' meant that fewer small
or personal films were being made. And of those that were,
fewer still were being afforded a chance to prosper from that
hallowed breed of goodwill known as word-of-mouth. A movie
opened big today, or else it closed tomorrow.

This commercial pressure affected the other directors pro-
filed in these pages, who proceeded with mixed fortunes (as opposed to Terrence Malick, who didn't proceed at all, at least
not for another twenty years). Brian De Palma began the 1980s
by firing off his wittiest thrillers, *Dressed to Kill* and *Blow Out*,
but by the end of a variable decade he had succumbed to the
lure of the blockbuster by making *The Untouchables*. From
there, *Mission: Impossible* was but a few sideways steps away.
Stanley Kubrick completed three more films before his death in
1999, of which *The Shining* is masterful, *Full Metal Jacket* is
largely unrewarding, and *Eyes Wide Shut* gets richer and funnier with each viewing. In *Zelig* and *Radio Days*, Woody Allen
made two further attempts to reconfigure the shape of cinematic storytelling, as he had done with the mix'n'match collage
style of *Annie Hall*. His most interesting later work came in the
1990s – the caustic comedy *Husbands and Wives*, the quick-
footed farce *Manhattan Murder Mystery* – but this was also the
decade that saw his most pronounced artistic decline, as he be-

gan to appear more than ever a man discarded by time, and ill-equipped to locate in that predicament the comic potential that might have reversed it.

None of these subsequent developments alters the calibre of the film-making quantified in this book, but it would be dishonest not to confess to a distant twinge of sadness at the general falling-off in quality. There have been exceptions. *E.T. The Extra Terrestrial* is like a spellbinding detail extracted from the broader canvas of *Close Encounters of the Third Kind*, while *Indiana Jones and the Temple of Doom* and *Minority Report* find Spielberg rolling up his shirtsleeves and delving deeper into the repugnant human horror that's so prevalent in his 1970s features. And Scorsese, who in 2000 took on his most daunting challenge by teaming up with Miramax's Harvey Weinstein to make *Gangs of New York*, produced yet more wild cards – *The Age of Innocence*, or 'Life Lessons' from *New York Stories*, the portmanteau film to which Coppola and Allen also contributed – that deserve to frustrate and complicate further his reputation.

But the only directors who consistently built on the promise of their 1970s work were Jonathan Demme and Robert Altman. Both men are toilers, grafters, whose modest films collectively amount to a study of human fears and foibles that is astonishing in its breadth and complexity. What's additionally heartening about Demme is that he has negotiated a move into the Hollywood mainstream that hasn't yet cost him his idiosyncrasies. It may be that Altman's scattershot approach to film-making, which typically results in several ugly misfires for every resounding bull's-eye, had better prepared us for the erratic direction that his career would take, than the patterns of some of his peers. When Coppola or Scorsese make a bad movie, the disappointment can be cataclysmic. With Altman, there's a sense that the hits couldn't happen without the misses. He has never stopped digging in the dirt and turning up wild, wonderful treasures, some of which were unfairly neglected (*Come*

Back to the 5 & Dime, Jimmy Dean, Jimmy Dean or *Kansas City*), while others were greeted with the kind of broad approval that felt like vindication, as with *Gosford Park*, a film for which no amount of praise would be too extravagant.

'Movies are like old girlfriends,' Coppola said in 1974. 'Once you've done them and you're finished with them, you don't go back.'[3] Twenty-seven years later, *Apocalypse Now Redux* premiered at the 2001 Cannes Film Festival. This was one of the more excusable instances of directorial tampering – a kind of post-post-post-production to which numerous films are now routinely subjected, even if it extends no further than a deluxe DVD edition complete with director's commentary and a bonus disc of extra features (out-takes and audition tapes that would previously never have seen the light of day; excerpts from the on-set catering menu). The extent of this tampering with pictures originally released in the 1970s speaks volumes about how the film-makers themselves view the work from that period. Their continued attention seems to acknowledge that it's their best, but the word of the fans and the history books isn't enough. Fans grow old and die, history books go out of print. Better to have those old movies in pristine twenty-first century condition, ready to compete for the favour of a new generation.

You can understand Ridley Scott crafting a version of his 1982 film *Blade Runner* more faithful to his original conception than had originally been allowed. But George Lucas updating the special effects in *Star Wars* to meet modern standards? That's more like retouching your old school photographs, replacing that threadbare tank-top with something from Duffer, or putting a 2005 haircut on a 1975 head. Similarly, Steven Spielberg can't keep his hands off *Close Encounters of the Third Kind*. He seems to spend a quarter of his life tinkering with the movie to produce new versions, each one proclaimed to be more definitive than the last, as though finality exists in gradations (and as though there was anything in the 1977 version that cried out for reparation).

This trend for revision smacks of the kind of opportunism that buzzes around the work of 1970s American directors. You won't need to wander the streets of London or New York for too long before you find yourself a gloating Travis Bickle t-shirt or a full-size *Taxi Driver* poster. The local supermarket will have plentiful supplies of the five-disc *Godfather* DVD box-set with gold-embossed lettering. While you're there, you could pick up a *GoodFellas* pizza, and the latest edition of a glossy monthly filling you in, once more, on the production history of *Apocalypse Now*, or the top ten all-time great 'Robert De Niro with a gun' movies. From the 1990s onwards, magazine editors and advertising executives have adopted those films, and their stars and directors, as talismanic icons for the fresh demographic group they had identified and on whom they wanted to foist new products. The popularity of movies like *Pulp Fiction*, *Lock, Stock and Two Smoking Barrels* and *The Matrix* revealed an insatiable hunger for anything cinematic, moderately violent and approximately male-oriented. Where better to draw from in the pursuit of marketing opportunities than the deep well of 1970s film-making, where it all began (or, at least, began again)?

As disheartening as the commercialization of this film culture has been, it does testify to the enduring hold that 1970s cinema has over audiences and practitioners alike. We are now far enough from that decade to view it with more objectivity and generosity than the dissenting voices at *Film Comment* found themselves able to do in 1980. We know that cinema suffered in the 1980s as a direct result of the trends set in motion by the success of Coppola, Lucas and Spielberg. But we can also see that the 1980s were not at all the listless, barren years for US cinema that they had promised to be. How could that be true when the decade saw the debuts of Kathryn Bigelow, Tim Burton, the Coen brothers, Todd Haynes, Jim Jarmusch, Spike Lee, Steven Soderbergh and Gus Van Sant? And we know too that film-makers continued to challenge the reign of the blockbuster. It remains the dominant species of movie, but in the wake of disastrous efforts like *Pearl Harbor*, *Godzilla* and *Batman and Robin*, and the widespread popularity of works that would once have been marginalized or considered difficult or experimental – *Crouching Tiger, Hidden Dragon* or *The Blair Witch Project* or *Memento* – the form has lost some of its erstwhile lustre.

There has undoubtedly been a dramatic divergence in the distinctions between art and entertainment since the 1970s. No one regards Michael Bay as a figure of unique vision, as the similarly bankable Spielberg was considered in the 1970s. The enduring visions now are coming from more modest sources. It is hardly possible to feel depressed about a culture in which pictures as challenging as Wes Anderson's *The Royal Tenenbaums* or Alexander Payne's *Election*, David Lynch's *Mulholland Drive* or Spike Jonze's *Being John Malkovich*, can be greeted not only with official commendation (these features all earned Oscar nominations) but the approval of audiences unperturbed by the prospect of cinema acting as a stimulant rather than a balm.

Despite the emergence of this band of forthright auteurs, the most consistently innovative and experimental narratives to be found at the start of the 21st century are almost exclusively televisual. The medium, publicly maligned for so long by cinema, and roundly trumped in the 1970s by the arrival of the blockbuster, has once again become a plausible rival for the attention of intelligent audiences. Shows such as *The Sopranos* and *Oz*, *Six Feet Under* and *The West Wing*, have graduated to that privileged position in popular culture occupied in the 1970s by the films of Scorsese, Coppola and Spielberg. The impact of those series may not be as immediately visible as a stellar opening weekend or a mile-long queue down Hollywood Blvd, but they have permeated ordinary life to an extent that 'event' movies – a *Lord of the Rings*, say – can only occasionally match. In the 1970s, US television was a dwindling force that depended on the current movie hits for its sporadic transfusions of creativity. As of the early 21st century, it has never been mightier or more full-blooded.

American cinema will need artists capable of the feral abandon of Altman, the day-glo daydreams of Demme, the toothsome vitality of early Spielberg, if it is to be insulated against accusations of irrelevance or frivolity. In a world fractured by its own wealth of available entertainments, cinema can no longer take supremacy for granted. It will always be the biggest medium, but whether it can remain the deepest is down to those film-makers who have not yet bellowed their first 'Action!'

Notes

Introduction

1 *How I Made a Hundred Movies in Hollywood and Never Lost a Dime* by Roger Corman with Jim Jerome, p. xi (Random House, New York, 1990).
2 *Take One*, v4, n8, Nov/Dec 1973, p. 29, by Michael Goodwin.
3 *Film Comment*, v11, n2, Mar/Apr 1975, pp. 43–6, by Marjorie Rosen.
4 *Take One*, v4, n10, Mar/Apr 1974, pp. 8–12, by David Helpern.
5 Figures from *Hollywood Reporter Book of Box-Office Hits* by Susan Sackett, pp. 202–7 (Billboard Books, 1990), reprinted in *Easy Rider* by Lee Hill, p. 30 (BFI Publishing, 1996).
6 Figures from *Hollywood, England* by Alexander Walker, p. 442 (Harrap, 1986), reprinted in *Sixties British Cinema*, p. 274, by Robert Murphy (BFI Publishing 1992).
7 *Film Facts* by Patrick Robertson (Aurum Press, 2001).
8 Statistics from *Film Comment*, v16, n1, Jan/Feb 1980, pp. 35–8, by Richard Corliss.

1. Francis Ford Coppola

1 *Sight and Sound*, v41, n4, Autumn 1972, pp. 217–23, by Stephen Farber.
2 *Filmmakers Newsletter*, v7, n7, May 1974, p. 30, by Brian De Palma.
3 Corman, p. 97.

4 *Film Comment*, v14, n1, Jan/Feb 1978, p. 49, by Mitch Tuchman.
5 *American Film*, v4, n10, Sept 1979, pp. 55–60, by Audie Bock.
6 Ibid.
7 *Sight and Sound*, Farber, as above.
8 *Sight and Sound*, v43, n3, Summer 1974, p. 131, by David Denby.
9 *Sight and Sound*, Farber, as above.
10 *Filmmakers Newsletter*, De Palma, as above.
11 *Sight and Sound*, Farber, as above.

2. George Lucas

1 *Film Comment*, v17, n4, Jul/Aug 1981, p. 52, by Mitch Tuchman and Anne Thompson.
2 *The Making of American Graffiti*, Universal DVD 2000.
3 *American Film*, vII, n6, April 1977, p. 11, by Stephen Zito.
4 *George Lucas* by John Baxter, p. 10 (HarperCollins, 1999).
5 *Steven Spielberg* by Joseph McBride, p. 137 (Faber and Faber, 1997).
6 Baxter, p. 104.
7 *Scorsese on Scorsese*, ed. David Thompson and Ian Christie, p. 69 (Faber and Faber, updated edition, 1996).
8 *Film Comment*, Tuchman and Thompson, as above.
9 *The Making of American Graffiti*, as above.
10 *Filmmakers Newsletter*, v7, n5, March 1974, p. 22, by Larry Sturhahn.
11 *Film Comment*, v11, n2, March/April 1975, p. 48, by Madeline Warren and Robert A. Levine.
12 *Filmmakers Newsletter*, Sturhahn, as above.
13 Ibid.
14 *American Film*, Zito, as above.
15 Ibid.
16 *Film Comment*, Tuchman and Thompson, as above.
17 *Cinefantastique*, v7, n3/4, Aug 1978 double issue, by Don Shay.

3. Steven Spielberg

1 *American Film*, v3, n10, Sept 1978, pp. 43–53, by James Powers.
2 *Sight and Sound*, v46, n2, Spring 1977, p. 111, by Richard Combs.
3 *Close Encounters of the Third Kind Diary* by Bob Balaban (Paradise Press, 1978).
4 *Film Comment*, v14, n1, Jan/Feb 1978, pp. 49–55, by Mitch Tuchman.

5 *American Film*, Powers, as above.
6 *Film Comment*, Tuchman, as above.
7 *Robert Altman Jumping Off the Cliff* by Patrick McGilligan, p. 372 (St Martin's Press, 1989).
8 *Take One*, v4, n10, Mar/Apr 1974, pp. 8–12, by David Helpern.
9 *Cinema Papers*, July–Aug 1975, pp. 107–190, by John Moran.
10 *Take One*, Helpern, as above.
11 McBride, p. 200.
12 *Filmmakers Newsletter*, v11, n2 Dec 1977, pp. 28–30.
13 *Film Comment*, Tuchman, as above.

4. Terrence Malick

1 *Film Comment*, v18, n1, Jan/Feb 1982, pp. 46–9, by Mary Corliss, Richard Corliss and Carlos Clarens.
2 *Sunday Express*, 5 Dec 1999, author interview.
3 *Sight and Sound*, v44, n2, Spring 1975, p. 82, by Beverly Walker.
4 Ibid.
5 Ibid.
6 *American Cinematographer*, v60, n6, June 1979, p. 562, by Nestor Almendros, translated by Hal Trusell.

5. Brian De Palma

1 *The Cinema of Alfred Hitchcock* by Peter Bogdanovich. p. 4 (New York: Museum of Modern Art Film Library, 1963), reprinted in *The Birds* by Camille Paglia, p. 64 (BFI Publishing, 1998).
2 *Cinefantastique*, v4, n2, Summer 1975, p. 8, by David Bartholomew.
3 *Film Comment*, v35, n5, Sep/Oct 1999, by Gavin Smith.
4 *Take One*, v7, n2, Jan 1979, p. 14, by Gerald Peary.
5 *American Film*, v2, n9, Jul/Aug 1977, by Royal S. Brown.
6 *The Movie Brats: How the Film Generation Took Over Hollywood* by Michael Pye and Lynda Myles, pp. 154–5 (Faber and Faber, 1979).
7 *Filmmakers' Monthly*, v13, n11, Sept 1980, p. 35, by Ralph Applebaum.
8 Pye and Myles, p. 142.
9 *Filmmakers Newsletter*, v8, n4, Feb 1975, p. 26, by John Coates.
10 *Film Comment*, Smith, as above.
11 *Filmmakers Newsletter*, Coates, as above.

6. Robert Altman

1 McGilligan, p. 435.
2 McGilligan, p. 344.
3 McGilligan, p. 381.

7. Stanley Kubrick

1 *Millimeter*, v3, n12, Dec 1975, p. 32, by Mark Carducci.
2 *Sight and Sound*, v41, n2, Spring 1972, pp. 62–6, by Philip Strick and Penelope Houston.
3 *Kubrick* by Michael Herr, p. 37 (Picador, 2000).
4 *Sight and Sound*, v46, n2, Spring 1977, p. 111, by Richard Combs.

8. Woody Allen

1 *Cult Movies 3* by Danny Peary, p. 24 (Fireside, 1988).
2 *Take One*, v6, n12, Nov 1978, p. 18, by Ira Halberstadt.
3 'Lovborg's Women Considered' from *Without Feathers* by Woody Allen, p. 31 (Sphere Books, 1978).

9. Jonathan Demme

1 *Film Comment*, v16, n5, Sep/Oct 1980, pp. 56–9 by Carlos Clarens.
2 *The Badger Herald*, 9 Sept 1988, by Rob Nelson, reprinted in *Conversations with Pauline Kael*, ed. Will Brantley, pp. 105–7 (University Press of Mississippi, 1996).
3 *American Film*, v9, n4, Jan–Feb 1984, pp. 44–7, by Michael Sragow.
4 *Film Comment*, v13, n5, Sept/Oct 1977, pp. 6–15, by Dave Kehr.
5 'Demme on Demme' from *Projections 1*, ed. John Boorman and Walter Donohue, p. 195 (Faber and Faber, 1992).
6 *Film Comment*, Clarens, as above.
7 *Cult Movies* by Danny Peary, p. 46 (Delta, 1981).
8 *American Film*, Sragow, as above.

10. Martin Scorsese

1 *American Cinema/American Culture* by John Belton, p. 302 (McGraw Hill, 1994)
2 *Film Comment*, Rosen, as above.

3 *Millimeter*, v3, n5, May 1975, pp. 12–6, by Mark Carducci.
4 Ibid.
5 *American Film*, Sragow, as above.
6 *Sight and Sound*, v7, n2, Feb 1997, p. 18–20, by Quentin Curtis.
7 *Filmmakers Newsletter*, v7, n3, Jan 1974, p. 29 by Andrew C. Bobrow.
8 *Scorsese on Scorsese*, p. 31.
9 Author interview, November 1996.
10 *Film Comment*, Rosen, as above.
11 *Millimeter*, Carducci, as above.

Conclusion

1 *Film Comment*, v16, n1, Jan/Feb 1980, by Stuart Byron.
2 Statistics from the same piece, by Richard Corliss.
3 *Film Comment*, v10, n4, Jul/Aug 1974, pp. 43–9, by Marjorie Rosen.

Acknowledgements

Sincere thanks to the following people, each of whom contributed criticism, advice, encouragement and/or some unclassifiable magic during the writing of this book: David Benedict, Anne Billson, Walter Donohue, Leslie Felperin, Cathy James, Richard Kelly, Stefan Ketelsen, Cat Ledger, Charlotte O'Sullivan, Matthew Sweet and Mark Wilson. Thanks to Jon Riley for the idea. For help with research, I would like to thank Edward Lawrenson, Marc Morris, James Mottram and Brian Robinson. Thank you also to my parents and my brother and sister for unstinting love and support; and to Rosie, Barney, Edith and Fred for providing happy distractions.

Index